Intimacy and Responsibility

The Criminalisation of HIV Transmission

In what circumstances, and on what basis, should those who transmit serious disease to their sexual partners be criminalised? In this book Matthew Weait provides a critical analysis of the response of the English criminal courts to those who have been convicted of transmitting HIV during sex. He argues that the cases provide us with an important insight into the way in which the criminal constructs the concepts of harm, risk, causation, blame and responsibility, and – more generally – how it is impossible to understand the law in this area without also engaging with the socio-cultural dimensions of HIV/AIDS and sexuality.

Matthew Weait is Senior Lecturer in Law and Legal Studies at Birkbeck College, University of London. He studied law and criminology at the University of Cambridge and was awarded a DPhil from the University of Oxford, where he was a Research Officer at the Centre for Socio-Legal Studies. After being called to the bar he worked at the Open University and at Keele University, where he was an active member of the AHRB Centre for Law, Gender and Sexuality. His research into the impact of law on people living with HIV and AIDS is informed by work he has undertaken for a number of local, regional, national and international HIV/AIDS organisations.

Intimacy and Responsibility

The Criminalisation of HIV Transmission

Matthew Weait

Routledge·Cavendish
Taylor & Francis Group
a GlassHouse book

First published 2007
by Routledge-Cavendish
2 Park Square, Milton Park, Abingdon, Oxon OX14 4RN

Simultaneously published in the USA and Canada
by Routledge-Cavendish
270 Madison Ave, New York, NY 10016

A GlassHouse book

Routledge-Cavendish is an imprint of the Taylor & Francis Group,
an informa business

Typeset in Times by
RefineCatch Limited, Bungay, Suffolk
Printed and bound in Great Britain by
TJ International Ltd, Padstow, Cornwall

British Library Cataloguing in Publication Data
A catalogue record for this book is available from the British Library

Library of Congress Cataloging-in-Publication Data
Weait, Matthew
Intimacy and responsibility : the criminalisation of HIV transmission
/ Matthew Weait.—1st ed.
    p.   cm.
Simultaneously published in the USA and Canada.
ISBN-13: 978–1–904385–71–4
ISBN-10: 1–904385–71–0
ISBN-13: 978–1–904385–70–7
ISBN-10: 1–904385–70–2
[etc.]
    1. HIV-positive persons—Legal status, laws, etc.—Great
Britain.   2. AIDS (Disease)—Transmission—Great Britain.
3. Sexually transmitted diseases—Law and legislation—Great
Britain.   4. Liability (Law)—Great Britain.   I. Title.
KD3368.A54W43 2007
344.4104′369792—dc22
                                              2007024937

ISBN10: 1–904385–71–0 (hbk)
ISBN13: 978–1–904385–71–4 (hbk)

ISBN10: 1–904385–70–2 (pbk)
ISBN13: 978–1–904385–70–7 (pbk)

eISBN10: 0–203–93793–7
eISBN13: 978–0–203–93793–8

This book is dedicated to my partner in life
Robert Walker Hanwell
and to the memory of my father
John Geoffrey Buckland Weait (1939–2000)

Now I am ready to tell how bodies are changed
Into different bodies.
Ted Hughes, *Tales from Ovid*
(London: Faber and Faber, 1997)

Contents

Foreword

by Mr Justice Edwin Cameron

Matthew Weait begins the final chapter of this book with a quotation from Cindy Patton, who pleads powerfully that to deal effectively with HIV and AIDS, to stop needless illness and death, we need theory as much as action. We must theorise because we need to understand. And we need to understand not only the experience of people with HIV and AIDS, but also the social, political, economic and legal context in which they live.

Understanding each of these dimensions is important, for discrimination and prejudice disfigure our attempts to grapple with the epidemic. And stigma prevents many people from accessing care, treatment and support (where these are available). Politically and economically, HIV is a fraught factor in debates about asylum and immigration, disability rights, drug pricing, and the allocation of healthcare resources. We know that many of those who have not tested positive for HIV resent the 'burden' that those with HIV place on others – something often underscored by the media.

And legally – how do we best theorise the role of the law in the epidemic? The law can do good. It can provide protection against discrimination, reduce the prices of – and ensure the availability of – life-saving drugs, protect confidentiality and privacy, shield against human rights violations. But the law can also be hazardous for those with HIV – nowhere more sharply than where the criminal law is used against those who transmit HIV to others, or who expose them to the risk of transmission.

Criminal law has vital functions in a democracy – to deter conduct that adversely affects others, and to incapacitate and to rehabilitate offenders. Most fundamentally, the law speaks values. In his book, Matthew Weait critically analyses how moral sentiment about those who recklessly transmit HIV to their sexual partners is expressed in English criminal law.

He argues that the criminal law is ill-suited to deal with reckless transmission, and that it can harm more than help. Weait never denies that it may be necessary to condemn those who disrespect their sexual partners, and who fail to practise safer sex, or to disclose their HIV status. What he confronts us with is the argument that the criminal law need not be the best means to respond. Weait's premise is that criminal law and criminal justice should be used for the public good rather than as means of securing reparation for particular individuals.

I approach Weait's reasoning not merely with the focus of an African, in whose sub-continent many millions have suffered and died, and more face suffering and death, from AIDS (and who have myself been saved from death by privileged access to anti-retroviral treatment), but with the political consciousness of a proudly gay man, whom history reminds of the law's dismal role in persecuting and humiliating those seen as sexually transgressive. I also reflect on his argument with the professional hopefulness of a judge who is privileged to hold office under one of the world's most enlightened and humane constitutions.

If his argument is correct, then we must question criminal laws that may discourage people from HIV testing, or from being candid about their sexual history when confiding in health care workers. We must question whether it is good to impose criminal liability when media coverage is often sensational and inaccurate – with the effect of demonising all with HIV, and marking them as potential aggressors. We must question whether such laws acknowledge the difficulties that some living with HIV – particularly women, who may risk violence and expulsion from the home – have in negotiating safer sex. And we must question the public 'good' that comes from ascribing sole responsibility for transmission (as such laws do) to the person with HIV, thus attenuating the partner's responsibility for avoiding transmission – especially in an epidemic when all should be aware of the risks of unprotected sex.

Many believe strongly that those who recklessly infect others with HIV should be publicly condemned and punished, and that their condemnation and punishment by the criminal law is defensible and legitimate. I hope they will reflect on and engage with the arguments presented here. Those who take a primarily moral stand against people who violate the interests of others (and believe that this should be reflected in the law) may approach with scepticism Weait's arguments about public health, stigma, and the importance of shared responsibility for sexual health.

But even if such readers are not convinced, the book will enable them to understand the possibly negative impact of these laws on the spread of HIV and on those living with HIV and AIDS. And such reflection and debate is ample affirmation of the importance of Weait's book.

Mr Justice Edwin Cameron
Judge of Appeal of the Supreme Court of Appeal of South Africa
Professor of Law, Centre for Applied Legal Studies,
University of Witwatersrand

Acknowledgements

This book has been a long time in the gestation, and there are many people to whom I owe a debt of gratitude. I would first like to thank the people in the many UK-based HIV and AIDS organisations who have helped me understand the epidemic and its effects and whose dedication is a continuing source of inspiration. I should like especially to thank the paid and unpaid staff of George House Trust, the Terrence Higgins Trust, the National AIDS Trust, the African HIV Policy Network, the National AIDS Manual, the Global Network of Positive People, the UK Coalition, Sigma Research and Positively Women. It is invidious to name individuals associated with these organisations, but I should like to acknowledge (in no particular order) the support provided by Angelina Namiba, Bernard Forbes, Rhon Reynolds, Michelle Reid, Chris Morley, Yusef Azad, Catherine Dodds, Edwin Bernard, Jack Summerside and Lisa Power. If there were a particular order, one person would be at the front of the list: thank you Catherine. Thanks are also due to colleagues and friends working to combat the epidemic and promote understanding of the impact of law on people living with HIV and AIDS both in the UK and abroad, whether directly or indirectly: Richard Elliott of the Canadian HIV/AIDS Legal Network, Jane Anderson of Homerton Hospital and the British HIV Association, Yannick Delord of AIDES, Peter Smit of the Dutch HIV Association, Ronald Brands of SOA AIDS, Nikos Dedes of the European AIDS Treatment Group, Susan Timberlake of UNAIDS and Pivot Legal Society, Vancouver.

This book is an attempt to raise some of the difficulties associated with the criminalisation of HIV transmission. Many of those difficulties are political and practical, but some are intellectual and academic. I have benefited substantially from conversations and dialogue (sometimes heated, but always civilised) with many, but in particular James Chalmers, John Spencer, Gillian Calder, Daniel Monk, Anna Worrall, and Scott Burris. I was also sustained throughout this project by the untiring support of all my academic and other colleagues in the Law School and Research Institute for Law, Politics and Justice at Keele University, and the AHRC Centre for Law, Gender and Sexuality. Particular thanks are owed to Marie Fox, Jane Krishnadas,

Zoe Pearson, Tony Dugdale, Ruth Fletcher, Nicola Barker, Andrew Francis, Jill Gordon, Robert James and Peter McTigue. My undergraduate students at Keele never failed to challenge me, sometimes with reason.

For my interest in, and understanding of, criminal law and criminal justice, I am particularly indebted to Alison Morris, Nicola Lacey, Ngaire Naffine, Celia Wells, Alan Norrie and Lindsay Farmer. Any errors of law or judgment in this book are mine, not theirs. Keith Hawkins impressed upon me the importance of using semi-colons wisely. Antony Lester explained the politics of law to me. Michael Prichard gave me the opportunity to study law in the first place and told me (on more than one occasion) that I might one day understand it.

Some of the arguments presented in this book have been developed during conferences, seminars, and visits to other institutions the financial support for which has been provided by academic and other funding bodies. I would like to acknowledge the support of the ESRC, for the Research Seminar Series, *HIV/AIDS and Law: Theory Practice and Policy*; the AHRC Centre for Law, Gender and Sexuality; the British Academy for an Overseas Conference Grant; the Government of Canada for a Faculty Research Program Scholarship, and the Law Faculty at the University of British Columbia for a Visiting Research Fellowship. I have also benefited from participating in events organised by the British HIV Association, the British Psychological Society, the European AIDS Treatment Group, the World AIDS Conference, and the World Health Organisation.

At the time of writing I am a member of the Expert Advisory Group on AIDS, a group that exists to advise the UK Government's Chief Medical Officer on AIDS-related issues. I have learned much from discussion with colleagues on this group, but the views expressed in the book are my own and should not be attributed to them either individually or collectively.

Without friends and family the book would not have been possible. I owe special thanks to Emily Jackson, Miranda Hill, Shona Peel, Elizabeth Frazer, Marjorie Jones, Lynn Errey, Suzanne Shale, Adam Bourne, Kay Taylor, Michael Delaney, Philippe Mangeot, Mavis Maclean, Dave and Jude Harris, Christine Biggs, George, Lily and Ellie (RIP). If Nicky Priaulx did not exist it would be necessary to invent her – immediately. Many of the ideas expressed in this book are ones that have evolved in discussion with her. My family know who they are!

Finally, I should like to thank Colin Perrin of Glasshouse Press for his patience – a necessary virtue.

This book is dedicated, first, to Robert Hanwell. Without his unfailing love, understanding and tolerance this book would not have happened. It is dedicated also to the memory of my father, John Weait – never one to accept received wisdom.

I should also like to thank the following for their permission to include published material in the text:

Blackwell Publishing for:
Weait, M. (2005) 'Criminal law and the sexual transmission of HIV: *R v Dica*', *Modern Law Review*, 68(1): 120–133.
The National AIDS Manual and the National AIDS Trust for:
Bernard, E. Azad, Y., Geretti, A.-M., van Damme, A.M. and Weait, M. (2007) *HIV Forensics: The Use of Phylogenetic Analysis as Evidence in Criminal Investigation of HIV Transmission*, London: National AIDS Manual and National AIDS Trust.
Routledge-Cavendish for:
Weait, M. (2007) 'On being responsible', in V. Munro and C.F. Stychin (eds) *Sexuality and Law: Feminist Engagements*, Abingdon: Routledge-Cavendish.
Springer for:
Weait, M. (2005) 'Harm, consent and the limits of privacy', *Feminist Legal Studies*, 13: 97–122.
Sweet and Maxwell for:
Weait, M. (2005) 'Knowledge, autonomy and consent: *R v Konzani*', *Criminal Law Review*, 763–772.
Taylor and Francis for:
Weait, M. (2001) 'Taking the blame: criminal law, social responsibility and the sexual transmission of HIV', *The Journal of Social Welfare and Family Law*, 23(4): 441–457.

I should also like to thank the following for permission to reproduce previously unpublished material:

Bernard Forbes, for the letter to him from the Home Office, an extract from which is quoted in Chapter 1.
Neil Gerrard MP, for correspondence between him and Home Office Ministers, extracts from which are also quoted in Chapter 1.

Table of cases

Chapter 1

The terrain: the state, criminal justice and HIV

> The criminalization of HIV has been a strange, pointless exercise in the long fight to control HIV. It has done no good; if it has done even a little harm the price has been too high. Until the day comes when the stigma of HIV, unconventional sexuality and drug use are gone, the best course for criminal law is to follow the old Hippocratic maxim, 'first, do no harm.'
>
> (Burris *et al*, 2007: 49)

Introduction

HIV and AIDS[1] have been the subject of academic interrogation since the first cases of AIDS were diagnosed in the early 1980s. The nature of that interrogation has been extraordinarily diverse, reflecting a wide range of intellectual and practical concerns. For sociologists, economists, psychologists, social historians, philosophers, political and cultural theorists, writers, artists and – importantly people living with HIV and with AIDS (PLHA), the virus and its effects (both physiological and social) have provided an opportunity to question and explore from a novel perspective the nature of identity, stigma and dignity, the impact of globalisation, the right to health, the parameters of responsibility, and relations between people of different genders, ethnicities and sexualities. We have come, in short, to understand that HIV and AIDS is as much an 'epidemic of signification' (Treichler, 1988) as it is an epidemic that blights bodies.

From a specifically legal perspective, HIV and AIDS have also provoked a range of interventions. Some, reflecting the fact that – above all – HIV and AIDS have had stigmatising and discriminatory effects on those who live with the virus, have had a practical orientation. 'AIDS law' guides and handbooks were critically important in the early years of the pandemic, providing both

---

1 A note on terminology: in the book I refer to, and distinguish between, HIV and AIDS where appropriate. The commonly used term 'HIV/AIDS' is one that conflates two inter-related, but different phenomena. HIV infection no longer leads inevitably to AIDS, and it is people living with HIV and/or AIDS who may transmit the virus to others.

the means by which PLHA might know their rights in areas such as housing, employment, insurance, and immigration, and also a means by which legal practitioners might be alerted to the particular needs of a new and growing client base (see, for example Burris *et al*, 1993; Haigh and Harris, 1995; Rubenstein *et al*, 1996). Other interventions have been more academic, focusing in particular (though not exclusively) on the human rights, civil liberties and public health implications of HIV and AIDS (for example Sullivan and Field, 1988; Monk, 1998; Elliott, 2002; Lazzarini *et al*, 2002; Watchirs, 2003; Gostin, 2003).[2] Still others have been professedly theoretical in their orientation, albeit grounded in the case law (for example Rollins, 2004).

This book is an attempt to make a sustained and critical contribution to a particular, but important, area of legal scholarship in the field of HIV and AIDS: the criminalisation of HIV transmission. This is a topic that has not only generated a vast amount of literature in jurisdictions with a common law heritage,[3] but has also engaged the attention of international human rights and health organisations (Elliott, 2002; WHO, 2006). The reasons for the interest in the subject are discussed in detail in subsequent chapters. Here, it is sufficient to note that they are relatively self-evident. Most people are HIV negative. Many, if not all, HIV negative people are afraid of HIV and AIDS; many, if not all, people are aware that HIV is a transmissible disease; and many, if not all, people think that those who transmit HIV to others – especially to those with whom they have an intimate sexual relationship – have by definition done something wrong and should be punished for it.

The purpose of this book is not to deny the validity of those who hold these views, although they are not ones I share. Rather, it is an attempt – focusing on the law in England and Wales – to problematise the way in which the criminal law has responded to the transmission of HIV, to question the justifications for using the criminal law against those who transmit HIV to their sexual partners, and – I hope – to provide some original insight into the way criminal law constructs us as responsible subjects before the law.

---

2 For an excellent bibliography of legal materials (to June 1998, and with a US bias) see Leonard, 1998. For a wide-ranging collection of essays discussing the ways in which jurisdictions across the world have responded to the pandemic, see Frankowski, 1998.

3 It would be impossible to refer to all of the relevant contributions. For an excellent, if now slightly dated, review of the international literature see Elliott, 1997. For a recent, policy-oriented, account of the issues see WHO, 2006. For discussions of the way in which the law relating to disease transmission in general, and HIV transmission in particular, has developed in England and Wales over the past 30 years, see Lynch, 1978; Bronitt, 1991; Smith, 1991; Alldridge, 1993; Bronitt, 1994; Ormerod and Gunn, 1996; Dine and Watt, 1998; Weait, 2001; Chalmers, 2002; Spencer, 2004a, 2004b; Warburton, 2004; Weait, 2005a, 2005b, 2005c; Weait and Azad, 2005; Ryan, 2006, 2007.

Context

This may be a book about the response of the English criminal law to the sexual transmission of HIV, but it would be foolhardy to begin that discussion without locating the particular subject matter within its broader political and historical context. A fundamental part of the argument I attempt to present about the criminal law's response to HIV is that it has failed to acknowledge the fact that HIV and AIDS are, and should be understood as, public health issues first and foremost, rather than as problems necessarily capable of effective legal resolution through the criminal law. Although the UK has been fortunate in the relatively low number of people living with HIV infection and with AIDS-defining illnesses (as a percentage of the total population, and compared with both other Western European countries and – more obviously – many African countries), it is nevertheless a public health crisis on a grand scale. To explore and attempt an analysis of the response of the criminal law to isolated incidents of transmission between individuals would be possible; but a purely juridical analysis would be equivalent to attempting to understand the principles of English contract law without acknowledging their development and functions within a capitalist economy. We might be able to learn the rules, but we would not understand why they exist, or how they are interpreted and to what end.

In order to give some background, this chapter therefore provides, first, a brief overview of the HIV epidemic in the UK, the relationship between the nature of the epidemic and the characteristics of the prosecutions that have been brought. It then explores the way in which the epidemic has informed international human rights principles, and how those principles have been articulated within the context of the epidemic. This discussion is important, since debates surrounding the criminalisation of HIV transmission have, in large part, been set against that human rights background.[4] The chapter then considers, in a little more detail, the way in which the use of criminal law, as a coercive power of the state, interrelates with public health law. Here I suggest that public health law may – rather than being a 'soft option' – amount to criminalisation by the back door, and that its coercive potential not only threatens the human rights of PLHA but may actually impede the effective management of the epidemic. The final part of the chapter sets out, in brief, the relevant legislative and policy history immediately preceding the first cases in which people were convicted for transmitting HIV in England and Wales, and a summary of the cases that have been decided so far.

---

4 For a discussion of the relationship between international law and HIV/AIDS see Mameli, 2000.

HIV/AIDS in the United Kingdom: an overview[5]

Epidemiology

2006 marked the twenty-fifth anniversary of the first reported case of AIDS (in the United States), and the beginning of HIV surveillance in the UK. By the end of March 2007 there had been a total of 86,738 HIV diagnoses in the UK, 45 per cent of which were among men who have sex with men (MSM), 40 per cent among heterosexuals, and 5 per cent among injection drug-users (IDUs). Of those diagnosed, 70 per cent have been male and 30 per cent female. Although many initiatives aimed at limiting the spread of HIV within the population have been successful and beneficial (for example blood- and ante-natal screening, voluntary and confidential HIV testing, the provision on the NHS of highly active anti-retroviral therapy (HAART), targeted HIV and AIDS information and needle-exchange programmes for IDUs) the number of reported cases of HIV infection continues to rise. In 2005 there were an estimated 63,500 people living with HIV in the UK, one-third of whom were ignorant of their HIV positive status. This increase in the number of reported HIV cases has been mirrored by an increase in the rate of other sexually transmitted infections (STIs). Between 1996 and 2005 the number of people presenting with an STI at genito-urinary medicine (GUM) clinics in the UK increased by 60 per cent, and 790,000 acute STIs were diagnosed. Of particular concern in recent years has been the clinical management of people with HIV and other STIs who present for care and treatment with multiple infections (including tuberculosis (TB), and hepatitis B and C). Not only are those with HIV and TB co-infection – most of whom come from minority ethnic populations – harder to treat, since the first line drug used to treat TB reacts adversely with some drugs used in HAART, but also the increased prevalence of HIV and syphilis, or HIV and LGV (lymphogranuloma venereum), co-infection indicates a significant link between infection and high-risk (unsafe) sexual behaviour.

Until 1984 only those people whose HIV infection had resulted in the development of AIDS were subject to reporting, since until that time there was no test for HIV itself. That year therefore saw a substantial increase in HIV diagnoses (to just over 3,000). The annual number of diagnoses has more than doubled since then (7,450 in 2005), though that number has remained relatively stable since 2003. The number of AIDS-related deaths, however, reached a peak in 1995 and has been in decline since then as the result of the availability of HAART. Since 1998 there have been fewer than 1,000 AIDS diagnoses annually (with most being of people who had been

5 The information presented here is drawn largely from Health Protection Agency, 2006. For more general discussion of the history of AIDS in the UK see Porter and Porter, 1988; Garfield, 1994; Berridge, 1996. For a more general account see Marks and Ellison, 2003.

diagnosed HIV positive late in the course of their HIV infection), and even fewer deaths.

These bald figures do not, though, illustrate the way that the HIV epidemic has progressed in different population groups. The increase in diagnoses in the early to mid-1980s was largely among men who have sex with men (MSM), those who needed blood products (such as haemophiliacs), and IDUs. As the rate of diagnoses in these groups stabilised, so the number of heterosexuals testing positive increased. Between 1996 and 2005 there was a 52 per cent increase in new diagnoses among MSM, but an almost 500 per cent increase among heterosexuals, with a greater increase among heterosexual women (partly as a result of routine ante-natal screening). The rise in heterosexual diagnoses generally is largely attributable to the number of heterosexual men and women in the UK who were infected in countries with a high HIV prevalence (primarily sub-Saharan Africa). Of the 1,374 HIV diagnoses of MSM in 2005 where the country of origin of infection was reported, 84 per cent were infected in the UK, whereas among heterosexuals it was 15 per cent. The increase in infections acquired heterosexually outside the UK correlates significantly with the ethnic distribution of HIV. Of heterosexuals living with diagnosed HIV in the UK in 2005, 70 per cent were of black African ethnicity, 18 per cent were white, just under 4 per cent were black Caribbean, and 1.4 per cent were Indian, Pakistani or Bangladeshi. This distribution is in marked contrast to MSM, where 88 per cent were white, 1.3 per cent black African, and less than 1 per cent Indian, Pakistani or Bangladeshi.

Epidemiology and criminal cases involving HIV transmission

The epidemiology of HIV in the UK is thus a complex one. It impacts differently on people depending on their sexuality, their ethnicity, and their gender. It is a virus that does not distinguish between people at the molecular level, but at a socio-economic one. For the purposes of this book, what is particularly significant is that the vast majority of onward transmissions occur as the result of sexual contact between adults. While it would, in theory, be possible to convict women who recklessly transmit HIV to their newborns through breastfeeding, or diagnosed IDUs who allow others to share their needles, there have been no cases in the UK on these facts. Instead, and to this extent at least the cases that have been brought so far reflect the epidemiology, prosecutors have focused on those who have consciously taken unjustified risks (as the law views these) in the context of lawful consensual sex.[6] There is,

---

6 It has been established by the Court of Appeal that non-disclosure of known HIV status is not relevant to the question of whether a complainant consented to intercourse (and is thus irrelevant to the question of consent in the context of a prosecution for rape: *R v B* [2007] 1 Cr App R 29).

however, a marked negative correlation between HIV epidemiology in the UK and the gender, sexuality and ethnicity of the defendants in cases involving HIV transmission (James, Azad and Weait, 2007). Thus, whereas 45 per cent of HIV positive diagnoses to March 2007 were among MSM, only 2 of the 14 cases to date (less than 20 per cent) have involved same-sex transmission (contrasted with 40 per cent heterosexually caused diagnoses and over 80 per cent of the cases). Similarly, whereas approximately one-third of those accessing HIV care in the UK are heterosexual men, 10 out of the 14 cases concern men in this group. Lastly, whereas less than 20 per cent of heterosexuals accessing HIV care in the UK are white, this group constitutes the majority of heterosexual defendants. There are too few cases in the UK to be able to engage in anything other than conjecture about the possible significance of these differences. As for the sexuality of defendants, it is possible that gay men (to now at least) have, in general, been more willing to treat HIV infection as a matter of shared responsibility than, say heterosexual women, and thus less willing to go to the police if they discover that they have been infected. Alternatively, it is possible that more gay men who discover that they are HIV positive are unable, as the result of multiple sexual partners, to be sure about the identity of the person who transmitted the virus to them. As for ethnicity, it was initially of concern to some that the first three defendants in England were of black African origin, but now the proportion of those from minority ethnic communities is more representative of the epidemic as a whole. What can be said with some degree of certainty is that, as far as the criminal law is concerned, every HIV positive person who recklessly transmits HIV – irrespective of the ways in which their cultural or ethnic heritage, their gender, or their sexual orientation may have affected their subjective understanding of responsibility or their ability to negotiate safer sex – is fair game.[7]

HIV/AIDS, human rights and criminal law

Having provided some epidemiological context, it is now appropriate to consider the more immediate legal background against which the cases have taken place. The mid-1990s was a critically important period for people living with HIV and AIDS. Not only did it see the introduction of HAART, a form of therapeutic intervention which has enabled millions of people living with HIV to manage their infection and live longer, it saw a renewed commitment on the part of the international community to ensuring that PLHA should not, by virtue of their HIV status, suffer in their enjoyment of basic human rights. That commitment had first been articulated in Oslo in 1988, when the World Health Organization hosted the International Consultation on Health Legislation and Ethics in the Field of HIV/AIDS. This Consultation,

---

7 The relevance of these considerations is discussed further in Chs 4 and 6.

consistent with its occurrence in a period still characterised by profound ignorance on the part of many about HIV itself, and by the vilification of, and prejudice against, those living with HIV and AIDS, advocated the 'bringing down of barriers between people who were infected and those who were not infected, and placing actual barriers (for example condoms) between individuals and the virus' (UNCHR, 1998: annex 1, para 1). This dual theme marked many subsequent international initiatives,[8] and was driven by the belief – one still in evidence today – that discriminatory legislation and practices make it harder to combat the epidemic, since it makes those living with HIV and AIDS harder to reach.

The international movement towards the promulgation and adoption of international human rights standards in the field of HIV/AIDS continued during the late 1980s and 1990s, with the UN Sub-Commission on Prevention of Discrimination and Protection of Minorities and the Commission on Human Rights adopting annual resolutions against discrimination. In 1995 these resolutions were complemented by an even more concrete commitment when the UN Secretary-General recommended to the Commission that it consider the introduction of guidelines to this end. That recommendation stated that:

> The development of such guidelines or principles could provide an international framework for discussion of human rights considerations at the national, regional and international levels in order to arrive at a more comprehensive understanding of the complex relationship between the public health rationale and the human rights rationale of HIV/AIDS. In particular, Governments could benefit from guidelines that outline clearly how human rights standards apply in the area of HIV/AIDS and indicate concrete and specific measures, both in terms of legislation and practice, that should be undertaken.
>
> (United Nations, 1995: para 135)

This recommendation led, in 1996 and at the request of the Commission, to the Second International Consultation on HIV/AIDS and Human Rights in Geneva – an event convened in collaboration with UNAIDS, and comprising a range of stakeholders and interested parties.[9] The Consultation produced a number of guidelines:

> to assist States in creating a positive, rights-based response to HIV/AIDS

---

8 For a good, brief, overview see UNCHR, 1998: Annex 1.
9 The first Consultation, which also proposed the development of guidelines, had been organised in 1989 by the then UN Centre for Human Rights and the World Health Organization (UNCHR, 1989).

that is effective in reducing the transmission and impact of HIV/AIDS and consistent with human rights and fundamental freedoms.

(UNCHR, 1998: 3)

While recognising that States bring to the epidemic 'different economic, social and cultural values, traditions and practices' (diplomatic shorthand for variable commitment to the rights of PLHA), the Guidelines were nevertheless intended to ensure that all States ensure that local responses are informed by universal human rights standards.

Among the twelve Guidelines, which address both procedural and substantive responses, and deal with both civil and political and economic, social and cultural rights, Guidelines 3 and 4 are immediately relevant to the present discussion:

Guideline 3: Public Health Legislation

States should review and reform public health legislation to ensure that they adequately address the public health issues raised by HIV/AIDS, that their provisions applicable to casually transmitted diseases are not inappropriately applied to HIV/AIDS and that they are consistent with international human rights obligations.

. . .

Guideline 4: Criminal Law and Correctional Systems

States should review and reform criminal laws and correctional systems to ensure that they are consistent with international human rights obligations and are not misused in the context of HIV/AIDS or targeted at vulnerable groups.

Both of these Guidelines, as is the case with the others, are exhortatory rather than prescriptive – because they are Guidelines, they are not legally binding on States. Nevertheless, each concerns the potentially oppressive use of law against PLHA and each, in its further elaboration, is categoric and detailed about the ways in which States should avoid using the law in ways that would impact negatively on efforts to minimise onward transmission and the management of the epidemic. As the Commentary on the group of Guidelines of which these two form a part explains, law provides an essential framework for the observance of human rights:

Nevertheless, the role of law in the response to HIV/AIDS may also be over-emphasized and provide a vehicle for coercive and abusive policies. Although law may have an educative and normative role and may provide an important supportive framework for human rights protection and HIV/AIDS programmes, it cannot be relied upon as the only means by which to educate, change attitudes, achieve behavioural change or protect people's rights.

(UNCHR, 1998: 21)

Thus, the Guideline on Public Health Legislation suggests, *inter alia*, that States should ensure that, other than for surveillance and epidemiological purposes, HIV testing should be voluntary and only be carried out with the fully informed consent of the person concerned, that PLHA should not be subjected to isolation, quarantine or detention on the basis of their HIV status alone, that medical records be kept confidential, and that there be no requirement on the part of health-care professionals to inform partners of the HIV positive status of their patients. Where exceptions to these are made, it is affirmed that those exceptions should be necessary, proportionate and in accordance with due process principles. Similarly, the Guideline on Criminal Law and Correctional Systems advocates the review and repeal of laws that criminalise sexual acts between consenting adults (such as adultery, sodomy, fornication and prostitution), the regulation of sex work that does not involve victimisation, the legalised provision of needle and syringe exchange programmes for IDUs, and the appropriate care and surveillance of those in prison (whether HIV positive, or at risk of infection). As for the substantive criminal law the Guideline states that:

> Criminal and/or public health legislation should not include specific offences against the deliberate and intentional transmission of HIV but rather should apply general criminal offences to these exceptional cases. Such application should ensure that the elements of foreseeability, intent, causality and consent are clearly and legally established to support a guilty verdict and/or harsher penalties.[10]

(UNCHR, 1998: 14)

As we shall see in due course, the criminal law of England and Wales complies with the suggestion that there should be no HIV-specific transmission offences, though it is more debatable whether the general principles of liability that do apply have been, and are, sufficiently clearly and legally established to meet the UN Guidelines. What is equally worrying is that there appears to be a lack of commitment to the import and consequences of those Guidelines, at the heart of European politics. In 2006 the Social,

---

10 The argument that there should be no HIV-specific criminal offences, or unique legal treatment of PLHA, reflects other human rights principles such as the right to equal protection before the law, non-discrimination, and the right to liberty and security of the person (see Universal Declaration of Human Rights, Arts 2, 3, 14 and 26; European Convention on Human Rights, Art 14; International Covenant on Civil and Political Rights, Art 9).

Health and Family Affairs Committee of the Council of Europe's Parliamentary Assembly[11] appeared to demonstrate its understanding of the Guidelines when it stated:

> Comprehensive HIV prevention depends on good governance and a supportive legal environment nationally and internationally. The HIV/AIDS pandemic continues to be fuelled by human rights abuses, such as the denial of the right to education about safer sex, violence against sexual minorities and other marginalized groups such as women and children, and mandatory HIV testing. Human rights violations add to the stigmatization of people at highest risk of infection and thus marginalize and drive underground those who need information, preventive services and treatment most desperately. Human rights abuses also follow infection and make it more difficult for people living with HIV and AIDS to prevent further ill health and to protect against onward transmission. National governments *must adopt laws and policies that protect and enforce the human rights* of their citizens as they relate to HIV/AIDS, sexual and reproductive health and rights, gender and international law.
>
> (Council of Europe, 2006 (emphasis in original))

However, the Parliamentary Assembly's Resolution 1536 on HIV/Aids [*sic*][12] in Europe, which was based on the Report included the following statement. Drawing on the Report's recognition of the importance of law in the effective management of the pandemic, the Resolution called upon parliaments, *inter alia*, to:

> 11.1 draw up laws or amend existing legislation to define national standards of protection for those suffering from HIV/Aids [*sic*], especially for people in vulnerable groups, such as women and children,

11 The Parliamentary Assembly of the Council of Europe is an international parliamentary Assembly with a pluralistic composition of democratically elected members of parliament established on the basis of an intergovernmental treaty. The Assembly is one of the two statutory organs of the Council of Europe, which is composed of a Committee of Ministers and an Assembly representing the political forces in its member states. Its influence should not be underestimated in driving policy at the European level. As Andreas Gross, a Swiss member of the Assembly recently explained, its regular meetings and the obligation of the Committee of Ministers to respond to its Resolutions 'created not only in over 200 conventions a genuine pan-European space with a common understanding of human rights, democracy and the rule of law, but also a genuine transnational parliamentary discourse, exchange and learning process, which is able not only to bring legitimacy to transnational law and policy making but is also able to shape directly national legislations and governmental accountability' (Gross, 2006).

12 To use 'Aids' rather than AIDS is problematic because it renders an abbreviation into a noun, thus consolidating and reifying what is a very complex condition.

with particular attention being paid to the situation of anyone having lost a close family member as a result of HIV/Aids;

11.2 review and adjust legislation to ensure that it conforms to the
International Guidelines on HIV/Aids and Human Rights;

11.3 *enact legislation to punish those who wilfully transmit HIV/Aids.*
(Council of Europe, 2007 (my emphasis)).

It is odd, to say the least, that the Resolution could, at one and the same time,
affirm the importance of conformity to the Guidelines and the need for an
HIV specific transmission offence (quite apart from the vagueness of the term
'wilfully', which could be interpreted as both recklessly and intentionally, and
the suggestion that 'HIV/Aids' can be transmitted – which is simply inaccurate). What is clear is that, despite the recognition of the importance of
protecting HIV positive people, that protection is not seen to extend to those
who – in certain circumstances, and with a particular awareness or knowledge
– transmit HIV to others. The problems inherent in criminalising such people
are discussed in far greater detail in the remainder of the book. For now, it is
necessary to set out briefly why a public health law approach may not, despite
its apparent attractiveness as an alternative to criminalisation, be the answer
either.

Public health, public law and the criminalisation of HIV transmission

People accept the general idea that they should protect themselves and
others in their sexual behavior. The norm is out there, and probably
caused rather than resulted from criminal law. The problem for people
with HIV lies in knowing what to do and consistently doing it. Criminalization of sexual behavior does not help people in these two tasks. There
is no good public health reason to treat sexual behavior involving HIV
exposure as a crime, and we think it is very difficult or impossible to do
so fairly.

(Burris *et al*, 2007: 49)

Partly in response to the UN Guidelines, and partly in response to the
increasing number of criminal cases being brought against people for the
transmission of HIV in jurisdictions across the world, UNAIDS commis-
sioned and published *Criminal Law, Public Health and HIV Transmission: A
Policy Options Paper* (UNAIDS, 2002). This Paper, prepared by Richard
Elliott of the Canadian HIV/AIDS Legal Network, sought to identify the
principles and policy considerations that should inform the criminalisation
of HIV exposure and transmission. As a Paper grounded in the work of UN
organisations in the field of HIV/AIDS, it adopted a rights-based approach
and was informed by four basic principles (UNAIDS, 2002: 5):

- the best available scientific evidence regarding modes of HIV transmission and levels of risk must be the basis for rationally determining if, and when, conduct should attract criminal liability;
- preventing the transmission of HIV should be the primary objective and this, rather than any other objective, should guide policy-makers in the area;
- any legal or policy responses to HIV/AIDS, particularly the coercive use of state power, should not only be pragmatic in the overall pursuit of public health but should also conform to international human rights norms, particularly the principles of non-discrimination and of due process;
- state action that infringes on human rights must be adequately justified, such that policy-makers should always undertake an assessment of the impact of law or policy on human rights, and should prefer the 'least intrusive' measures possible to achieve the demonstrably justified objective of preventing disease transmission.

These principles are ones that, self-evidently, ignore – or deny the relevance of – moral or ethical principles as such. There is nothing here which would justify the imposition of criminal liability simply on the basis that the transmission of HIV is, in and of itself, *wrong*, or irresponsible. Rather, the appeal is, on the one hand, to a strongly positivist legal rationality in which laws that lack clear social objectives and a strong, empirically grounded, evidence base cannot be justified; and on the other (somewhat paradoxically) to an ethically informed natural law tradition in which there is something immanently important about treating people, whatever their particular attributes, status and qualities, with dignity and respect. There are, of course, a number of justifications that can be given for using the criminal law against those who infect others, including retribution, deterrence, incapacitation and rehabilitation (Gostin, 1989: 1056; Elliott, 1997; 2002). Here, I want to focus specifically on the relationship between the use of criminal law and the use of public health legislation; for while both of these engage the coercive powers of the state (Sullivan and Field, 1988), the appropriate balance between the two is critical if the law is to serve a socially beneficial, proactive function rather than a purely symbolic, condemnatory, and reactive one.

The relationship between public health law and the HIV/AIDS epidemic is a fraught and enduring one.[13] The principal reason for this is that, whereas sexual health promotion professionals have long advocated an emphasis on voluntarism, individual agency and shared responsibility in combating onward transmission, this approach (measured both by increased prevalence

---

13 For further discussion and analysis see Bayer, 1989; Gostin, 1989. For a more general account see Gostin, 2000. In the context of TB see Coker, 2003; 2006.

and an increase in the rate of infection, at least within some population groups) has not met with unqualified success. As a result, claims that HIV should be treated differently from infectious and contagious diseases – over which those infected have little if any agential control – have been met, at least by those with an eye to the populist majority, with calls to 'get real' and 'get tough'. This reactionary stance, further fuelled by the fact that the principal modes of transmission are sexual activity (particularly anal intercourse) and injection drug use, has ensured that law – with its near-monopoly on the public regulation of moral matters in secular democracies – is seen as a, if not the, critical mechanism for solving the problem which the epidemic represents.

This unreflective approach to the use of public health law in the context of HIV and AIDS is profoundly problematic. Jonathan Mann – one of the most influential figures in the field – was, perhaps, the first person fully to articulate the difficulty. In an influential article (Mann, 1997), he drew attention to the fact that whereas it was legitimate to frame the relationship between individual clinicians and their patients in ethical terms, this was inappropriate when thinking about the health of populations:

> Not surprisingly, medicine has chosen the language of ethics, as ethics has been developed in a context of individual relationships, and is well adapted to the nature, practice, settings, and expectations of medical care. The language of medical ethics has also been applied when medicine seeks to deal with issues such as the organization of medical care or the allocation of societal resources. However, the contribution of medical ethics to these societal issues has been less powerful when compared, for example, with its engagement in the behavior of individual medical practitioners.
>
> (Mann, 1997)

In contrast:

> Public health, at least in its contemporary form, is struggling to define and articulate its core values. In this context, the usefulness of the language and structure of ethics as we know it today has been questioned. Given its population focus, and its interest in the underlying conditions upon which health is predicated (and that these major determinants of health status are societal in nature), it seems evident that a framework which expresses fundamental values in societal terms, and a vocabulary of values which links directly with societal structure and function, may be better adapted to the work of public health than a more individually oriented ethical framework.
>
> (Ibid)

Thus, while it is possible to frame the (legal) obligations of individual clinicians towards PLHA (as regards, for example, medical confidentiality) and the obligations of PLHA towards others within an individualised ethics of care and responsibility, this approach will not necessarily produce beneficial effects at the societal level. So, for example, legal requirements on PLHA to inform sexual partners of their HIV positive status, or the compulsory isolation, detention or quarantine of PLHA may have the unintended (and negative) consequence of reducing the number of people willing to come forward for HIV testing, thereby contributing to increased onward transmission through ignorance, and so to morbidity and mortality.

The point is that, while the criminalisation of conduct that has – or may have – an adverse impact on public health sends out a clear denunciatory message, the use of public health law may, even though it has a different objective, have the same negative consequences. As Larry Gostin has explained:

> Absent evidence that personal control measures change behaviour more effectively than voluntary education and counselling, government cannot justify their use. The behaviors sought to be controlled or punished are highly ingrained, intimate, and deeply human activities. Coercive state action is a particularly crude tool to compel change in these behaviors.
>
> (Gostin, 1989: 1019–20)

It follows from this that the imposition of measures designed to regulate the conduct of people living with PLHA cannot, and should not, be deployed simply because they satisfy the desire of electorates, their representatives, and public officials to 'do something'. As Gostin further explains:

> Compulsory public powers are justified only if they meet the following criteria: there is a significant risk of transmission of the AIDS [sic] virus; the public health response is efficacious in preventing a primary mode of transmission of the virus; the economic, practical or human rights burdens are not disproportionate to the public health burdens; and the public health power is the least restrictive alternative that would prevent viral transmission.
>
> (Gostin, 1989: 1019–20)[14]

Two recent examples, from the European Court of Human Rights and from

---

14 The criteria that Gostin applies here in the context of public health derive from more general internationally accepted human rights law principles: that any departure from a human right (where this is permitted) must be in the pursuit of a legitimate aim, and be necessary, proportionate, and the least restrictive means of achieving that aim. He might also have added that the departure must legally sanctioned, and that the relevant law is clear, certain and non-discriminatory in its application. For further discussion of the limited utility in deploying criminal law in the service of public health see Wolf and Vezina, 2004.

domestic UK public health policy may serve as concrete illustrations both of the tensions that the legitimate objective of controlling the spread of HIV versus the importance of ensuring the human rights protection of PLHA generates, and the extent to which apparently beneficent public health policy may lapse all too easily into the criminalisation of people living with disease. The first example is that of *Enhorn v Sweden*.[15] Mr Enhorn was a Swedish national living with HIV who had infected a young man with the virus during sex. At the time of his diagnosis Mr Enhorn was given instructions, pursuant to the Infectious Diseases Act 1988, as to how he was to conduct himself thereafter. In particular, he:

> was not allowed to have sexual intercourse without first informing his partner about his HIV infection. He was required to use a condom. He was to abstain from consuming such an amount of alcohol that his judgment would thereby be impaired and others put at risk of being infected with HIV. If the applicant was to have a physical examination, an operation, a vaccination or a blood test or was bleeding for any reason, he was obliged to tell the relevant medical staff about his infection. Also, he was to inform his dentist [about it]. Moreover, the applicant was prohibited from giving blood and donating organs or sperm. Finally, he was to visit his consulting physician again and to keep to appointments set up by the county medical officer.[16]

In 1995 the County Administrative Court held that Mr Enhorn was not being compliant with the measures that had been imposed and subjected him to a period of three months' compulsory isolation. This period was subsequently extended to six months and renewed on a rolling basis. While in detention, Mr Enhorn absconded a number of times. In 1999, as the result of further concerns about the risks that he posed to others, the isolation order was again renewed. The final application to detain in late 2001 was refused and Mr Enhorn brought an action against Sweden, alleging that his compulsory isolation was in breach of his right to liberty and security of the person under Art 5(1) of the European Convention on Human Rights.[17] In particular, he argued that his detention under s 38 of the Infectious Diseases Act 1988 was unlawful because its provisions were too vague and imprecise. Although he admitted not attending some of the appointments he had been required to

---

15 *Enhorn v Sweden* (2005) 41 EHRR 633. For an incisive commentary see Martin, 2006.

16 Ibid, at para 9.

17 Art 5(1) provides that 'Everyone has the right to liberty and security of person', and that 'No one shall be deprived of his liberty save in the following cases and in accordance with a procedure prescribed by law'. One such case is, 'the lawful detention of persons for the prevention of the spreading of infectious diseases, of persons of unsound mind, alcoholics or drug addicts, or vagrants'.

keep, there were no grounds upon which it could reasonably be concluded that he posed a 'manifest risk' to others. He also argued that the rolling periods of compulsory isolation were, even if he did pose a risk, a disproportionate response to that risk. The European Court of Human Rights, in its judgment, held that while Mr Enhorn's isolation did have basis in Swedish law, it was important that such isolation should have been necessary for it to be lawful. In so holding the Court stated that:

> the essential criteria when assessing the 'lawfulness' of the detention of a person 'for the prevention of the spreading of infectious diseases' are whether the spreading of the infectious disease is dangerous for public health or safety, and whether detention of the person infected is the last resort in order to prevent the spreading of the disease, because less severe measures have been considered and found to be insufficient to safeguard the public interest. When these criteria are no longer fulfilled, the basis for the deprivation of liberty ceases to exist.
>
> (Para 44)

Although HIV was an infectious disease that posed a threat to public safety, the Court held that the seven-year period of compulsory isolation, notwithstanding the times that Mr Enhorn had absconded during that period, was – because of the failure to consider other possible measures – not the last resort. Furthermore:

> the authorities failed to strike a fair balance between the need to ensure that the HIV virus did not spread and the applicant's right to liberty.
>
> (Para. 55)

There was thus a violation of Art 5(1).

The decision in *Enhorn v Sweden* is not one that makes it unlawful for signatory states to the Convention to impose restrictions on the liberty of those who pose a risk of spreading disease. Indeed, Art 5 expressly allows for such restrictions (see above, n 17). It does, however, make it clear that they must respect fundamental human rights principles: that the default position is liberty of the subject – whatever his disease status – and that the burden is on the state to justify in accordance with those principles any limitations that it may wish to impose.

It is this aspect of the decision that is of particular relevance to the second example I wish to discuss – the UK Government's proposals on the reform of the Public Health (Control of Disease) Act 1984 (PH(CD)A 1984). This Act, which despite its date is an amalgam of earlier legislation and therefore not as contemporary as it might seem, is complex and incoherent. It is for this reason that the Department of Health has, at the time of writing, put out to consultation a set of suggestions as to how it might best be reformed

(Department of Health, 2007). The Consultation document, while stressing that the vast majority of treatment and prevention work is undertaken by a National Health Service that is accessed by a large number of people voluntarily, explains that some people infected with an infectious disease may pose problems if their behaviour places others at risk of infection. In those cases where a voluntary approach is not adopted by such people it is necessary, in order to protect those others, to use coercive powers. As the law currently stands, those powers may be exercised (by means of a Magistrates' Court Order) in relation to notifiable diseases[18] so as to require a person's medical examination,[19] and their removal to,[20] and detention in,[21] hospital. Although HIV is not included in the list of notifiable diseases to which the Act applies, the Public Health (Infectious Diseases) Regulations 1988[22] provide that the same powers may be exercised in relation to those with AIDS. In other words, the fact that someone is HIV positive is insufficient to allow the powers to be deployed.

It would be foolhardy to dispute that the PH(CD)A 1984 is in need of reform. As a piece of consolidating legislation it contains many anachronistic provisions that reflect a nineteenth-century understanding of diseases and their modes of transmission. The powers it contains tend to focus on infectious diseases over whose transmission an infected person can exercise little or no control; and, given its origins, the Act does not reflect on its face more recent concerns about data protection, medical confidentiality and – more generally – human rights.[23] Equally importantly, the Act manifests the Victorian legislator's obsession with the particular, and with tightly circumscribed executive powers. Rather than adopting an 'all-hazards' approach (by referring generically to 'infectious disease') it deals with specific diseases, and rather than allowing a Minister the power to deal with novel problems as they arise through the promulgation of regulations, it specifies in relatively narrow detail the powers that he has and so constrains the potential for government action in the face of changed circumstance.

In the light of these, and other difficulties, the Consultation Paper makes a number of recommendations for modernisation. Most critically, for the purposes of the present discussion, it proposes the repeal of Part II of the Act, to be replaced by:

18 S 10 of the PH(CD)A 1984 sets out the notifiable diseases as being cholera, plague, relapsing fever, smallpox and typhus.
19 S 35 PH(CD)A 1984.
20 S 37 PH(CD)A 1984.
21 S 38 PH(CD)A 1984.
22 SI 1988/1546.
23 In this context human rights relate especially to the right to respect for private life (Art 8), freedom of liberty and security of the person (Art 5), the right to freedom of association (Art 11) and the right to non-discrimination (Art 14).

some specific powers in primary legislation to require action of individuals (for example, that they undergo medical examination or stay in quarantine). The primary legislation would include some powers for the Secretary of State to make regulations in connection with the use of these powers; and

a general regulation-making power for the purposes of making provision to prevent, protect against, control, and provide a public health response to, the spread of disease. Regulations under this power would be of a more general nature, unlike the specific powers.

(Department of Health, 2007: 3.1)

The Consultation Paper is alive to the importance of respect for human rights ibid: 3.5),[24] due process (ibid: 4.3–4.4), and the need to keep narrow the contexts in which action may be taken (ibid: 4.9). However, this principled stance is arguably undermined elsewhere in relation to the circumstances in which magistrates would be able to make orders. For example, the Paper rightly acknowledges that because the PH(CD)A 1984 provides for the making of orders where a person is suffering from a disease, this is inconsistent with the objectives of a legislative regime that is intended to prevent onward transmission (for the simple reason that people may be infectious without showing symptoms of the disease caused by their infection). Its suggested remedy, logically enough, is that:

. . . it should be possible for a justice of the peace to order actions not, as now, only where a person is suffering from a disease, but where a person poses, or may pose, a risk of infecting or contaminating others.

(Ibid: 5.7)

Furthermore:

Other things being equal, the arguments for using the power are likely to be stronger where a person is known to pose an *immediate* risk to others. But there could be cases where use of the power might be justified even if there is no immediate risk to others, or even no certainty that there will be a risk to others in future.

(Ibid: 5.7)

---

24 The same is true of other Department of Health policy documents. For example, its national strategy for sexual health states its guiding principle to be that 'Sexual health is an important part of physical and mental health. It is a key part of our identity as human beings together with the fundamental human rights to privacy, a family life and living free from discrimination. Essential elements of good sexual health are equitable relationships and sexual fulfilment with access to information and services to avoid the risk of unintended pregnancy, illness or disease.' (Department of Health, 2001: para 1.2)

This approach self-evidently widens the potential use of coercive powers considerably. It would mean, for example, that an HIV positive person could forcibly be removed to, and detained in, a hospital on the basis that he may pose a risk of infecting another person, even if there is no evidence whatsoever upon which to base that assessment. The issue here is not – at one level – whether the exercise of such a power is likely or probable in the case of a person living with HIV (as opposed to the case of a person infected with a highly contagious disease), but rather the fact that such an approach could ever be contemplated as a matter of principle in respect of HIV infection. For what this approach demonstrates is precisely the slippery-slope implicit in the warnings of Larry Gostin, Michael Kirby and others. It is an approach that, on its face and despite the nod to human rights, ignores the fact that sexual health is matter of shared responsibility. It is an approach that constructs the person with disease, whatever their infectiousness, their state of mind, or their behaviour, as the appropriate target of coercive intervention. Nowhere in the Paper (and I recognise that it is a Consultation that is general in scope and purpose) is there any acknowledgement of the fact that some people may voluntarily expose themselves to the risk of infection or disease, or be prepared to run that risk. More immediately, some HIV negative people want, and practise, risky sex. Such people are not only an irrelevance within a model of public health that identifies diseased people as the responsible agents, the legitimate focus, and the object of power – they are, quite literally, invisible.

The Consultation Paper does not, however, stop there. It further proposes that existing criminal offences within the PH(CD)A 1984, which are specific, out-dated and fail to reflect contemporary understanding of the nature of disease transmission, should be repealed. In their place two more general offences should be introduced, of:

> knowingly or recklessly putting others at risk of infection or contamination contrary to provisions made in or under the Act; and
>
> failing to comply with a requirement created in or under the Act (for example, failing to comply with directions under an order by a justice of the peace to observe home quarantine, or with a requirement in regulations to provide information in certain circumstances).
>
> (Ibid: 8.3)

In addition:

> there would be a power in secondary legislation to make further detailed provision in relation to these offences: for example, to identify behaviours that would count as putting others at risk for the purpose of the first offence.
>
> (Ibid)

If enacted these provisions could, for example, criminalise HIV positive people merely for having unprotected sex with an HIV negative person or (theoretically) for leaving their homes if they had been ordered to remain there. It is not just that the first offence would, at a stroke, introduce exposure liability (where none in English law currently exists), and (arguably) further extend liability by criminalising those positive people who merely know their status – as opposed to those who are aware of the risk of transmission; it is the proposal for a power to determine the conduct that would attract liability that is of equal concern. It is not, for example, inconceivable that HIV positive gay men could be required not to frequent saunas, or other places where they may meet to have sex, or be required to disclose their HIV status to existing or potential partners.

Some will no doubt suggest that these possibilities are fanciful; and, further, that these are merely recommendations that are not even elements of a bill, *let alone* an Act of Parliament. But this, I think, is beside the point. Apart from the fact that the financial penalties which the Consultation Paper proposes[25] will be beyond the means of many people living with HIV (and whom, it may be supposed, could be sent to prison for default in payment), what is worrying is the underlying policy logic behind the proposals, at least so far as they would apply to HIV positive people. That logic, which one must assume is indicative of current Department of Health and hence government policy, is one informed by risk-management, dangerous populations, and a technocratic faith in the power of law effectively to regulate human behaviour.[26] The Consultation Paper asks for the views of those with expertise and an interest in the subject; but there is no apparent evidence base for the proposals. Ignoring, it would seem, the UNAIDS position that any legislative proposals regarding HIV (or here, proposals that could well apply to HIV) should be based on the best scientific evidence, and that they should be the least intrusive possible consistent with the goal of securing public health and minimising onward transmission (which was the view of the European Court of Human Rights in *Enhorn*), the Consultation Paper's recommendations assert the importance of respecting human rights while providing the state with every possible means of ignoring or diminishing them.

It remains to be seen, at the time of writing, whether the proposals contained within the Consultation Paper ever reach the statute book; but whether they do or not, what remains clear is that there exists, at the heart of current government policy, the view that those who are suffering from a transmissible disease are legitimate objects of state regulation. That may be

25 The Paper proposes a maximum fine of £5,000 on conviction in a magistrates' court. If the level of custodial sentencing that the Crown Court has imposed on people for reckless transmission is any guide (see below, Ch 4, n 45) it is not unreasonable to believe that knowing or wilful exposure would attract fines at the top end.

26 The importance of risk discourse is explored further in Ch 4.

so, and in itself is a perfectly defensible position; but an approach to public health which deploys law in a way that allows both for the isolation and detention of people in the absence of any evidence of the risk that they pose to others and simply on the basis of some hypothetical risk, and for the criminalisation of those who are the targets of that is arguably a very different matter indeed. The core problem is that it is an approach which – in the context of HIV prevention at least – not only fails to reflect the lived experience of PLHA, but ignores evidence-based policy developments. To give a concrete example: while it may seem logical and justifiable, on public health grounds, to impose a legal obligation on people to disclose their known HIV positive status to prospective sexual partners, or (as a deterrent) to impose substantial fines on those who expose others to the risk of infection, such measures would be based on (i) a misunderstanding of the dynamics of, and barriers to, disclosure, (ii) a (false) assumption about the correlation between disclosure and safer sex, and – more generally (iii) a model that identifies PLHA as the only participants in a potentially risky encounter who bear any responsibility for the risk-taking itself or for any unwanted consequences that ensue. The points are critically important, and are developed in more detail later in the book.[27] For now, I want to return to liability for transmission itself and to provide an account of the recent legal and policy background to the cases that have been brought.

Criminal liability for HIV transmission: the legal and policy background

In February 1998 the Home Office published *Violence: Reforming the Offences Against the Person Act 1861* (Home Office, 1998). The purpose of this Consultation Document was to set out, and invite comments on, the Government's proposals for the reform of what it referred to as 'out-moded and unclear Victorian legislation' (Home Office, 1998: 3) and was based on the proposals put forward five years earlier by the Law Commission (Law Commission, 1993). The fact that the Government had taken the initiative in this area of the law so soon after coming to power in 1997 reflected the view, widely shared in the professional and academic legal communities, that after 137 years the OAPA 1861 (itself an Act which consolidated even earlier legislation) was archaic, unclear and unable to deal effectively with contemporary manifestations of violent behaviour. True to its concern with presenting itself as committed to efficiency in the public sector, the Government also emphasised the fact the lack of clarity in the existing legislation gave rise to 'unnecessary and expensive appeals arising from wrong decisions on questions of law' (Home Office, 1998: 6).

27 See, especially, Ch 5.

Although it praised the Law Commission's work in this area, and was particularly positive about its attempts to provide a 'clearer and more coherent statement of the law',[28] the Government did not accept the Commission's reform recommendations wholesale. Nowhere was this more apparent than in the area of criminal liability for the transmission of disease. The Law Commission's 1993 Report had been unequivocal in its view that the OAPA 1861 could be used to prosecute alleged cases of transmission. It had also recommended that the new offences proposed in the Draft Bill should enable the prosecution and conviction of those who transmitted disease whether serious or not, provided that the fault requirements (of intention or recklessness) were satisfied. The Government was resistant to such an inclusive approach. Critical of the Law Commission's view that only 'appropriate' cases would be prosecuted (such appropriateness to be determined by the Crown Prosecution Service (CPS)), the Home Office's view was that – so far as 'normally minor illnesses such as measles or mumps' was concerned – it would be wrong 'to make the range of normal everyday activities during which illness could be transmitted potentially criminal' (Home Office, 1998: para 3.15). As for the transmission of more serious diseases, the Government explained its concerns in the following terms:

> An issue of this importance has ramifications beyond the criminal law, into the wider considerations of social and public health policy. The Government is particularly concerned that the law should not seem to discriminate against those who are HIV positive, have AIDS, or viral hepatitis or who carry any kind of disease. Nor do we want to discourage people coming forward for diagnostic tests and treatment, in the interests of their own health and that of others, because of an unfounded fear of criminal prosecution.
>
> (Home Office, 1998: para 3.16)

The Government's welcome recognition that the issue of criminalising disease transmission was one that had to be situated within a broader policy framework did not, however, prevent it from concluding that those who transmit serious disease to others intending them to suffer serious harm should face the prospect of a criminal conviction. Such people, the perpetrators of 'evil acts', could, by virtue of the mental state accompanying their actions, legitimately be distinguished from others for whom criminalisation was not justified. For the Government, this distinction was one that aimed:

> . . . to strike a sensible balance between allowing very serious intentional acts to be punished whilst not rendering individuals liable for prosecution

---

28 Hansard Written Answers 31 Jul 1997, col 578(HC) (Rt Hon Jack Straw MP).

for unintentional or reckless acts, or for the transmission of minor disease.

(Home Office, 1998: para 3.18)

What, then, was the thinking behind this 'sensible balance'? On the face of it, the language of 'evil' deployed in the Consultation Document might be thought of as an effective political ploy. Within the context of a public document, it allowed the Government to condemn and censure a morally distinct category of bad people intent on wilfully harming others and so forestall any populist criticism that it was being 'soft' on crime. Furthermore, it was a distinction that enabled it to deflect attention from those (no doubt far more numerous) individuals whose conduct might produce the same consequence, the same kind and degree of harm, but whose behaviour was better categorised as careless or thoughtless and whose criminalisation would be against both their own, and the wider public's, best interests.

This is an interpretation that is certainly borne out in contemporary correspondence between the Home Office and the All Party Parliamentary Group on AIDS (the APPGA). The Chairman of the APPGA, Neil Gerrard MP, had, since the autumn of 1997, been in correspondence with the then Home Secretary, Jack Straw MP, and his ministerial team. In that correspondence he had emphasised the negative public health impact which criminalising HIV transmission could have, and urged the Government not to pursue a policy that might have this effect. In the first of a number of letters on this topic Mr Gerrard wrote to Mr Straw in the following terms:

I would be very concerned at any proposals to criminalise the transmission of HIV. Clearly one wants people to behave responsibly and every encouragement should be given to people to do so. What I very much fear is that if there were any criminalisation of transmission of disease, this would inevitably deter some people from having tests. It would obviously be difficult to prove intentional transmission of a disease if the person concerned could deny any knowledge that they themselves [sic] were infected and in the case of HIV, where no symptoms may be shown for a considerable period of time, it might well dissuade people who may well be at risk from having tests. The result could well be more infection rather than less, which is obviously the complete opposite of one of the effects that a change in the law might be intended to produce. There is also the aspect with HIV, unlike some other infectious diseases, the stigma of prejudice which is still attached and which undoubtedly has an effect on very many people.[29]

---

29 Excerpt of letter from Neil Gerrard MP to Jack Straw MP, October 22, 1997.

In his reply, the Home Secretary emphasised that the Government's concern with the criminal law's application in cases of disease transmission was not an opportunistic response to the Jeanette Pink case,[30] but was part of a genuine desire to reform the law concerning non-fatal offences. He was also sympathetic to the concerns which Mr Gerrard's letter raised. In his words:

> We have considered this issue most carefully, from what ought to be in the criminal law to what the requirements of public health policy are, and hence what we think would be appropriate. Our conclusion is that it is important to enable the most culpable behaviour to be capable of prosecution . . . A reform of the law on violence should never inadvertently cause infection to go untreated because of misconceptions about the law.[31]

The substance of Jack Straw's letter was reiterated, even more forcefully, in a subsequent letter from Alun Michael MP, Minister of State at the Home Office, which accompanied the copy of the Consultation Document sent on its publication to Neil Gerrard:

> In reforming and clarifying the law we have been at pains to ensure that our proposals are directed at genuinely blameworthy behaviour. That is why we are proposing that only the intentional transmission of disease that causes serious injury should fall within the criminal law, not as a separate offence but as part of a broad offence of intentionally causing serious injury. It would be wrong for the law to ignore the transmission of a disease as a potential weapon. That would mean if a serious incident occurred there would be no remedy and evil people could get away with wicked acts. The law must be able to deal with genuinely evil behaviour – spreading anthrax, or infecting jars of baby food with salmonella as well as more direct means of transmission. Nor should illness be excluded simply because it was sexually transmitted. That too would leave an unacceptable gap in the law. Our proposal that the deliberate transmission of an illness that causes serious injury should be an offence is not new: it clarifies and limits the present law. People who are, or think they may be, HIV positive would be at less risk of prosecution than they are at present.[32]

It appears from this correspondence, and from Mr Straw's minuted evidence

---

30 Jeanette Pink (who was living in Cyprus at the time) was the first reported Briton to be infected by a person who was subsequently convicted for an offence relating to the transmission. For discussion see Weait, 2001.
31 Excerpt of letter from Jack Straw MP to Neil Gerrard MP, December 22, 1997.
32 Excerpt of letter from Alun Michael MP to Neil Gerrard MP, undated, 1998.

at the meeting convened by the APPGA to discuss the Home Office proposals, that the Government had, in 1998, a very clear view both of what the scope of the criminal law should be and why that scope should be a narrow one. This position can in part be explained by the Government's understanding, presumably the result of legal advice, that it simply was not possible – under the criminal law as it then was – to criminalise the reckless transmission of disease. In this they were no doubt correct, since it was not until the decision in *R v Ireland; R v Burstow*[33] that a person could be convicted under s 20 of the OAPA 1861 for harming someone in the absence of an assault (an infliction of force that viral transmission did not represent).[34] But, as is evident in the correspondence quoted above, the Government's position was not simply based on the law as it stood – it was one that affirmed (for reasons set out earlier in this chapter) the potentially negative public health consequences of extending liability beyond those who intentionally infected others.

For those of us who were actively involved in the discussions that resulted in the Consultation Paper,[35] this seemed a significant victory – one which suggested that the Government was prepared to listen to reason and to the voice of expert HIV community organisations. In the event, though, it was no victory. Not only did the Government decide not to modernise the OAPA 1861 (a Bill was never put before Parliament), it retreated from its principled position on liability for disease transmission. In reply to a letter from the Chair of the UK Coalition which had expressed concern over the prosecutions that had taken place despite the Government's assurances, the Home Office acknowledged that new legislation had been promised but regretted that it had not yet been possible to find parliamentary time. The letter continued:

> We of course continue to support the position that we do not wish to discriminate against people with diseases of any sort, and we would not want the criminal law to have the effect of discouraging people from coming forward for vital diagnostic tests and treatment. We are also aware of the sensitivities where the criminal law covers any sexual activity. As one of our consultees put it, sexual acts should not be treated as acts done by one person to another, but as acts done together. This is a

---

33 [1998] AC 147.
34 See further below, Ch 3.
35 I was, at the time, a volunteer with the Terrence Higgins Trust. As a member of its Legal Services Group I attended meetings with the Department of Health and the Home Office and gave evidence to an All-Party Parliamentary Group on AIDS meeting at which the Home Secretary (Jack Straw MP) also spoke. The Terrence Higgins Trust, along with other groups including the UK Coalition, had been lobbying against criminalising the reckless transmission of HIV.

cogent argument for suggesting that the law should not interfere in sexual acts between consenting adults in private.

But the question of disease transmission does raise other issues. There is a degree of individual responsibility required in dealing with serious transmissible diseases. And the law should reflect this. It needs to balance protecting individuals from being prosecuted for acts which were unavoidable or excusable, and protecting others from avoidable spread of disease. This is clearly a difficult balance to maintain.[36]

The Government had evidently decided, in light of the successful prosecutions so far initiated by the CPS, that the balance the courts had established was the right one and should not be disturbed. Furthermore, not only were the degrees of harm and fault high ones to establish when bringing a case under s 20 (thus providing a degree of protection for potential defendants), but the absence of informed consent to the risk of transmission in the cases that had been brought showed that the criminal law could be justified where mere recklessness was established. In the words of the Home Office:

All these are very sensitive issues, and it is important that we do not hastily change the law in ways which may have unforeseen and undesirable consequences.[37]

The Government's change of position on the criminalisation of HIV transmission was, thus, one led by the judiciary. It no doubt thought (and in this they would surely have been correct) that actively to legislate so as to make it impossible to prosecute the kind of cases that, by then, were subject to widespread and condemnatory media coverage, would have been politically impossible. A failure to seize the legislative initiative and to emphasise the importance of prioritising public health concerns resulted in judicial ownership of the principles that should apply in cases of reckless HIV transmission. Consequently those principles were ones informed not by public health considerations but by the criminal law's dominant logic of individual moral responsibility.[38] It is true that the Sexual Health Independent Advisory Group (SHIAG) established a sub-group to consider the issues that the cases raised, and that the CPS set up a consultation process to establish the policy which should be applied when deciding which cases of alleged transmission

36 Extract from a letter dated May 23, 2005 from the Home Office to Bernard Forbes, Chair of the UK Coalition

37 Ibid.

38 The Court of Appeal did give leave for a number of HIV organisations to intervene on the public health issues when it granted leave to appeal to the House of Lords in the case of Mohammed Dica – but the House of Lords refused to hear the appeal, and so the arguments were never heard.

to pursue; but to date (May 2007) SHIAG's deliberations have produced no change in policy, and – despite being set up in 2005, the CPS has still not determined what that policy should be.

Criminal HIV transmission cases in the UK (to May 2007)[39]

That, then, is the context within which the criminalisation of HIV transmission has taken place. In subsequent chapters we will engage with the many of the issues touched on here in more detail. Before going any further, however, it will be useful to get a sense of the kinds of cases that have been brought, and the popular reaction to them. This is not, after all, a book about a theory – it is a book about real people.

To date, 14 people have been tried for, or pleaded guilty to, charges relating to the transmission of HIV in the United Kingdom. In all cases the charges have related to transmission, or alleged transmission, that occurred in the context of sexual intercourse. The following is a brief summary of each.

England and Wales

Mohammed Dica (November 2003/March 2004)

Mohammed Dica was an HIV positive man of Kenyan origin, living in the UK with refugee status. Married with children, he was initially prosecuted under s 20 of the Offences Against the Person Act 1861 (OAPA 1861) for having infected two female partners with HIV. He was convicted on both counts in November 2003 and sentenced to a total of eight years' imprisonment. Mr Dica appealed against his conviction on the basis that the judge had been wrong as a matter of law in refusing to allow his defence (that his partners had consented to the risk of transmission) to be considered by the jury. He did not deny that he had failed to disclose his HIV status to those partners. The Court of Appeal quashed the conviction and ordered a retrial.[40] It held that a distinction had to be drawn between consenting to the deliberate infliction of actual or serious bodily harm (which may not operate as a defence, other than in certain limited contexts such as recognised contact sports), and consenting to the risk of such harm (which may be raised as a defence). In so holding, the Court indicated that risk-taking of this kind was not something that it could, or should, outlaw – and that if it was felt

---

39 I have been assisted in compiling this list by Catherine Dodds. For a discussion of the cases up to its date of publication, see the Report produced by Sigma Research (Dodds *et al*, 2005).
40 *R v Dica* [2004] 2 Cr App R 28.

appropriate to change the law this was a matter for Parliament. It also held that for a person to be reckless for the purpose of a charge under s 20 where HIV transmission was involved it was necessary that the defendant should have known his HIV positive status at the relevant time. (In other words, a person who merely thought he might be HIV positive could not be legally reckless in this context.) After two abortive retrials, Mr Dica was finally convicted on one charge of recklessly inflicting serious bodily harm on one complainant and sentenced to four and a half years' immediate imprisonment.

Such was the significance of Mr Dica's conviction that leave was sought to appeal against the Court of Appeal judgment to the House of Lords. The Court of Appeal certified the point of law to be one of public importance, but the House of Lords refused to hear the case.

Kouassi Adaye (January 2004)

The details of Kouassi Adaye's conviction are sketchy. A male asylum-seeker living in Liverpool, thought to have originated from the Ivory Coast and with a wife in South Africa, Mr Adaye pleaded guilty in January 2004 to recklessly inflicting serious bodily harm by infecting a female partner with HIV. He also pleaded guilty to a number of fraud charges and one of bigamy. Newspaper reports at the time suggested that Mr Adaye's wife had, prior to his arrest and prosecution, informed him of her own HIV positive status, though this was never confirmed. Mr Adaye's 'knowledge' of his HIV positive status was never, it seems, confirmed by independent clinical diagnosis and to the extent that his plea of guilty to reckless transmission is concerned, it would appear that the judge was satisfied that he should have known his status on the basis of a recommendation to test that he had received from a doctor. In sentencing Mr Adaye the judge stated: 'you pleaded guilty on the basis you were reckless and did not intend to inflict this harm. It is recklessness of the highest possible degree . . . you went on and had unprotected sexual intercourse with this lady and you knew it was highly likely, if not certain, that you were HIV positive . . . I cannot imagine a greater degree of grievous bodily harm than infecting a person with a virus of this nature.' (BBC, 2004)

Feston Konzani (May 2004)

Feston Konzani was a Malawian national who had lived in the UK since 1998. He was convicted in May 2004 for recklessly transmitting HIV to three female sexual partners and sentenced to 10 years' immediate imprisonment. At trial he had argued that his partners' willingness to have unprotected sex equated to consent to the risk of transmission. He appealed against his conviction on the basis that the trial judge had misdirected the jury as to the meaning of consent. The Court of Appeal upheld the conviction.[41] In doing so, it agreed with the trial judge's conclusion that there was a difference between merely running a risk and consenting to a risk. The latter, if it was to operate as a defence recognised at law, had to be 'willing' and 'conscious'. In the absence of disclosure of known HIV status it was extremely unlikely (although not impossible) that a person would consent to the risk of transmission, and difficult for a defendant to argue that he *honestly believed* that there was such consent – which may also operate as a defence – because non-disclosure was incongruous with honesty. Feston Konzani's trial is discussed in detail in Chapter 2.

Paolo Matias (April 2005)

Paolo Matias was a Portuguese national who pleaded guilty to recklessly transmitting HIV to a female sexual partner in April 2005. He was sentenced to three years' imprisonment, but died before completing his term. Reporting on his death, the *Daily Mirror* commented, under the headline, 'Death of jailed HIV sex fiend':

> A man jailed for knowingly infecting his victim with HIV died before serving his full sentence, an inquest heard yesterday. Paolo Matias died at a Leicester hospice in January, nine months into a three-year prison term. The 38-year-old former soldier from Portugal had unprotected sex with the woman in 2002, despite being diagnosed with HIV on his arrival in the UK. Matias's victim was a grandmother in her 50s. He admitted biological GBH in April 2005 and his conviction was one of the first of its kind in the UK. The Leicester inquest heard Matias probably caught the virus injecting hard drugs in Portugal. He died from complications caused by HIV and Hepatitis C cirrhosis of the liver. Death by natural causes was recorded.
>
> (*Daily Mirror*, 2006)

Inaccurate and emotive reporting ('knowingly infecting' and 'biological GBH') has been a feature of many of the cases.

Anonymous female (July 2005)

In July 2005 a 20-year-old Welsh woman pleaded guilty to recklessly infecting her former male partner two years earlier. This was the first successful conviction in England and Wales of a woman for this offence, and she was sentenced to two years' youth custody. As with many of the other cases, it

41 *R v Konzani* [2005] 2 Cr App R 198.

was widely misreported that the woman had 'deliberately' or 'knowingly' infected her partner. As Edwin Bernard of the National AIDS Manual explains:

> The couple met in a nightclub in September 2002 when they were both 18 years old, and began a relationship. Condoms were used at first, but soon after they began living together, the couple began having unprotected sex, apparently in an attempt to conceive, according to a report in *The Sun*.
>
> The young woman tested HIV antibody positive in June 2003, but at the time did not disclose this to her boyfriend. The court heard she did not tell him because she feared that if she did, he would leave her. 'I just didn't want to believe I had HIV,' the young woman said in a letter to the court that was widely reported. 'I know I hurt you but I didn't know how to tell you. I just hoped and prayed you wouldn't catch it. I know it was a horrible thing to do.'
>
> (Bernard, 2005)

Sentencing the woman (who, to date, remains the youngest person to have been convicted for this offence) the judge is reported to have said:

> You never told your boyfriend and as a result he is now HIV-positive. You even sought to mislead him. His health is now devastated for life. In my judgement what you did to that man is so serious that only a custodial sentence can be justified. It is plain that no sentence I can impose will restore the health of that man, but I must impose a sentence which brings home to people the seriousness of this type of offence.
>
> (Ibid)

Derek Hornett (December 2005)

Derek Hornett pleaded guilty to recklessly transmitting HIV to an 82-year-old woman and was sentenced to three years and three months' imprisonment in December 2005. He was also made subject of a Sexual Offences Prevention Order[42], the effect of which was to ban him from associating, or working, with people over the age of 60. Sentencing Hornett, the judge stated:

> You were HIV positive. You knew that full well. Quite regardless of that knowledge you have infected this lady and that for her has had devastating mental and physical consequences.
>
> (BBC, 2005)

---

42 Such Orders are made under s 104 Sexual Offences Act 2003.

Sarah Porter (June 2006)

Sarah Porter was the second woman to be convicted of recklessly transmitting HIV. She pleaded guilty, and was sentenced to 32 months' imprisonment in June 2006. Porter's case was unusual, in that the man who originally made a complaint against her was not, in fact, infected by her. It was a result of enquiries that the police made following the complaint that an ex-partner discovered he was HIV positive, and it was in respect of this that the charge was brought. Speaking to the media about the case, the detective in charge of the investigation 'appealed for others to contact police if they thought they had been a sexual partner of the single mother from Kennington, south London' (Fenton, 2006). Commenting on the case and the police's approach, Deborah Jack, Chief Executive of the National AIDS Trust, commented:

> The prospect of the police investigating the sexual history of people living with HIV in this speculative way is profoundly stigmatising, and appears to treat everyone with HIV as a potential criminal. We seem to be back in the bad old days at the beginning of the epidemic when HIV had to be someone's fault. With only 46 per cent of people in 2005 always using a condom with a new sexual partner, it is time we stopped condemning some people living with HIV for majority behaviour. We must reassert the need for everyone to take responsibility for their own sexual health instead of instinctively trying to blame someone else.
>
> (Carter, 2006a)

Sarah Porter's case, which is discussed in more detail in Chapter 4, provoked a great deal of discussion and was subject to much sensationalist reporting. The *Daily Mail*'s headline to its on-line coverage was 'HIV test anguish for dozens of men after jailing of Aids [*sic*] attacker' (Sears and McIntyre, 2006). In a more measured response, Hannah Pool – writing in *The Guardian* – commented (under the banner, 'Porter's real crime: she slept with black men'):

> Porter has been vilified: she is the ultimate red-top baddie, given the kind of treatment usually reserved for child killers and paedophiles. The reporting of her character is strikingly one-dimensional: she is 'Pure Evil' (the Daily Mail), a 'Bitter Blonde' (the Sun), and a 'Heartless Blonde Maneater' (the Express). The subtext of her depiction is that she is a promiscuous white woman who has fallen so low as to sleep with black men; the implication being that her HIV status is also a punishment.
>
> (Pool, 2006)

Pool concluded:

Being HIV-positive is not in itself a criminal offence. Neither is promiscuity, whatever the motivation. The fact is that had any of the men Porter is reported to have had unprotected sex with insisted on taking safe-sex precautions, they would have much less to worry about. They, too, had the sex, remember.

Yes, she concealed the truth from her partner, but she's not being vilified for that. Her real crime is that she is an attractive woman who unleashed her diseased self upon helpless men. In fact, forget Ruth Ellis; in the tradition of folk demons and moral panics, this is more a case of Mary Mallon – otherwise known as Typhoid Mary.[43]

(Ibid)

Mark James (August 2006)

Mark James, who was sentenced to 40 months' imprisonment in August 2006, was the first gay man to be convicted for recklessly transmitting HIV to a partner. His case was complicated by the fact that he sought to change his guilty plea to one of not guilty, on the basis that there was insufficient proof that he was the cause of his partner's infection. The trial judge refused to accept the change of plea, and Mr James failed to attend court for sentencing, which had been deferred. A warrant was issued for his arrest, although at the time of writing he was still at large. The sentence given in this case was in line with that given in cases involving reckless heterosexual transmission, suggesting that the courts will not treat 'gay cases' any differently. (Carter, 2006b).

Matthew Collins (August 2006)

Matthew Collins, the second gay man to be charged with reckless transmission, was also the first person in the UK to be acquitted at trial. Unlike the earlier cases in which a not guilty plea had been entered, in which the defendants had argued that their respective partners had consented to the risk of transmission, Mr Collins' defence was that there was insufficient proof that he was the cause of the complainant's infection. (There was evidence before the court that the complainant had been sexually active with other men, some of whom were HIV positive.) A crucial determinant of his acquittal, which was directed by the judge, was the evidence of an expert virologist, Dr Anna-Maria Geretti. When called to say whether, in her opinion, Mr Collins was the source of the complainant's infection Dr Geretti indicated that on the

---

43 'Typhoid Mary' was the popular name given to Mary Mallon (1869–1938), an American woman who was the first person to be identified as a healthy carrier of the disease. A cook, who refused to acknowledge her responsibility for infecting 47 people – three of whom died – she died in quarantine. See, further, Bourdain, 2001.

basis of the evidence before her it was not possible to say. That evidence, based on phylogenetic analysis of the HIV in the defendant's and complainant's bodies, could not – without more – indicate the source, route or timing of transmission (each of which is critical if the prosecution is to establish liability under s 20 of the OAPA 1861 in HIV transmission cases) (O'Connor, 2006; Williams, 2006). The role of phylogenetic analysis is considered in greater detail in Chapter 3.

Clive Rowlands (September 2006)

Clive Rowlands pleaded guilty to recklessly infecting a female partner, who had psychiatric problems, in September 2006. Mr Rowlands' counsel told the court that his client was in denial about his HIV status as the result of post-traumatic stress disorder he had developed after being a soldier in Bosnia. This did not impress the judge who, when sentencing Mr Rowlands told him: 'It is absolutely no excuse for the arrogant selfishness you displayed years later.' As for the complainant's family's reaction, her brother is reported to have said, 'It was a low, callous and dirty trick. It's his time to suffer now in jail. We hope he goes through hell.' (Traynor and Roughley, 2006.)

Anonymous man (January 2007)

A man of Zimbabwean origin, who was not identified for legal reasons, was sentenced to 36 months' imprisonment in January 2007 after pleading guilty to recklessly infecting a female partner. The man, who discovered that he was HIV positive in 2000, had lied about his status and pressured his partner into having unprotected sex. It appears that the man pleaded guilty in the absence of phylogenetic analysis evidence to support the other evidence brought by the prosecution. (Bernard, 2007).

Scotland

Stephen Kelly (February 2001)

Stephen Kelly was the first person in the United Kingdom to be convicted of an offence related to HIV transmission. Mr Kelly had been infected with HIV while an inmate at Glenochil prison in Scotland in the early 1990s as the result of sharing injection drug equipment with other prisoners (see, generally, Yirrel et al, 1997). On his release, Mr Kelly had a sexual relationship with a female partner, during which HIV was transmitted to her (Bird and Leigh Brown, 2001). At his trial for recklessly causing injury, his partner gave evidence that she had been aware of Mr Kelly's history of imprisonment and injection drug use, but that he had denied being infected with HIV when asked. Mr Kelly was convicted of the Scots law offence of reckless endangerment and sentenced to five years' imprisonment in February 2001 (Robertson, 2005). The Kelly case was significant for reasons other than its legal novelty. The reason the police knew his HIV positive status was because they had seized, under warrant, research that had been undertaken into the Glenochil HIV problem. Mr Kelly had voluntarily participated in that project, and concerns were expressed about the impact the police's actions might have on subsequent epidemiological research (Dodds *et al*, 2005: 30).

Christopher Walker (May 2005)

Christopher Walker was charged with culpable and reckless conduct as a result of continuing to have sex with a female partner when he knew or believed he was infected with HIV. He did not stand trial, on grounds of insanity, and was detained in a psychiatric institution in May 2005.

Giovanni Mola (February/April 2007)

Giovanni Mola, an Italian national living in Scotland, was convicted in February 2007 of the Scots criminal offence of culpable and reckless conduct, having infected a female partner with HIV and hepatitis C (Robertson, 2005a). He was sentenced in April 2007 to nine years' imprisonment, certified under the Sexual Offences Act 2003, and recommended for deportation upon his release.[44] In sentencing, Lord Hodge was categoric in his disapproval of Mr Mola's behaviour:

> '. . . what you did to Miss X was chillingly callous and showed an utter indifference to her welfare. In reaching their verdict, the jury must have accepted Miss X as credible and reliable. Her evidence was unequivocally that she repeatedly asked you to use a condom and repeatedly you refused to do so. This was not a one off incident. You had sex with her on nine or ten occasions, on your evidence. On Miss X's evidence you used a condom only on the first and last occasions and then only reluctantly. Thus you repeatedly refused her request that you should wear a condom. And you did so in the knowledge that you had the viruses and could transmit them to her.
>   You did not tell Miss X that you were infected with HIV and Hepatitis C. Standing the advice that you had received from medical practitioners that you did not have to disclose your viral status if you took care to wear and use a condom properly, I do not consider that you can be judged to

---

44 *HMA v Giovanni Mola* (Court of Session, High Court of Justiciary) April 5, 2007 (http://news.bbc.co.uk/1/shared/bsp/hi/pdfs/05_04_07_mola.pdf).

be criminally culpable and reckless on the ground only that you did not disclose your viral status. It is not for me to judge whether the medical advice which you received was appropriate. Non-disclosure of viral status and then sexual intimacy when using a condom may expose a partner to a relatively small risk of infection to which she has not consented. But medical practitioners are no doubt very aware of the damage to an infected individual caused by social isolation. As I say, it is not for me to judge the medical advice that you received.

But you did not follow the explicit medical advice which you were given. You repeatedly did not use a condom despite there being condoms available to you and despite Miss X's requests that you use one. You explained to her that it was not necessary to wear a condom and that men did not like wearing condoms. This repeated refusal is a significant aggravation of your offence.

Lord Hodge's explicit reference to the distinction that needs to be drawn between failing to disclose known HIV status (which does not attract criminal consequences, either in Scotland or in England and Wales), and the need to practise safer sex is a particularly important aspect of this case. It suggests that, in Scots law at least, the failure to disclose known HIV positive status is not in and of itself something that can or should be used when determining whether someone has been reckless or not.

This chapter has attempted to set out the epidemiological, human rights, public health and policy background to the criminalisation of HIV in England and Wales. It should be apparent that far from being a simple, technical, local matter, decisions to prosecute people for transmitting HIV to their sexual partners are ones that take place against a complex political background in which the role of criminal law has been, and remains, contested. The chapters which follow are an attempt to explore in greater detail the contours of that contest, starting with the Crown Court trial of the second person to be convicted in England, Feston Konzani.

Chapter 2

The trial of Feston Konzani

Do you think these women would have consented to not using condoms if they had had the slightest suspicion he was HIV positive? It is a
simple question to ask and I would submit that whilst it is an important
question you can give it a pretty simple answer. The answer is 'No', isn't
it? Do you think those three women, if they had thought there was a
possibility that he would have the HIV virus, he was HIV positive, do
you really think they would have consented to having unprotected sex
with him? The answer is, 'No', isn't it?[1]

This case is not about his knowledge; it is about their consent to the
risk of infection. This case is not about morality; it is about taking risks
with your health. This case is not about broken hearts, disappointment
and broken promises in pursuit of love; it is not about consent to having
sexual intercourse; it is about consent to a risk of infection.[2]

Introduction

It is an unfortunate consequence of the way academic legal education is
conducted in this country that students gain little, if any, knowledge of the
law in practice. The emphasis on substantive legal doctrine, and on the application of legal principles to hypothetical fact situations, means that their
understanding of what law is will often be limited to an understanding of the

---

1 This quotation (from prosecuting counsel's closing speech, at 6), and all the other quoted
extracts used in this chapter, are taken from the official transcript of the trial of Feston
Konzani in the Crown Court at Teesside, May 6–14, 2004 (Ref: T20037605). The abbreviations
I use to denote the source of the extracts are as follows: E:A, B, C (evidence of complainants
A, B and C respectively); E:X (evidence of female witness who was not the subject of a count
on the final indictment); E:Y (evidence of female witness, the count in respect of whom was
dropped during the course of the trial); P:CS (Prosecution closing speech); D:CS (Defence
closing speech); S (submissions prior to swearing in of the jury); R:SU (Recorder's summing-
up). The page numbers in the footnotes after the abbreviations refer to the page numbers of
the different documents in which the various quoted extracts are to be found.
2 D:CS at13.

decisions and reasoning of the appellate courts. Add to this the fact that evidence and procedure (if they are taught at all) are not required for the purposes of a qualifying Law degree,[3] and we are left with a situation where law students' knowledge of the process of adjudication is at best partial and fragmented, and at worst non-existent. The same is true, though for different reasons, of the general public's understanding. Unless a person has undertaken jury service, or has been involved in litigation, knowledge of the law is typically limited to the making of wills, the conveyance of property, the signing of leases, the purchase of goods and services, or the payment of parking fines. Such routine and bureaucratic engagement with the law provides little insight into the tensions, complexities and passions that are often manifest in the courtroom, and such insight as is gained about the nature of a trial frequently comes not from dispassionate reporting but either from fiction, drama or sensationalised media accounts.

This absence of engagement with the nature of the trial process is regrettable, because it is in the trial process that we are able to see most vividly the way in which life and law interact. It is in the language that is used, the questions that are asked, the answers that are given, the assumptions that are made, the implications that are drawn, and in the verdicts that are reached, that we may come to understand the way an event, or events, in the world are translated into a set of discrete legal problems to which a legal resolution (and only a legal resolution) is reached. The judgment of an appellate court after reviewing a trial may provide legal theorists and legal textbook writers with the raw material they need to explain, analyse and criticise 'the law', but it cannot, by definition, give us a comprehensive account of how or why that decision was reached. The arguments, counter-arguments and evidence that provide the foundation for the development of legal principle in a particular area of law are, as is typically the case with foundations – and nowhere more so than with the foundations of law – buried deep and unexcavated.

The purpose of this chapter is to undertake just such an excavation. Using extended extracts from the trial transcript of the case against Feston Konzani, my aim is to provide as full an account as possible of a trial concerning the reckless transmission of HIV. In doing so, my aims are essentially three-fold. First, I want to provide the reader with an opportunity to reflect on the range of issues that are at stake in such a trial and to become acquainted with the complex, multi-faceted human stories with which it must deal. Second, I want to show the way in which those complex human stories are translated into simpler legal narratives of guilt and innocence in order that a verdict may be reached. Third, I want to highlight the way in which that process of

---

3 Such a degree is one that allows a student in England and Wales to continue to the professional stage of training.

translation entails particular modes of representation – of HIV and its transmission – of a person accused of transmission and of those whom he has infected, of responsibility, blame, harm, trust and consent, and of the nature of risk. The exploration of these themes in the trial will then provide a basis for the more detailed discussion in subsequent chapters of the substantive doctrinal, and legal theoretical issues that this and other similar cases raise.

A caveat: all cases are, of course, unique and fact-specific. I am not arguing that the case of Feston Konzani is typical or should be treated as such, or that the issues his case raises will be common to all those involving the reckless transmission of HIV. I am, though, suggesting that the issues raised exemplify the kind of problems with which the law will frequently have to deal when confronted with accusations of reckless transmission, and also that the way in which the issues are framed manifests certain common understandings about the meaning of HIV transmission, ones whose reiteration one might anticipate in analogous or similar cases.

Preliminaries

The trial of Feston Konzani: a summary

Feston Goodwell Konzani, a 28-year-old black African asylum-seeker from Malawi, was tried at the Crown Court in Middlesbrough in May 2004. He was charged on an indictment containing four counts. On each count he was charged with unlawfully and maliciously inflicting grievous bodily harm against a female complainant, contrary to s 20 of the Offences Against the Person Act 1861 (OAPA 1861), which provides that:

> Whosoever shall unlawfully and maliciously wound or inflict any grievous bodily harm[4] upon any other person, either with or without any weapon or instrument shall be guilty of [an offence triable either way] and being convicted thereof shall be liable to imprisonment for five years.[5]

Mr Konzani pleaded not guilty to each of these counts. During the course of the trial he made written admissions to the effect that he had recklessly infected each of the women concerned with HIV, thereby conceding that both the *actus reus* and the *mens rea* of the offence were established. His not guilty

---

4 The term 'maliciously' means recklessly, and is explored in detail in Ch 4. The phrase 'inflict any grievous bodily harm' means 'cause any serious physical or psychological harm', and is discussed further in Ch 3.
5 For further explanation and discussion see Ormerod, 2005: 553–559.

plea was based instead on the assertion that the complainants had, by agreeing to have unprotected sex with him (i.e. sex without a condom), consented to the risk of transmission of HIV. He did not give evidence in his defence during the trial, and the only evidence about his state of mind and conduct in respect of the charges against him came from interviews he had given to the police during detention after his arrest. Mr Konzani was found guilty on three of the four counts, the fourth having been dropped after it became apparent that the complainant concerned might have been infected with HIV prior to having unprotected sex with him, and before he learned of his own HIV positive diagnosis. Mr Konzani was sentenced to a total of 10 years' immediate imprisonment on the three remaining counts.

The role of the prosecution and defence

The role of the prosecution in a criminal case is to put the case for the Crown (McBarnet, 1981; McConville *et al*, 1991; Sanders, 1997). It is not for the prosecution to get a conviction at any cost, but to prove on the basis of the evidence admitted at trial, that the defendant is guilty of the offence charged. To do this, it must prove each and every element of the offence and, if necessary, disprove any valid defence raised by the defendant. Where there is more than one count on an indictment, the particulars of each count must be proved if a guilty verdict is to be reached. The counts against Feston Konzani alleged that he had unlawfully and maliciously inflicted grievous bodily harm on the complainants. As explained above, the prosecution was – during the course of the trial, and as a result of admissions – relieved of the burden of having to prove causation (that it was Mr Konzani who infected the women concerned), that the harm inflicted was grievous (i.e. really serious), and that he was reckless as to (i.e. aware of the risk of) causing that harm. This meant that the role of the prosecution, at least at the conclusion of the case, was simply to disprove Mr Konzani's claim that the complainants had consented to the risk of transmission. This it was required to do to the criminal standard, which meant that it had to convince the jury beyond reasonable doubt (or, put another way, so that they were sure) that there was no such consent. If they were sure of this, they would be obliged to convict. If they were unsure, they would have to acquit.

The role of the defence is very different. It is not under any obligation to prove anything. The defence's role is to challenge the evidence brought against the defendant, to raise questions in the jury's mind about both the reliability of that evidence and about the credibility of prosecution witnesses. A successful defence is one that – in a Crown Court trial – causes the jury to doubt the evidence to such a degree that they cannot be sure either that the elements of the offence are proved, or that a defence raised by the defendant has been disproved. In the context of the present case this meant that the defence was seeking to argue that the complainants had, by agreeing to have unprotected sex, consented to the risk of transmission and that this was not disproved by the prosecution.

The role of the judge and jury

The roles of the judge and jury in a Crown Court criminal trial are, needless to say, very different. The judge's function is to try the case according to law. This means that she or he is responsible for making rulings as to, for example, the admissibility of evidence, for directing the jury on such matters as the inferences they are entitled to make from the defendant's decision not to give evidence, for directing the acquittal of the defendant on counts for which there is no case to answer,[6] and for advising them about the weight they should give to the evidence of particular witnesses. The trial judge's decisions on points of law are final, open to challenge only on appeal. During the summing-up the judge explains the law to the jury, reviews the salient evidence, and makes any directions she sees fit. The trial judge is also responsible for imposing the sentence of the court in the event of a guilty verdict. In the context of the present case the judge was required to make a number of important rulings and decisions, among which were the direction he would give the jury as to the relevance of Mr Konzani's failure to give evidence, the directed acquittal on one of the counts that had originally been included on the indictment, and the explanation of the defence of consent.

Whereas the judge tries the case according to the law, the jury try it according to the facts. Although they must take the law in the way the judge directs them to, it is they who decide whether the case against the defendant is proved. It is they who decide, ultimately, what evidence they consider to be relevant or irrelevant for the purposes of reaching a verdict on counts included in the indictment. The judge may suggest that they treat certain evidence as particularly important, but they may ignore that suggestion if they wish to. They are also entitled to treat evidence as critical which the judge considers less so. The jury's only obligation is to use their own common sense in their evaluation of the evidence, to try the case and reach a verdict according to that evidence alone, and not to be swayed by emotion, passion, or views expressed by others outside the court. In Mr Konzani's trial the jury were evidently confused by some aspects of the case, and by the law they were required to apply, because they asked, after they had retired to consider their verdict, for clarification from the judge as to the meaning of consent. It was only after the

---

6 I.e. where the prosecution leads insufficient evidence to establish the commission of the offence. This is what occurred in the case of Matthew Collins because of the limitations of the scientific evidence upon which the prosecution was based (see above, Ch 1). It is my understanding that although the judge allowed the case to go to the jury, he subsequently recalled the jury and directed them to acquit (source: personal communication with observers at the trial).

judge had responded to this note in open court that they reached a verdict of guilty on each of the three counts.

Some observations on the use of the trial transcript

This chapter relies almost exclusively on an analysis of trial transcript material.[7] A trial transcript is, although verbatim, a text – and texts have their limitations. In the present context the most obvious of these is that although we are concerned to understand the way in which the verdict was reached *via* an exploration of the representation and construction of HIV/AIDS, its transmission, the person infecting and the people infected, that process of representation and construction took place over an extended period of time, by people with different roles speaking in the formal confines of a courtroom. These oral, temporal, visual and spatial dimensions and qualities of the trial cannot be adequately captured in the written word, however substantively faithful to the original this may be. There also exist other, more embedded, difficulties.

For example, when a defendant chooses not to give evidence in open court the jury's evaluation of her is based on visual cues (her behaviour in the dock, her reaction – or absence of reaction – to questions of, and answers by, witnesses), narratives provided about her conduct and state of mind by others during the course of the trial, and by the reading out of any statements made by her during the course of police questioning. Each of these sources of information is used, to a greater or lesser degree and with or without formal legal approval, to determine the kind of person the defendant is, her credibility, and whether she is guilty of the offences with which she has been charged. Feston Konzani did not give evidence, and so what we know about him from the trial transcripts is provided solely by the prosecution witnesses. What the jury came to know and think of him and of what he was alleged to have done and thought, however, was framed not by the text which we have to work with here, but by the testimony provided orally by witnesses – particularly those of the complainants (who themselves were of course subject to the same kind of evaluation). Although the text occasionally provides us with evidence about the way in which the witnesses' testimony came across (about their use of, and facility with, language) and their emotional state (as when questioning is stopped to allow them to recover themselves), the written word can only ever approximate to what must have been the lived experience of the trial for the jurors, and only ever suggest what the effect of that testimony must have been on them. Similarly, we may gain our own impression of the defendant and the complainants from their characterisation by prosecution and defence counsel in the questions they ask, and in the language of their

---

7 A transcript is produced in order that evidence, directions etc may be referred to accurately in the event that there is (as there was in this case) an appeal.

closing speeches; but without having ourselves heard the way in which that questioning and those speeches used the rhetorical devices of pause and emphasis, of stridency and eminent reasonableness, of varied pace and pitch, we cannot fully appreciate the way these influenced the jury's perception of Mr Konzani and his behaviour, or of his accusers.

Despite these limitations, and so long as those limitations are recognised, it is a worthwhile endeavour to explore the ways in which the participants in the trial, and the offence which forms its basis, are represented and constructed in the text. Firstly, because the transcript (or certain parts of it) provided the raw material for the Court of Appeal when it subsequently came to review Mr Konzani's conviction and sentence.[8] It is therefore, in a very meaningful and powerful sense, authoritative. Secondly, and more importantly in the context of the present discussion, the transcript does give us the language that was used, even if not as it was heard and experienced by the participants, and this is, in itself, a useful and valuable resource.

The prosecution case

The prosecution called 16 witnesses to testify on behalf of the Crown, of whom 14 were examined in court and two had statements read. The defence called none. Because my principal concern is to explore issues of fault and responsibility, and because of the amount of material, I concentrate in particular on the evidence of the three complainants whose HIV infection formed the basis of the counts on which he was found guilty, on the speeches of counsel, and on the words of the judge. I also organise this material thematically, rather than following the exact chronology of the case. My aim is not to provide the reader with a blow-by-blow account of what happened, but with a sense of the ways in which the case against Mr Konzani was built, and how his guilt was established.

Feston Konzani as blameworthy defendant

The defendant is at the heart of the criminal trial. It is she who has most to lose or gain from the process. It she who provides the focus of the narratives constructed from the questions of counsel, and the answers of witnesses. It is she about whom claims are made and rebutted, whose behaviour is the subject of scrutiny, whose mental state is evaluated and judged. She is the subject of the trial, and at the same time its object. In the trial of Feston Konzani, as I have earlier explained, the defendant gave no evidence in court. He was merely an observer of the proceedings. More than this, because the only disputed issue was the availability of a defence – that the complainants

---

8 The Court of Appeal's response to Mr Konzani's conviction is discussed in more detail in Ch 5.

consented to the risk of HIV transmission – his guilt was the product of the conclusions which the jury drew about him and his conduct *via* the accounts provided by others.

In this section I want to explore the way in which the accounts of those others constructed the defendant as someone whose blameworthiness was such that he deserved to be convicted. This, it should be noted, is a rather oblique and peculiar exercise as far the specific facts of this case are concerned. Feston Konzani's admission that he had been the cause of the complainants' infections and that he had been reckless meant that, in strictly legal terms, his conduct and fault were not in question. Indeed, defence counsel sought to argue – when making submissions about the way in which the judge should direct the jury as to the relevance of his failure to give evidence – that no adverse inference should be drawn because the defendant could contribute nothing of relevance so far as the complainants' consent or otherwise was concerned. Nevertheless, it was a central part of the prosecution case that Feston Konzani was a man whose conduct towards the complainants was such that there was no way they could reasonably be thought to have consented to the risk to which he exposed them. Put another way, the prosecution strategy was to emphasise that the risk of HIV transmission was something to which *he* exposed them, rather than something to which *they* exposed themselves. It was critical that he should be seen as the active agent of infection, and that they were his passive victims – that responsibility for the consequences was wholly his, and that they bore none. In the words of prosecuting counsel addressing the jury at the start of his closing speech:[9]

> What this case boils down to now and what you will be centrally concerned with is whether or not at the time these women had sex with this man they were consenting to the risk of catching this virus or some other really serious injury and, of course, the only evidence about whether they were consenting to this came from them, didn't it, and you know that in each of their cases, [the names of complainants] said, 'I wasn't consenting to this risk, I was not consenting to this'.

Knowledge and responsibility

The reason Feston Konzani was found guilty on only three counts, rather than on the four originally included in the indictment, was that only three of the complainants had been infected after it was established that he had himself received a positive HIV diagnosis (in November 2000).[10] This knowledge

---

9 P:CS at 1.

10 In *R v Dica* [2004] 2 Cr App R 28 the Court of Appeal had held that only those who know their HIV positive status may be reckless as to whether (i.e. consciously aware of the risk that) HIV may be transmitted. See below, Ch 4.

was critical to the question of whether he had been reckless with respect to transmission, but was also central to the way in which the prosecution sought to present the defendant to the jury for the purposes of disproving the existence of the complainants' consent. It was his knowledge of his own HIV positive status that made it possible to represent him as an irresponsible risk-taker and therefore, somewhat paradoxically, as someone who could and should be held responsible for the consequences of his actions. Consider, for example, the following exchanges between prosecuting counsel and complainant A (who was 15 years old at the time she and the defendant met, and whose evidence was that prior to sex with him, she had been a virgin):[11]

Q: Did he know how old you were?
A: Yeah, I told him.
Q: And what was his reaction?
A: He wasn't very much bothered.
Q: I think you have said that you had sex with Feston?
A: Yeah.
Q: How often did that take place?
A: Er, when I moved in with him it was every night.
Q: And how did you find that?
A: Me, I was all right with it at first but then I just, I didn't like it no more.
Q: Why didn't you like it?
A: Because he was going too hard and it was hurting.
Q: Did anything happen as a result of it hurting?
A: Erm, I started bleeding.
Q: Did you tell Feston about that?
A: Yeah.
Q: Now, at this time when you were living with Feston did you have sex with anyone else?
A: No.
Q: And the sex that you had with Feston, did he use protection?
A: No.
Q: Do you understand what I mean by that?
A: Yeah.
Q: Did he wear a condom?
A: No.
Q: And when you had sex did he ejaculate inside you?
A: Yeah.
Q: Did you worry about becoming pregnant?

11 E:A at 3–4.

A: Not at first, no.
Q: Did you have any discussion about any other risks?
A: No.

This examination reveals a man who was prepared to have sex with a girl under the legal age of consent, concerned with his own physical pleasure at her expense, apparently oblivious to the fact that she was not enjoying the experience, and who (even though she, too, seemed to recognise at least one kind of consequence) failed to use protection that would have minimised the risk of pregnancy and the transmission of disease. The impression of a man who fails to take responsibility for his conduct is reinforced in counsel's examination of complainant B. Because she is a far more experienced woman (who had in police interview disclosed having eight sexual partners including the defendant), counsel instead emphasises Mr Konzani's failure to disclose his HIV positive status when he might be thought to have had the opportunity to do so[12]:

Q: Now, you say you talked to him about Africa?
A: Yeah.
Q: Did you talk to him about any of the problems in Africa?
A: Yes.
Q: What specifically did you talk to him about?
A: About HIV and AIDS and children in Africa, orphans.
Q: Do you remember what was said about that?
A: I said that I really want, would like to go to Africa and help the children and we talked about general orphans as well and [name of organisation] which is set up for children with HIV and AIDS who are orphans and we also spoke about his country and I was interested to know if I was with him and maybe we could do something in Malawi and I asked what HIV, how widespread it was in Malawi and Feston told us it wasn't very common.
Q: During that discussion about HIV and Africa and Malawi at any stage did he tell you about him being HIV positive?
A: No, never.
Q: Did he tell you subsequently at any point that he was HIV positive?
A: No, never.

[There then follows an account of how their friendship developed after the meeting when this discussion took place]

Q: How did that friendship develop?
A: It developed the night we came back from church.

12 E:B pp 5–7.

Q: How long had you spent in Feston's company until that point?
A: We were together the whole time until he left for Middlesbrough.
Q: You say that it developed the night you came back from church?
A: Yeah.
Q: What happened?
A: We had sexual intercourse.
Q: Was there anything unusual about sexual intercourse on that occasion?
A: No.
Q: Did he wear a condom?
A: Yes.
Q: Did you have any conversations with Feston after that?
A: Yes, I says to him, joking, joking, I said, 'I hope you haven't got any diseases'.
Q: And what did he say?
A: He said, 'Don't be stupid.'

I return later in the chapter to this particular evidence, as it is explored in cross-examination. Here I want simply to note the way in which counsel draws attention to a conversation about HIV and AIDS (which, presumably, he intends to suggest provided a perfect but ignored opportunity for the defendant to disclose his own status), and his active deceit – which though not strictly relevant to the question of whether there was consent on the complainant's part to the risk of transmission (and which in any event occurs after protected sexual intercourse) is clearly intended to demonstrate his irresponsibility and lack of concern given the knowledge he had about his own health.

The importance of Mr Konzani's knowledge to the prosecution case is emphasised by its early appearance in counsel's closing speech. Referring to the people the defendant saw at the time of his diagnosis he addresses the jury thus:

You have heard from those others, and he was specifically advised, wasn't he, about a number of things: the fact that he was infected and what this was going to mean to him, how this would be monitored, the treatment he would receive, the future for him, and, of course, crucially, the risk that he posed to others. He was specifically told that he must always have safe [sic][13] sex and he was also specifically advised, wasn't he, and you will remember this, that he should tell people he was going to have sex with. He must tell these people that he was HIV positive.

Now, in interview, of course, the defendant said, and perhaps I need not refer to the passage, but he said, 'Well, I can't remember what I

13 The conventional term in sexual health is 'safer' rather than 'safe' sex.

was told'. Well, we would say that is not right, members of the jury, because in the same passage in his interview he seemed to be able to remember the doctor's name, albeit not what the doctor said to him, but it wasn't just the 28th November when he was spoken to about this, was it? He was told again on the 4th December, the 8th January the following year, the 5th February, the 12th April. You remember the doctor saying, 'We take a specific approach to these people. We repeat the same things over and over again to make sure it gets through to them', and he was also being seen by others, wasn't he, [name of health adviser], for instance, and they were telling him exactly the same sort of things, so he knew amongst others that he posed a substantial risk of passing this on and he also knew of the need that he should tell potential partners.[14]

This passage merits careful scrutiny. For the clinician and health adviser, the importance of disclosure is that it can serve to minimise the risk of HIV spreading within the population. In so far as disclosure is expressed as being an obligation (and there is a noticeable slippage from 'should' to 'must' to 'should tell' in counsel's speech), it is to emphasise the importance of informing potential partners in order that the risk of onward transmission is reduced. To the extent that it is advice which may be interpreted as placing a burden on the person with a positive HIV diagnosis, this is because such a person provides an obvious and immediate *locus* for such advice. It is not intended as a message whose purpose is simply to impose (unenforceable) constraints on a person diagnosed with HIV, but to stress the importance of taking care. But if this is the underlying reason for the clinician's prescription, the prosecuting lawyer uses the provision and reiteration of health advice, provided to the patient for public health reasons, as the basis for suggesting a specifically legal responsibility on the defendant's part. This is without foundation in legal terms. There is no legal obligation on a person to disclose known HIV positive status to a partner. This fact appears to be unimportant to prosecuting counsel, who continues (without any apparent awareness that, in addressing the jury, he may not be speaking hypothetically):[15]

> . . . Put yourself in the shoes of somebody told that they are HIV positive.
>   He knew what it meant, of course, didn't he? It means you have got a future ahead of you of serious illness followed by an early death, because HIV is a terrible thing, isn't it, members of the jury? It doesn't get much worse, you might think, and that is in reality simply not the sort of thing you consent to catching, is it? Again, you may think about

14 P:CS at 1–2.
15 P:CS at 2.

it yourselves but it is at the top of the list of things you would want to be told by a prospective sexual partner, isn't it, 'I am HIV positive. Have sex with me and you're taking your life, or putting your life in very substantial risk indeed.'

Pursuing his theme, counsel makes the transmission of HIV (in strictly legal terms, equivalent to breaking someone's arm) a signifier of imminent mortality, emphasises the defendant's knowledge of his own HIV status (in strictly legal terms, irrelevant to the question of a partner's consent to the risk of transmission), suggests that 'it' is not what one would consent to catching (where, in strictly legal terms, the relevant consent is to the risk of transmission, not to the infection itself), constructs an almost unimaginable form of disclosure (which even if made in these terms would amount at most to morally laudable, not legally required, transparency), and ignores the fact that it is only certain kinds of sexual practice that carry with them a risk of transmission. Such, then, is the way in which Feston Konzani's (ir)responsibility is characterised by the Crown, whose duty is – it should be recalled – to put the *legal* case against the defendant before the jury.

This (ir)responsibility extends, of course, beyond prior disclosure, into the realm of sexual practice. While the emphasis on the absence of disclosure is intended to convince the jury that there was no willing consent to risk, the prosecution seeks also to emphasise his failure to take care by insisting on the use of condoms. Counsel stresses the culpability of this failure by referring to the time that Mr Konzani was given his HIV positive diagnosis. This he received at the same time as the woman whose infection did not form the basis of a count against him. Here is her account of how she felt on being given the news, and how the defendant reacted:[16]

Q: You were very angry. How did Feston seem?
A: Feston . . . He did not say anything and, most strangely, when somebody realises they are HIV positive you feel the world falling to, on the top of your head. He did not show anything, not one tear, nothing. He was just not speaking and blanking [sic] at the wall.

After receiving their respective diagnoses Mr Konzani met up with this woman and apologised to her. Counsel pursues the theme in his closing speech:[17]

You know that there was a meeting in London in March of 2001 and he apologised at that for infecting her and it is important not because it

16 E:X at 23.
17 P:CS at 5.

shows any criminal responsibility on him, and I stress the fact that no charges are brought in relation to [name of woman], but, of course, it illustrates very well that he must be aware of the effects that he can have on people. He knew, didn't he, how she felt, knew the effects of his actions, and, of course, again what happens after November 2000 [the month of his diagnosis] is in that light, isn't it? It is with that background. He knows what happens when this gets passed on to people and it happened to him and it happened to somebody he seems to have cared very deeply for and yet he goes on and does the same to others.

Put yourself in his shoes, members of the jury. If you had been told this, if you had this devastating news, this appalling future, I would suggest you would not want to put somebody else in that position, put somebody else in the position of having to be told this and having to realise what lay ahead of them.

And yet, so the prosecution asserts, this is precisely what the defendant himself did. Despite his awareness of the effects of HIV infection, he not only fails to disclose his status to sexual partners but fails to do anything to minimise the risk of transmission:[18]

You perhaps may think to yourselves, 'Well, if he was going to keep it quiet that he had HIV surely you would at least use a condom with these women', but, of course, he didn't, did he? Did he really care about these people? Did he really care about what risk he posed to them and was he bothered about infecting them? I hope I do not put it in a flippant way like that but, of course, he was having unprotected sex with these people, wasn't he?

You see, you might want to ask yourselves, if he was really that bothered about passing this infection on to them, because, of course, wearing a condom was really the easiest thing in the world to do, wasn't it, from his position? He had condoms, there was no shortage of them, he confirms that in his interviews. He was being offered them from a number of sources. Do you remember [name of health adviser] saying, 'Well, whenever I saw him I offered him condoms but he said, "I don't need any"', and he had obviously within him this terrible virus that he could readily pass on to people through having unprotected sex with them. Of course, wearing a condom would have been the easiest thing to do, he had them, they were available, yet he chose not to, and you may think that is really a window on the way this defendant thought towards these people, and a window on the way perhaps he behaved towards them.

18 P:CS at 6.

It is important to remember when reading this that Mr Konzani had admitted being reckless as to transmission. He was not asserting that he was unaware of the risk he posed to the complainants, or that he was not the cause of their infection. This, however, is not something to which the prosecution refers the jury. Instead, counsel seeks to suggest that in deciding whether the complainants had consented to the risk, it is relevant to emphasise the defendant's failure to deploy preventive measures. This contributes to the construction of Feston Konzani as an immoral, feckless person who should bear the full brunt of any responsibility judgment the jury might wish to make.

Trust and deceit

Just as the prosecution sought to emphasise Mr Konzani's knowledge of his HIV positive status, his failure to disclose this, and his failure to use prophylaxis as a means of demonstrating (ir)responsibility, so it sought to drive home that (ir)responsibility as being his alone by locating it within a relational context of trust. Such trust was initially induced, according to the prosecution, by the way in which the defendant presented himself to the complainants. In one of the more striking passages in his closing speech, counsel characterises Mr Konzani as follows:[19]

> . . . he is in a position of some success with women, he can have sexual intercourse with women if he wants to, he knows the risk to them and, of course, over this period of time, 2000, 2001, 2002 and into 2003 he is described as far as people could tell when they met him, when they spoke to him, as the picture of health. Women described him as being in good health, well-presented, you remember them saying he was very smart. He is not somebody who looked like you would imagine somebody looks when they've got AIDS. He had a very active social life. He was very into the music scene. He seems to be a committed churchgoer and heavily involved in the church, and you may think – it is a matter for you – but you may think somebody who puts themselves forward as a committed religious person, that carries with it certain sureties, doesn't it, you might think.
>
> He impressed his religion on these women and really in these circumstances, somebody of good health, very outgoing, very sociable, a churchgoer, a committed churchgoer, there is no way on earth any of these women can have had any reason to guess there was anything wrong with him. That must follow, mustn't it?

The strategy is clear. The prosecution want to suggest that the women who

19 P:CS at 5.

agreed to have unprotected sex with the defendant during this period should not be thought consciously to have consented to the risk of HIV transmission, because there was no reason for them to have adverted to this possibility. The prosecution does this by drawing attention to Mr Konzani's appearance and behaviour, even though there was no reason at all why these should have been any different from that of an HIV negative person, and implying that someone with an AIDS diagnosis (which in any event he did not have) would not be expected to be outwardly healthy, 'smart', or have a social life. By playing on the common prejudices and misunderstanding people have of HIV infection, ones that had been central to many safer sex advertising campaigns in the years prior to 2000, the prosecution is able to suggest that it was perfectly reasonable for the women concerned to assume that there was no risk of HIV transmission. Similarly, the emphasis on the defendant's church attendance, the fact that he 'put himself forward' as a committed person of faith, is used to suggest that he thereby gave certain implicit guarantees about himself on which the complainants were entitled to rely. The fact that the sexual relationships he had with them all took place outside marriage and soon after meeting them (something with which the complainants themselves, irrespective of their own religious beliefs, were content) is – unsurprisingly – not averred to.

Even though the legal question at stake in the case is whether the complainants had consented to the risk of transmission when they agreed to have unprotected sexual intercourse with the defendant (a question whose answer does not depend on the quality or kind of relationship two people have), the question of whether there had in *fact* been consent is one to which the prosecution sought a negative response by emphasising not only his appearance and conduct, but also the fact that the sex which resulted in transmission took place within relationships (notwithstanding variations in commitment, duration and intensity) rather than casual sexual encounters. In relationships, so it is argued, partners are entitled to trust each other, and the breach of that trust through deceit (whether that be active, by lying, or through omission, by failing to tell the truth) is particularly culpable.

Consider the following account of the developing trust relationship given by a woman with whom Mr Konzani had a relationship prior to being diagnosed, and in respect of whom no charge was brought. Her evidence is being given via an interpreter:[20]

> Q: I think you told us that you became his girlfriend in about May or June, 2000.
> A: I think I remember, yes.
> Q: Was it at that time when you started having sex with him?
> A: Yes.

20 E:X at 20.

Q: Could you describe for us, please, the nature of your sex life with this defendant?

A: We used to have sex four or five times a day. At the beginning he would use condoms and then we stopped doing that. We used to have sexual intercourse even when I had my period.

. . .

Q: . . . You have told us that to start with Feston wore condoms and after a while he didn't wear condoms. Whose idea was it to wear condoms?

A: I prompt the use of condoms at the beginning. This is the way I'm educated, been educated and used to. The first sexual relations with somebody I always use condoms when the relationship becomes, evolves, I can decide not to, and also Feston was asking me not to use it.

Q: When you say 'not to use it' do you mean not to use condoms?

A: Yes.

Q: You said that when the relationship evolves, the use of condom stops. What do you mean by 'evolves'?

A: Because we were, I mean we were together, I had feelings towards him and he had feelings towards me.

There is, of course, no question of disclosure here because there was no proof that the defendant was at that time aware of his HIV positive status, but the exchange illustrates well the way in which sex which carries little or no risk can become risky as relationships change over time. A developing intimacy prompts a desire to eliminate any barrier to that, something which condoms exemplify.[21] Another woman (the one in respect of whom one of the four counts was dropped) gave the following account of her relationship with the defendant[22]:

Q: . . . did you have an ongoing relationship with him, would you say?

A: On/off, on and off, on and off.

. . .

Q: Was there a period when it was on to start with?

A: It was in the beginning.

Q: And how long was that initial period, how long would you say it lasted for?

A: About four weeks.

21 The decision to desist from using condoms is positively correlated with the desire for intimacy and the development of trust within a relationship. See, for example, Moatti et al, 1997, and the other essays in van Campenhoudt et al, 1997.

22 E:Y at 32–34.

Q: About four weeks, and you say it was then on and off after that?

A: Yeah.

Q: Was there anything in particular that had caused it to go off the boil or go off?

A: It's mainly he used to say he was busy or he had to go to Newcastle or, he was always making excuses so I just believed him. He said, you know, he can't make it or he has to go to London or . . .

Q: Right. When you say 'On/off', what do you mean by that? Just describe for us?

A: Well, when we met each other, you know, we both didn't want commitments and at the time having a child, which I wasn't with other partners, it was only Feston for a long time because it was easier, having a child, to have a relationship like that. It was better for me if I knew today that he would be there and if he wanted me I was there but most of the time he did the 'phoning and come.

. . .

Q: . . . This on and off period, how long do you think that lasted for in total?

A: About two year.

Q: About two years, something like that. When you met up with Feston on these times when it was on, what would happen?

A: Well, he used to come round late when the child was in bed and he'd always 'phone before he came if it was okay to come and when he used to come it wasn't that long before we were just having sex or . . . We hardly had much communication, but it was sex mainly.

. . .

Q: Do you yourself know of other people he was seeing?

A: I know two girls that while he was with me but again he said [name of 'girl 1'], the first girl who lived . . . He said, 'She's a neighbour [. . .] on [name of street where the defendant lived], and another girl, [name of 'girl 2'] . . .

Q: Right.

A: . . . and he said [name of 'girl 2'] was nothing to him.

Q: Right.

A: He said, 'The other one's just a friend', so I believed him.

Here the complainant acknowledges a primarily sexual relationship, one that is long-term but occasional and pursued for its convenience. Although she is aware of other women in the defendant's life, and conscious of his 'excuses' for not being around, she accepts his account of these other relationships at face value and admits that physical satisfaction was more important than communication.

As for the complainants in respect of whom counts remained on the indictment, their relationships with the defendant were similarly different from one another. Consider, for example, the way in which complainant B describes certain aspects of the evolution of her relationship with him:[23]

Q: Now, you have told us that the first time you had sex with Feston you used a condom?
A: Yes.
Q: Did that position change?
A: Yeah.
Q: When did it change?
A: Not . . . Well, we discussed me using contraception because me or Feston wanted to have any more, well I didn't want to have any more children and Feston didn't want any children so I, we discussed it and we, I said, 'The, probably the best route to take is for me to get some sort of injection or the pill', and I chose to have the Depot injection because it was just once a month, er, once every three months and I couldn't forget, unlike pills and things, and that would protect me.
Q: So you were using a contraceptive injection?
A: Yeah.
Q: And when did Feston stop using condoms?
A: Within, it wasn't a long time that we used condoms for.
THE RECORDER:[24] I didn't quite understand that answer.
A: Sorry. It wasn't for a long period of time we used condoms. We just sort of, it just fizzled out cos . . .
Q: I see, soon after . . .
A: Yeah, I wanted to be with him, he wanted to be with me, so we made that decision together.
PROSECUTING COUNSEL: At the time when he stopped using condoms, did you have any further conversations in relation to HIV?
A: Throughout the relationship we had conversations about HIV.
Q: And what was the upshot of the conversations you had stopped using condoms?
A: Just generally like before, about the children in Africa and people living with HIV and AIDS, the effect it has on people and how we can help and just general, general discussions.

Contrast that account of a relationship, in which the decision to stop using condoms took place as the result of open negotiation, with that of complainant

---

23 E:B at 8–9.
24 The Recorder is the title the judge had in Mr Konzani's trial.

C, a Christian graduate student who had been introduced to the defendant in church, and who was a reluctant witness for the prosecution. Here she is answering questions about the way her relationship developed with Mr Konzani around the time she moved in with him. I set out almost all the relevant dialogue, because this is necessary to show how difficult it was for the complainant to express the way she felt:[25]

> Q: What was your relationship with Feston at that time?
> A: Good.
> Q: Did your relationship develop?
> A: Yeah, it was developing.
> Q: It was developing. How did it develop?
> A: We were just talking about the Bible, that's all.
> Q: You were just taking about the Bible?
> A: Yeah.
> Q: But how did your relationship with Feston develop? You say you were friends with him?
> A: Sort of, but I became more than friends with him when I went to his house.
>
> . . .
>
> Q: And did your friendship develop into anything else?
> A: We were good friends.
> Q: How did you feel towards Feston?
> A: Good.
> Q: Did you ever have a relationship with Feston that was more than a friendship?
> A: We were friends.
> Q: I understand you were friends. Did you have a relationship . . .
> A: Yes.
> Q: . . . that become [sic] more than a friendship?
> A: Yes.
> Q: When you say 'more than a friendship', what do you mean? What happened?
> A: We were good friends.
> Q: You say that your relationship became more than a friendship?
> A: Yes.
> Q: What do you mean by 'more than friendship'?
> A: We were lovers.
>
> . . .

---

25 E:C at 3–5.

Q: Did you have sexual intercourse with Feston?
A: Yes.
Q: Had you had sexual intercourse with other people before Feston?
A: Yes.
Q: How many?
A: One.
Q: One. How often did you have sex with Feston?
A: Several.
Q: Several? Several times in what period of time?
A: I can't remember.
Q: How often did you have sex with Feston?
A: Several.
Q: Sorry?
A: Many times.
Q: Many times. How many times in a day?
A: I don't know.
Q: You don't know. Was it every day, was it once a day, was it more than once a day?
A: I can't remember.
Q: Did you have vaginal sex?
A: Yes.
Q: Did you have anal sex?
A: No.
Q: What was the sex like?
A: I can't remember.
Q: Did you use protection?
A: No.
Q: No. Do you understand what I mean by that?
A: Yes.
Q: Did Feston use condoms?
A: No. At times.
Q: At times?
A: Yeah.
Q: When did he wear condoms?
A: Sometimes.
Q: When he didn't wear condoms did he ejaculate inside you?
A: I can't remember.
Q: When Feston didn't wear condoms were you concerned about any risks?
A: No.
Q: Why weren't you concerned?
A: I trusted him.
Q: Did Feston tell you he was HIV positive?
A: No.

> Q: How long were you together with Feston once you had moved in
>   with him?
> A: Three or four months.
> Q: Three of four months. What happened at the end of those three
>   or four months?
> A: I moved out.
> Q: You moved out. Was there a reason you moved out?
> A: I wasn't happy.

In questioning this witness, who did not want any charges brought against the
defendant, prosecuting counsel emphasises the sexual dimensions of their
relationship in a way that the complainant clearly feels deeply uncomfortable
with. He also ensures that the jury understand the relationship as one in
which, with hindsight, she only took risks because at the relevant time she had
no reason to suspect that she was taking any. This, given what the prosecution
must prove, is all counsel needs her to admit.

Prosecuting counsel draws together the theme of trust and deceit in these
relationship narratives in his closing speech, drawing in particular on the relationship which brought Feston Konzani to England in the first place. While
still in Malawi he had met, through his brother who worked as a security
guard at the British Embassy in Ilongwe, a diplomat. The diplomat provided
Mr Konzani with the opportunity to train as a steward at the Embassy, and
a sexual relationship between them began when Mr Konzani came to live at
his flat. Subsequently, the diplomat provided assistance to Mr Konzani when
he sought asylum in the United Kingdom, and the sexual relationship continued intermittently after that. This relationship, which because of its political implications was the focus of much media discussion at the time, was
used in the trial as an opportunity to explore the defendant's character.
For the prosecution, the relationship was important because it provided
an insight into how Mr Konzani expected other people to behave towards
him. Referring to part of his police interview, prosecuting counsel quotes
Mr Konzani's response to the suggestion that coming to the UK, coming to
terms with this, would have been unsettling[26] (Mr Konzani's words are in
italics):

> 'What do you mean "Come to terms with it"? Didn't you, I don't quite
> understand what you're getting at there', he [Mr Konzani] replies. 'First of
> all, I didn't understand what the word "gay" meant. Secondly, I did not
> understand anything about this asylum seeking process. I was only doing
> what I was told because I trusted the guy'. It is that section I am
> emphasising, 'I trusted . . .' 'He knows my parents, he knows every one of

*my family, he's visited my family, so I trusted him, and I was just doing, I
mean what he told me'.*

 . . . He goes on to say the following, '*I trusted this guy and to me he
was a completely different white man*', so, again, you have got the
defendant emphasising the trust element to their relationship, and he
says the same, and I will just read this out . . . he said the same sort of
thing in his next interview and I will read the part from the summary.
'*He said he trusted* [name of diplomat] *as his white friend*', because,
members of the jury, I refer to those because trust is a theme of this
case, I would submit. These women trusted this defendant and that is
what they told you. They said they never thought he would have the
HIV virus or anything like that and they trusted him.

 . . . he can't have it both ways, can he, members of the jury? He can't
complain about his trust relation to [name of diplomat] being
breached and then really ignore the trust that was built up by him
with these women, because that is what they said to you, wasn't it?
'Well, I trusted him. I had a relationship with him and I trusted him'.
They were not consenting to this, were they? They trusted him, he
never said a word.

The complainants' accounts of their relationships with Mr Konzani are here
homogenised and simplified by counsel through paraphrase. They are, of
course – as their own individual testimonies demonstrate – far more complex.
At one level they may be thought of as simply descriptive of the infinitely
various ways in which people express their desire for each other. And at the
time they were happening, they were simply that – complicated human relationships. But the trial process entails the production of a certain kind of
narrative. It imposes a form of inverse reductivism in which the particular is
rendered general, the specific universal. So there is a need for these stories –
of developing relationships, of platonic friendship leading to constant sex, of
immediate physical passion followed by rationalisation, of intermittent and
inconsistent precaution, of communication and silence, of fidelity and open-
ness, care and carelessness, risk-taking and risk-aversion – to be characterised
as ones that *each* manifest the clear and incontrovertible irresponsibility of
one partner and the ignorant passivity of the other. In particular, because it
serves to distinguish the HIV transmission that happened to them from that
which might be thought of merely as 'bad luck' were it to have occurred
between casual partners, the prosecution seeks to emphasise the breach of
trust such transmission represents, and the deceit upon which that breach
is built. From being – from one perspective – simply the risk of producing
adverse physiological change in the body of another human, exposing a person to the risk of HIV transmission, and failing to alert her to this possibility,
transmission is represented as a symbolic breach of commonly shared values
and expectations. It undergoes a translation from the factual and descriptive

(which would be sufficient were the case to have turned simply on causation), to the symbolic and normative (which is necessary if the jury are to be convinced that they did not willingly consent to the risk of transmission). Because even though this latter state of mind is also technically only a question of fact, the prosecution needs the jury to believe there is no reason why the complainants *ought* to have been aware of the risk; and it does this by establishing the meaning of their relationships, and how they might be expected to have been treated. And that, put simply, is how Mr Konzani might have wanted to be treated himself.

The defence case

The knowledge of the complainants

Because the burden on the prosecution in the Konzani trial was to disprove that the complainants had consented to the risk of HIV transmission, the defence strategy was largely concerned with establishing that they were aware of this risk. In doing so, the defence hoped to persuade the jury that, despite Mr Konzani's failure to disclose his known HIV positive status to them, they had – in effect – consented: not to the transmission of HIV itself (a defence that was not legally available), but simply to the risk of its transmission. In the absence of disclosure by Mr Konzani, the only way of persuading the jury to reach this conclusion was to emphasise the knowledge that each complainant had of the risks associated with unprotected sex with someone about whose HIV status they were ignorant. Here is the relevant testimony of complainant A, who is being cross-examined by defence counsel:[27]

> Q: . . . did you get sex education classes at school?
> A: Yeah.
> Q: It's a long time ago now but do you remember them?
> A: Sort of, yeah.
> Q: Did they teach you about contraception?
> A: Yeah.
> Q: About how to practise safer sex?
> A: Yeah.
> Q: Did they tell you about sexual infections?
> A: Yeah.
> Q: And were you aware that if condoms are worn it reduces the risk of spreading a sexual infection?
> A: Yeah.
> Q: Did they tell you anything about HIV? Did you know anything about AIDS?

27 E:A at 6.

A: No.

Q: Either from those lessons at school or from what you heard on the news?

A: Er, well, they told us about it in school but I still didn't get to grips with what it was about.

Having established the extent of A's knowledge of risk, which although general appears to be limited so far as the risk of HIV transmission itself is concerned, defence counsel focuses on the extent to which she was aware of the risks associated with having sex with Mr Konzani, whose girlfriend she had agreed to be at his request the second time they met:[28]

Q: What did you know about [Feston Konzani] at that stage?

A: Not much.

Q: But what had you asked him about himself?

A: Well, I asked him where he was from.

Q: And where did you understand him to be from?

A: Well, he said 'Africa', so I just . . .

Q: And where you aware that there is an AIDS problem in Africa?

A: Not really, no.

Q: Did you think about that?

A: No.

Q: Did you ask him about his previous sexual partners, whether he had had any girlfriends before?

A: No.

. . .

Q: What did you know about him before you agreed to have sex with him?

A: Not much.

Q: Why did you have unprotected sex with him when you had been taught about the safety of using a condom at school?

A: I don't know.

Q: Did you realise you were taking a risk of becoming pregnant?

A: Yeah.

Q: Were you prepared to take that risk?

A: Yeah.

Q: Did you realise you were taking a risk of catching a disease?

A: Yeah.

Q: And were you prepared to take that risk?

A: [No reply.]

28 E:A at 7–8.

> Q: Are you able to answer that question, please, [name of witness]?
> A: Yeah.
> Q: What is your answer?
> A: Yes, I was, yeah.
> Q: You knew you were taking a risk?
> A: Yeah.

Having established an evident awareness on the part of A of the risk of contracting a sexually transmitted disease through unprotected sex, defence counsel then seeks to demonstrate to the jury her willingness to run that risk with others whose 'riskiness' is greater than in the general population. He does this by referring to her relationship with a subsequent boyfriend 'P'.[29]

> Q: Did you know that people who inject drugs are at greater risk of having HIV?
> A: Yeah.
> Q: Because of sharing needles.
> A: Yeah, I know.
> Q: So why did you have a relationship with somebody who you knew was injecting drugs and might have . . .
> A: Well, I didn't know at first. When I first got with him he wasn't injecting.
>
> . . .
>
> Q: . . . but you came to know that he was injecting, didn't you?
> A: Yeah, I found him in the bedroom injecting.
> Q: How soon after you had started going out with him was that?
> A: About two month.
> Q: But you were going out with him for three months, weren't you?
> A: Yeah.
> Q: So is it true, [complainant's name], that you carried on having sex with him knowing that he was an injecting drug user?
> A: Yeah.
> Q: So what risk did you know you were taking doing that with P?
> A: I knew it was a big risk.
> Q: You also told [the complainant's doctor] that P might be gay or bi-sexual?
> A: Yeah.
> Q: Do you know what risk there is of HIV in people who are gay or bi-sexual?
> A: Yeah.

---

29 E:A at 8–9.

Q: Is it a greater risk or a smaller risk than people who are
heterosexual?
A: I don't know, I only know it's a risk.
Q: So P was both an injecting drug user and gay or bi-sexual.
A: [No reply.]

The impression the jury would have gained of A's knowledge of risk from
these exchanges is a complex one. She was a young woman (15 at the time of
meeting Mr Konzani), who had gained some understanding at school about
the risks associated with unprotected sex, but apparently understood little
about HIV or AIDS. She was aware of the greater HIV transmission risk
associated with having such sex with injecting drug users, and with gay or
bi-sexual men (although she is ignorant of its magnitude relative to those
who identify as heterosexual). With this knowledge, such as it was, she was
prepared – apparently – to take on the general risks of unprotected sex as
they were understood by her.

The complicated, partial and fragmentary knowledge which complainant
A had about the risks associated with unprotected sex was unique to her, the
product of her youth, limited education, and experience. With complainant
B the story was somewhat different. She, it will be recalled, had had substantial contact with Africans. By her own admission she had had eight sexual
partners, of whom two (including Feston Konzani) were African. She also
had a son whose illness meant that she was particularly careful about infections. The defence used this knowledge to try and elicit admission by her that
she would have been aware of the consequences of having unprotected intercourse with the defendant, with whom she had sex soon after their initial
meeting:[30]

Q: And how did the idea of having sex together come about?
A: Well, it just happened.
Q: Did you give any thought to it before it happened?
A; No.
Q: You see, you had a particular anxiety about infections on behalf of
your son, didn't you?
A: Yes.
Q: You had a particular knowledge of HIV and AIDS in Africa
through your interest?
A: Yes.
Q: And you spoke to Feston about the predicament in Africa?
A: Yes.
Q: Did it not occur to you to ask him if he had ever had a test for HIV?
A: No.

30 E:B at 15.

Q: But you were actually on the subject of talking about HIV in Africa. Would it have been easy to ask him if he . . .

A: No, it would have been easier for him to tell me. That's what I think. He had . . . I didn't have the responsibility to ask him. He had the responsibility to tell me.

Q: You had experience of working with Africans before, hadn't you?

A: Yes.

Q: And as I understand it, you had formed the view that many Africans you had met would tell lies?

A: Yes.

Q: That is something which you put in your statement to the police?

A: Yes.

Q: Was there not a reason then to take a little care and ask questions with this man that you were about to have sex with?

A: No.

Here, defence counsel attempts, by playing on her personal knowledge of both Africans and of HIV/AIDS in Africa, and on her maternal concerns, to get the complainant to admit that she had a responsibility to make inquiries about her prospective partner's health. This she rejects. In her view, despite her general knowledge, and these concerns, there was what appears to her to be a self-evident responsibility to disclose known HIV positive status. The defence strategy means that counsel is obliged, in a sense, to essentialise Africans, to construct the defendant as simply a member of a high-risk group, and by virtue of that alone, to suggest that the complainant was aware of the risk she was taking, and irresponsible for not taking precautions against transmission. Because she refuses to play this game, counsel tries once again in extensive questioning to suggest that she was careless with her health through failing to use condoms, especially with an African man:[31]

Q: And . . . the sexual intercourse which followed did not involve the use of a condom?

A: Well . . .

Q: Do you accept that or . . .

A: . . . I first had sex with Feston Konzani was the second night and he wore a condom when we had sexual intercourse.

Q: Where did the condom come from?

A: I've got loads of them in me drawers.

Q: Did you produce it?

A: Yes.

31 E:B at 16–17.

Q: Did you put it on?

A: No, I can't put them on.

Q: Are you sure one was worn?

A: Yeah, pretty much so.

Q: Well, are you sure or are you not sure?

A: Well, I'm not a hundred per cent sure.

Q: No, because afterwards there would be no reason for you to say to him, 'I hope you haven't got any diseases' . . .

A: No, that's wrong.

Q: . . . unless it had been unprotected sex.

A: No, that's wrong, because you can have, you can get sexually transmitted diseases even with wearing a condom. I am quite well aware of that fact.

Q: So it was in your mind immediately after you had sex with him that there was a question of disease being transmitted sexually?

A: No, it was just a joke, said in a joke, it was said with no malicion [sic] or whatever and if he had have took it that seriously then he would have told me that he was HIV positive.

Q: But you said in your statement to the police that you mentioned this light-heartedly due to the fact that Feston was African.

A: Mmmm.

Q: Is that correct?

A: Yeah.

Q: So you mentioned this, 'I hope you haven't got any diseases' because he was African?

A: Well, not only because he was African but that was part of it, yeah.

Q: So the risk you were taking by having sex with an African who you had recently met was that there might be a risk of sexually transmitted disease?

A: Well, but then again there's risk with anybody you have sex with sexually transmitted disease and I'm not willing to be prejudiced and say that just because he was African, just because he was black that I should have wore protection all the time. I wouldn't be in this situation if I'd wore protection all the time, I wouldn't have to stand here defending myself.

Q: I'm not asking you to defend yourself. I am asking you what was in your mind at the time.

A: It was just light-hearted. I'm just one of them people.

Q: The reason that there was a particular risk because he was African was because you knew about the HIV and AIDS epidemic in Africa.

A: Yeah.

Q: And so that is why being African as opposed to being from Iceland was important. Would you agree?

A: Mmmm, but on the first day we met we had discussed that and he had told me that the HIV and AIDS epidemic wasn't very big in Malawi, it was tiny, so I, he was from that country so I believed him.

Q: But you have told us that he . . .

A: No, he didn't actually, he told us it was Burundi, sorry, where he was from, didn't have a big HIV epidemic so I believed him then.

Q: So that did influence your decision to have sex with him?

A: Yes, of course it did.

Q: That you didn't believe the epidemic in Burundi was big?

A: Well, he told me that, yes.

Q: Well, did you know that for yourself?

A: No.

Q: And you have told us that from you experience in dealing with Africans they lie regularly.

A: Yes, but in situations they lie, not, I didn't mean, I meant they lie which country they're from, how old they are or why they are in England. That's what I meant. I didn't mean as a whole they were just liars.

This complainant's knowledge of the risk of HIV transmission is as complicated as that of complainant A, but in different way. It is composite, comprised both of her general understanding of risk-groups, human behaviour and sex, and her particular knowledge of the defendant. At one and the same time she demonstrates an (accurate) awareness that condoms do not provide total protection against disease, but also that she would not be in court if she had had protected sex all the time. She has 'loads' of condoms (demonstrating an awareness on her part of the need for precautions), but expects her male partner to put them on (demonstrating her expectation that he will take responsibility for their use).[32] She thinks condoms were used, but can't (which is reasonable) be sure. She suggests that 'African men' can't necessarily be trusted, and appears to be concerned about the risk of disease, but is unwilling to 'be prejudiced' and explains that her comment about disease was spoken in jest. She recognises that the risk of transmission depends on the kind of sexual intercourse that is had, rather than on the ethnic or national origin of a partner, but is influenced in her decision to have penetrative sex with the defendant by his claim that he came from a country with a relatively low prevalence of HIV in the population.

Whereas complainant A's testimony demonstrated a relative paucity of knowledge either about the risk of HIV transmission in general, or of the particular risk to which she was exposed by agreeing to have unprotected sex

---

32 It is interesting that she uses the construction 'if I'd wore' in the context of condom use, especially since she admits to being inept at using them. It would appear that she sees condoms as protection for her, worn 'by her'.

both with the defendant and others, and complainant B's testimony, in places feisty, self-confident and challenging, demonstrates a confused understanding, complainant C is very different. She is monosyllabic in her response to cross-examination and appears to accept that she was aware of the risks associated with unprotected sex, both in general and with the defendant:[33]

Q: Miss [name of complainant], you have told the police, haven't you, that you don't want any charge brought against Feston for what happened to you?

A: Yes.

Q: And you have told them you don't want to take part in any court proceedings, haven't you?

A: Yes.

Q: You are an intelligent young woman, aren't you?

A: Yes.

Q: You have a degree in [science subject]?[34]

A: Yes.

Q: From the University of [name of university].

A: Yes.

Q: And you are studying for a doctorate, a PhD?

A: Yes.

Q: In [science subject] as well?

A: Yes.

Q: And may I ask how old you are, please?

A: 27.

Q: You are 27, and you come from [sub-Saharan African country]?

A: Yes.

Q: And you are aware of the problem in [name of country] with HIV and AIDS?

A: Yes.

Q: And is that a problem also in Malawi?

A: Yes.

Q: And in all of Africa below the Sahara?

A: Yes.

Q: You met Feston Konzani in Middlesbrough.

A: Yes.

Q: And you shared a strong interest in the church and the Bible.

A: Yes.

Q: And you would often have long arguments about the Bible and discussion about the verse in the Bible.

33 E:C at 8 9.

34 To preserve the complainant's anonymity I have not identified the subject of her under-graduate degree, or of her PhD research.

A: Yes.

Q: Do you remember?

A: Yes.

Q: And there came a time when you moved into his house?

A: Yes.

Q: And soon after that you started to become lovers?

A: Yes.

Q: Did you discuss contraception at all before becoming lovers?

A: No.

Q: So you took the risk of becoming pregnant?

A: Yes.

Q: You knew you were taking that risk?

A: Yes.

Q: And you have, in fact, produced a baby, haven't you?

A: Yes.

Q: Is that [name of baby]

A: Yes.

Q: And she is HIV negative.

A: Yes.

Q: You also realised that by having unprotected sex you risked catching an infection.

A: Yes.

Q: You are after all a [scientist], aren't you?

A: Yes.

Q: A scientist, and that too is a risk which you took.

A: Yes.

Q: That risk included the risk of contracting HIV, didn't it?

A: Yes, but I didn't think about it at the moment.

. . .

Q: That means at the time that you had unprotected sex.

A: Yes.

Q: But you agree that you knew there was a problem with HIV and AIDS in Malawi.

A: Yes, I had had unprotected sex before that.

Q: You had had unprotected sex before.

A: Yes.

Q: This is with your previous partner?

A: Yes.

Q: And you knew that Feston Konzani was from Malawi before you had sex with him?

A: Yes.

Q: But there was no discussion about HIV or tests or anything before you had sex?

A: Yes.
Q: You agree that there was no discussion?
A: Yes.

The passivity of this reluctant witness is broken only when she asserts that she did not think about HIV at the time of having unprotected sex, and to explain that she had previously had unprotected sex with another man. It is, in the true tragic sense, pathetic testimony, with no obvious desire either to contradict what is put to her, or to assert the defendant's responsibility for what happened. And despite her intelligence she makes no attempt to challenge, as does complainant B, the implication that simply by virtue of having sex with a man whose origins lie in a country with an HIV/AIDS problem, she had exposed herself to a greater risk of infection.

These testimonies demonstrate, I think, the complex and multi-faceted nature of the knowledge people may have about the risks associated with unprotected sex, and the risks they are prepared to take with the knowledge that they do have. As for knowledge itself, this self-evidently is contingent on people's individual life experience, their education (whether at school or through the media), their awareness of the epidemiology of HIV/AIDS and of the prevalence of HIV in particular populations (so called 'risk groups'), their exposure to, membership of, and communication/socialising with, people within such risk groups, and their own ethnic and national origins. It is a knowledge which is also partial and selective, in the sense that the very same act (unprotected sexual intercourse) may be recognised as risky with respect to pregnancy, and even – in a generic, non-specific, way – as far as sexually transmitted infections are concerned, but not necessarily recognised as risky with respect to anything as serious as the transmission of HIV. One may only speculate as to whether the absence of such recognition on the part of the complainants represents a conscious or sub-conscious repression of a risk that was, because of its gravity and immensity, in some sense unthinkable and yet realised; and one may only speculate as to whether the stated absence of any such recognition at the time of infection represents a *post hoc* narrative, a strategy of rationalisation and self-justification deployed by the complainants to distance themselves from any responsibility they may have in fact felt for the consequences of their actions.

The important point here is not whether any lack of awareness, or any failure to think about the risk of transmission as the time, was true or false, rather it is that these accounts, these complex, confused, and sometimes contradictory narratives, are those that formed the basis of the evidence on which the jury concluded that there had been no consent on the part of any of the complainants. That conclusion was, however, reached not simply on that evidence. While that evidence was being given, the judicial direction as to how they should apply the relevant law had not yet been given. Nor, of course, had the closing speeches of prosecution and defence counsel, in which attempts were made to persuade the jury of the merits and demerits of the case against the defendant. In the next two sections I consider the way in which the factual issues of knowledge and risk awareness undergo their translation into the specifically legal question of consent, both *via* the advocacy of the barristers and the authoritative voice of the judge.

Consent

As has been explained, the key issue in the Konzani trial was whether there had been *consent* to the risk of HIV transmission. That this was the key issue was the result of the decision of the Court of Appeal in *R v Dica*,[35] which was handed down on May 5, 2004 – the very day that the Konzani trial started. Indeed, prior to the swearing in of the jury, there was much discussion between counsel and the Recorder as to the implications of the Court of Appeal judgment for the case in which they were about to be involved. The prosecution sought to persuade the Recorder that *Dica* should be read restrictively, so that the defence of consent to risk should mean only consent to the risk of HIV or another serious sexually transmitted disease, while the defence attempted to argue that it should be read more expansively, so that it would be a defence if there was consent to the risk of any sexually transmitted disease, serious or otherwise. The reason for these alternative submissions was obvious – it would be easier for the prosecution to prove beyond reasonable doubt that a person to whom HIV had been transmitted had not consented to the risk of *that* outcome, than it would be to prove that they had not consented to the risk of a less grave one (i.e. the transmission of a disease that could be cured). Conversely, it would be easier for the defence to suggest that, by agreeing to have unprotected sex, the complainants had consented to the risk of *any* disease that might result, and the fact that HIV was transmitted (rather than chlamydia, syphilis or gonorrhoea) was to all intents and purposes irrelevant.

The Recorder was not persuaded by the defence argument, which in his judgment failed to reflect the fact that the defendant had been charged under s 20 of the OAPA 1861. In his words:[36]

> My decision is that . . . the ambit of consent which the Crown must prove was absent on the part of any complainant in these four counts is that of being prepared to run the risk of suffering HIV or some other serious sexual disease. That, I think, is to be distilled from the decision given this morning in the Court of Appeal (Criminal Division) and the word 'serious' is a significant word in that formulation,

35 [2004] 2 Cr App R 28.
36 S at 26.

in other words not any sexual disease. I am assisted in coming to that conclusion by having regard to the specific charges which the defendant faces, namely under section 20 of the Offences Against the Person Act, 1861 where the subject matter is grievous bodily harm, or in other words serious harm.

We have seen how, in light of this ruling, the prosecution sought to show how the defendant's outward appearance and demeanour provided no reason for the complainants to suspect his HIV positive status, how he lied or failed to tell the truth about this when he had the opportunity to do so, and how he failed consistently to use condoms with his sexual partners. In doing so, prosecuting counsel's strategy was to suggest that there could have been no consent (in any meaningful sense of the word) to the risk of transmission. In contrast the defence strategy was to elicit from the complainants their awareness at the relevant time of the risks associated with unprotected sex – something with which he had some success. He then invited the jury, in his closing speech, to conclude that such awareness amounted to consent to the risk of HIV transmission. In doing so, a much-reiterated theme is that the prosecution have in some sense misled the jury as to the relevant issue(s):[37]

Time and time again in his closing speech for the Prosecution you were told that none of these women would have had sex with him if they had known. That is utterly irrelevant. It has no bearing on any legal principle here involved. It supports no aspect of any charge which is legally laid against Mr Konzani. It only serves to promote your moral censure of Mr Konzani, which is utterly beside the point, and to confuse two issues. We are not concerned with whether there was consent to sexual intercourse.

They have said, 'These women wouldn't have consented to having sex if they had known.' That is not an ingredient of any charge faced by Mr Konzani. We are concerned not with his knowledge of his condition, that is utterly beside the point. So we are not concerned with consent to sexual intercourse, we are not concerned with knowledge of his condition, we are not concerned with rewriting the criminal law and making it an offence to have sexual relations without disclosing an infectious disease. That is not the law, and we are not in this case about the business of rewriting the law. You could make a moral argument for rewriting the law. This is not Parliament. We are here to do justice according to what the law is and the only issue which you are here to decide is whether in each specific case of the three women with whom you are concerned the specific facts in each case show that she may have consented to the risk of being infected with

37 D:CS at 12–13.

HIV, consent to the risk, not consent to being given the disease – two wholly different concepts.

For the defence, it is critical that the ethical dimensions of the case are stripped away to leave a simple, technical, legal question. Aware, no doubt, of the emotional impact which the testimony of the complainants may have had on the jury, and of the possibility that their own prejudices, fears and moral judgement might affect the way in which they interpreted the evidence, defence counsel makes valiant attempts to emphasise their irrelevance in the present context. To do this he seeks to de-sexualise and de-moralise the issue, to frame the relevant question as one concerned not with the risks to which others may recklessly expose us, but to which we may willingly expose ourselves:[38]

> No one wants HIV. No one wants lung cancer, but how many people risk those conditions? On the way up to court I picked up a packet of cigarettes that had been discarded. 'Smoking seriously harms you and others around you'. You can go outside this court at lunch time and look at all the cigarette ends on the ground and if you trace the trail you will find groups of smokers puffing vigorously outside. They all have packets like this that tell them that smoking seriously harms them and people round them, people they love, their children, their wives, there is a serious health risk and yet these are sold all over the town in shops [sic] which say, 'Smoking kills you'. You go up to one of those smokers, you say, 'Do you consent to getting lung cancer?' They'll say, 'I'm more likely to get run over by the number 99 bus', 'My grandfather, Dave, lived till he was 99 and he smoked 20 Woodbine a day'. That's what they will say, I guarantee it. They are taking an obvious risk of serious harm to their health and deaths from smoking in this country are more significant a health factor than deaths from HIV.
>
> That shows you that people do take risks with their health and if you ask them whether they consent to taking the risk of lung cancer they will say 'No', but the question which they are actually answering is, 'Do you want lung cancer?' isn't it? That is what they are saying, 'I don't want it'.
>
> No one wants HIV, no one wants lung cancer, but the way people rationalise these risks is if they want something enough they are prepared to put those risks to the back of their mind. It does not mean when they go to the doctor they look at the X-rays and they are shown to have lung cancer that they have not consented to that risk.

---

38 D:CS at 13.

Despite its immediate appeal, this argument is not without its difficulties. It is hard to see, for example, how smoking cigarettes (which results from a physiological addiction to nicotine that may certainly cause a smoker to ignore health warnings) can be compared to the voluntary engagement in sex which carries the risk of HIV transmission. And even if it is true that the complainants wanted this so much they were prepared to put that risk to the back of their minds, there is (arguably) a fundamental difference between consenting to a risk in respect of which another person has the capacity to exercise agency, and consenting to a risk in respect of the ingestion of a noxious substance over which only the potential 'victim' has control.

Defence counsel's argument is stronger where he emphasises the fact that people may reasonably be expected to, and do in fact, modify their own (non-addictive) behaviour in light of known health risks associated with certain foods and behaviours at certain times (for example the salmonella in eggs, 'mad cow disease' and foot and mouth scares of the 1980s and 1990s). He is also on firmer ground when he talks about the risks that rugby players and boxers willingly consent to when they go on to the field or into the ring. In each of these contexts he asserts that people who are aware of, and take, the risks associated with certain activities have thereby consented to them. They may suppress their awareness of those risks, but such suppression does not equate to an absence of consent. The last thing they may want is to be harmed, but if they are this does not mean that there was no consent to the possibility of that happening. Counsel develops this argument in the particular context of the case by suggesting that the evidence of character and behaviour used by the prosecution to emphasise Mr Konzani's fault and the complainants' innocence is in fact evidence of the very opposite:[39]

> All that evidence perhaps helps you to understand is how many, many different women of different ages and from different origins seem to have had an immediate attraction for Mr Konzani. It shows in the history of some three or four years that we have looked at how women would meet him on the street and come to his house and be in bed with him, knowing almost nothing about him.
>
> No careful courtships in evidence here before entering into sexual relations. It just shows the speed with which these relationships started and helps to demonstrate how little thought is given by either party to engaging in sexual activity, because you will know from your experience of life that when people hit it off and they are strongly attracted and there is passion, reason goes out of the window. That does not mean that those people are not taking risks with their sexual health or as to whether they become pregnant or not. Because someone is overcome by passion and emotion and has unprotected sex,

39 D:CS at 17.

they can't say, 'Well, I didn't consent to the risk of becoming pregnant and having a baby.' They have consented to that risk. They have taken that risk. Of course, it was not in the forefront of their mind at the time and, of course, they didn't want it to happen but they took the risk.

There is a fundamental and fatal paradox here. Defence counsel want, as we have seen, to disaggregate the messy, affective and emotional aspects of the relationships between the defendant and the complainants in order to focus the jury's mind on the technical question of the existence or otherwise of consent to risk. This, it is argued, may be assessed on the basis that people use their common sense and general knowledge to modify their behaviour. The trouble is that the rationality allegedly underpinning such behaviour modification, and what makes it legitimate to find wanting those who carry on regardless, is – on his own admission – absent when passions are aroused. He wants, needs, the jury to conclude that, at the relevant time(s), the complainants were thinking clearly, exercising a voluntary willing consent; but the converse may be true precisely because of the emotional, passionate, uncontrolled context in which unprotected sex occurred. It is similarly difficult for him to assert convincingly that even if they were not aware, they should have been:[40]

> What this also demonstrates, doesn't it, and this is relevant because you have to consider what thought these young women gave to the risk, if he was prepared to sleep with them so easily, surely it must have been apparent to them that he must have slept with others in that way and that if he is someone who is therefore involved in casual sexual relationships he is someone who it is more risky to have unprotected sex with. Is that not a fair point?
>
> If he is in bed with woman A after 36 hours of knowing her is it not reasonable for her to think, 'Well, I wonder if he does this often? I wonder if he's married. I wonder if he's got a string of girls. I wonder if he'll come back next week.' If he has with them struck up such a passionate relationship leading to intimacy so quickly, ought they not be on guard that he might be someone who is at higher risk of transmitting sexual diseases? Is that not obvious?

It is striking how satisfying the legal test for consent to risk, which relies on a finding of fact about the existence of such consent, requires counsel to avoid direct reference to what was in fact in the complainants' minds at the relevant time and instead to focus on the normative question of what ought to have been. Given the strength and immediate appeal of the prosecution's

40 D:CS at 17.

suggestion that the women's ignorance of the defendant's HIV positive status meant that there was in fact no consent to the risk of transmission, the defence has to argue that there *was* because there *ought* to have been. There ought to have been because, according to the defence case, the complainants were agents with the capacity to make rational choices based on their intelligence and experience. Their failure to make the right choices renders them, rather than the defendant, the (ir)responsible parties.

The Recorder's summing-up

The problem with the defence strategy was that it implied, albeit indirectly, that it was the women who were on trial rather than the defendant – something which critics of rape laws have long criticised, and a suggestion with which the jury might very well have felt uncomfortable. It was, however, arguably the only strategy available on the facts of such a case tried under such a set of legal principles. Despite the fact that the legal and evidential burden was on the prosecution to disprove the existence of consent, the real burden – and it is a heavy one indeed – may reasonably be said to have lain squarely on the shoulders of the defence.

When it came to summing up, the Recorder had a complicated task. He had on the one hand to review the evidence which he thought would be of assistance to the jury (but at the same time making clear that they were entitled to give such evidence little weight, and treat as determinative evidence he ignored); he had to direct the jury on how they were to assess the evidence and credibility of each of the relevant witnesses and to explain the implications of Mr Konzani's failure to testify; and most important of all, he had to explain what the law was, and what it was the prosecution had to prove. These are, of course, specific examples of what every judge in every criminal trial must do; but the relative novelty of the facts of this particular trial, the fast-developing law, the media interest and the strong feelings which were aroused, meant that the Recorder's job in summing up was especially critical. He was particularly careful to emphasise the importance of reaching verdicts on the three counts using common sense and reason, and not being swayed by prejudice or passion:[41]

> Can I just say this, and it is an important matter. In drawing any inference be reasonable, be fair, be logical, use your common sense and your knowledge of the world. The subject matter of this case is a very human matter, isn't it? You will need to get to grips with people as they were behaving and as they were thinking – and that is an important element – some years ago now, so draw inferences that you think to be right and fair and proper but be fair in doing so . . .

41 R:SU at 5.

> You twelve people come from different walks of life, different life experiences and most importantly in a case like this you can apply your accumulated wisdom – if you will forgive the word, it is a bit of a pompous one – but do you see what I mean? You apply your experience of life to the questions that arise in this case. Do not shrink from drawing such inference as you might think right to draw but be careful not to jump to conclusions, illogical and unfair ones.
>
> I have said, 'Use your common sense and your knowledge of the world and of people.' Make sure that emotion does not enter into your judgment in this exercise that you must embark upon. There is an old saying that, 'When emotion comes in, sense moves out.' Emotion has its place, of course, but it can mislead judgment.

It is a nice irony that the jury are warned that emotion may mislead *their* judgement, when one of the very things they are being asked to evaluate objectively is the effect of emotion on the judgement of the complainants. They were to apply their reason to determine the existence of consent, the presence of which depends on the exercise of reason, and the absence of which may be explained by the effects of passion. It is no wonder then that the Recorder was at pains to explain precisely the legal and evidential burden:[42]

> ... the Prosecution must make you sure that at the time of being so infected with the virus the young woman in question, whichever it was, did not willingly consent to the risk of suffering that infection. Note that I use the phrase 'to the risk of suffering that infection' and not merely just to suffering it. That is an important point which [defence counsel] rightly drew to your attention in his speech to you this morning. He put it this way, it is whether she consented to that risk, not consented to being given the disease which is, as he put it graphically, a mile away from the former.
>
> That is right, but note that I use the word 'willingly' in the phrase 'willingly consent' and I did that to highlight that the sort of consent I am talking about means consciously, that is to say thinking about the matter at the time as opposed to either not giving it any thought at all or having a theoretical or general awareness of life's risks.

It is at this point, I would argue, notwithstanding the detailed review of the complainants' evidence and credibility,[43] and the faultless direction on the

---

42 R:SU at 9–10.

43 This was particularly relevant with complainant A who had been identified by the police as an unreliable witness.

inferences that could, and could not, be drawn from the defendant's failure to give evidence, that the prosecution to all intents and purposes ensured a conviction. In chapter 5 I explore the question of consent in more detail, suffice it to say here that there was no evidence from any of the complainants that they had consciously thought about the risk of HIV transmission at the time they had unprotected sex with Mr Konzani. Indeed, it was something they all denied in more or less categoric terms. The Recorder was particularly critical of the suggestion, put by defence counsel in his closing speech, that the complainants' knowledge of the defendant's HIV positive status was irrelevant to the question of consent:[44]

> One very significant matter . . . would be whether or not the young woman in question knew Mr Konzani was HIV positive at the time and here [defence counsel] was wrong to tell you that 'it is utterly irrelevant' – that is his phrase – that such a young woman would not have had sex with Mr Konzani if she had known he was HIV positive; it is relevant, for if she did know of his infection and in that knowledge had unprotected intercourse with him, one may well think she would have been prepared to run the risk.
>
> Of course, the uncontradicted evidence here in each case is that she did not know he was HIV positive, so although the two things, knowledge on the one hand and consent on the other, are inevitably linked in the way I have just demonstrated, the ultimate question for you is not any knowledge on her part of his infection or the lack of such knowledge on her part, but her consent to running the risk of being infected with the HIV virus.
>
> I would add only that although it is a matter entirely for you, you may think that unless she was consciously prepared to take whatever risk of sexually transmitted infection there may be, in other words have deliberately and completely abandoned care for her own safety, it is unlikely she would have consented to a risk of major consequent illness if she was ignorant of his having the virus, but I stress that is a matter for you.

It will be recalled that the point the defence had been seeking to make was that the central issue was consent to risk, not to sexual intercourse, and that this could exist despite the complainants' ignorance of the defendant's condition. Although it would have been possible for a jury to conclude that there was such consent, had the Recorder directed them in more general terms, it was arguably impossible for them to do so after receiving the direction he in fact gave, and the supplementary assistance he subsequently provided.

---

44 R:SU at 10–11.

Despite its general tenor, this part of the direction is, I would respectfully suggest, confusing; not because it is wrong, but because it is inherently contradictory. On the one hand the Recorder makes it crystal clear that the central question is consent to the risk of infection (something which it would not be *logically* impossible for a jury to find in the absence of knowledge about a sexual partner's HIV positive status), and on the other that their knowledge is both relevant *and* irrelevant: relevant because its presence might lead one to conclude that there *had* been consent (even though these are not the facts before the jury), and irrelevant because consent does not depend necessarily upon it. He then (using the language of the Court of Appeal in *Dica*) suggests – with appropriate warning that is a matter for them – how the jury might reasonably conclude that a person would be unlikely to consent to the risk of infection *unless* she had intentionally chosen to throw caution to the wind and *if* she was ignorant of the defendant's condition. The use of two conditions ('if' and 'unless'), which if met *may* lead to a particular conclusion would not, it is suggested, have made the jury's task an easy one. The Recorder himself appears to have been aware of this because he tries to sum up the issue, after indicating that defence counsel's arguments about behaviour modification and consent during health scares and in sport may help them, with the following supplementary assistance:[45]

> You give these arguments such weight as you think appropriate, but I am going to give you this one which is the best help that I can give you. Note the very clear and important distinction between running a risk on the one hand and consenting to run that risk on the other.
>
> You may not be willing to run the risk of falling through the ice on a frozen pond and drowning, you may believe it will support your weight, you may be wrong and go through because it may not be as thick as you believe or even hope. You are running that risk, but you have not consented to it just because everyone knows that such accidents happen.
>
> If, on the other hand, the farmer has put up a sign, 'Danger – thin ice' which you read but think you know better or at least are a good enough skater to whiz across unscathed, then that would be an example of your consenting to run the risk of falling through thin ice. Why? Because it has been drawn to your attention by the farmer's sign.

This too is confusing. The jury has already been told that the central question is consent, not knowledge. The Recorder seeks to reassert this through an analogy (literally concerning thin ice) which arguably muddies the water even further. First, he suggests that the general knowledge one may be expected to have about certain risky activities does not equate to consent to run that risk (and that wanting a good outcome does not mean you are unprepared to take the risk of a bad one). In making this suggestion there is the clear implication that even being conscious of a risk, and taking it willingly, should not be understood as consenting to it. Second, he contrasts that situation with one where a person consciously consents to the risk because, prior to running it, they have been warned by the person with relevant knowledge about that risk. In other words, the Recorder appears to be suggesting in the strongest possible terms that only the presence of a warning from such a person distinguishes the consensual taking of risks from the running of risks. Put simply, he seems to indicate that there can be no consent without knowledge gained *via* disclosure – the very thing he earlier sought to refute.

It is perhaps no wonder that the jury were confused, and that after retiring to consider their verdicts one of them sent up a note. That note, which was read out in court, was as follows:[46]

My teenage children regularly accept lifts in other people's cars from friends or taxi drivers. They willingly or knowingly consent to the very low risk of being involved in a serious accident.

If the driver was obviously drunk, smelling of alcohol, slurred speech, et cetera, the likelihood of accident would be very much higher and I would expect my children to refuse the lift. If they accepted the lift and were okay I would say they were foolish and lucky; if they regularly accepted such lifts I would say they were irresponsible and very lucky. They were consenting to increased risk of injury or death.

What if the driver was high risk but did not show any outward signs of being so, for example he might be a recreational drug user or an epileptic who has been told by his doctor not to drive or he may have been banned from driving? I could not reasonably expect my children to ask the driver to take a drugs test and to show his driving licence and his medical records. Unless the driver volunteers the information my children are not willingly and knowingly consenting to any increased risks.

In any of the above situations if an accident did lead to serious injury or death I would expect the law to take action but maybe the seriousness of the punishment would reflect the specific circumstances.

In summary, I suggest the HIV positive person who engages in unsafe sex is analogous to the persistently drunken and/or dangerous

46 R:SU at 48–49.

> driver. He might get away with this behaviour many times but eventu-
> ally he will cause serious harm to some innocent party. The law needs
> to punish this behaviour as a deterrent to others.

This note provides a fascinating insight into the response of at least one of the jurors to the evidence, speeches and summing-up. It demonstrates well the confusion that the application of this law to these facts may be thought to have provoked. There appears to be recognition of the complicated relationship between knowledge and consent, and that those who willingly take risks of which they are aware may be taken to have consented to them. At the same time the person with HIV seems to be characterised as someone who should be found guilty because they take unjustifiable risks with the safety of others. The note is an excellent example of the way in which the legal distinction between liability (which arises if the elements of an offence are established, and there is no valid defence) and culpability (which relates to the blameworthiness of the defendant) may be collapsed in the mind of someone responsible for determining guilt; and it is an equally good example of how the factual (whether this defendant is, on the evidence, guilty as charged) may be transposed into the normative (whether he should be).

Unsurprisingly, the Recorder took some time dealing with the content of this note, but in essentially the same terms as he had done previously. He reminded the jury that there was no legal duty to disclose known HIV status, that they were to apply the law as he had directed them it was, not on the basis of what they thought it should be, and he reiterates the frozen pond analogy, noting that they 'kindly nod' when he explains the distinction between running a risk and consenting to one. He concludes (one gets the sense, in some desperation) with one final thought which he hopes will nail the issue:[47]

> I leave you with this acid test which you may find of practical use. If a little bird had whispered in [the particular complainant's] ear as she was about to have unprotected sexual intercourse with Feston Konzani, 'Would you be doing this if you knew he was HIV infected?' and that little bird had gone on to describe what that meant . . . would she reply, 'No, I wouldn't' or would she reply, 'It doesn't matter, I'll be all right'?
>
>   If you are sure she would say, 'No, I wouldn't', then that would lead you to a guilty verdict. If it is your judgment that she would have said or may have said, 'It doesn't matter', then he is not guilty.

Unsurprisingly perhaps, the jury concluded that with this knowledge (which they didn't have, and which appears now to have become critical to explaining

47 R:SU at 53.

the presence or absence of consent) the complainants would not have agreed to have unprotected sex. After a trial lasting two weeks, and having heard evidence from 16 witnesses, the jury returned a unanimous guilty verdict on each of the three counts in less than four hours.

Concluding observations

The purpose of this chapter was three-fold. First, I wanted to explore in detail, using extensive transcript material, the kind of issues that may typically arise in cases of reckless HIV transmission. In doing this, I hope to have shown how complicated is the range of problems which the law has to confront when dealing with human relationships. These include, but are not limited to, the faultlines that may exist in communication between sexual partners, the way false and dangerous assumptions about health status are made, the ways in which the expression and fulfilment of desire may lead to the repression and denial of danger, the way willingness knowingly to engage in risky behaviours correlates (paradoxically) with growing intimacy, the way trust is experienced and abused, and the way general knowledge of the risks associated with certain conduct may cease to have application in the context of a particular relationship. In the evidence of the complainants, and the other women called to give evidence, we see a variety of experience, awareness, acceptance, ignorance, and a spectrum of risk-taking behaviour, unique to each of them; but each also shared, in some sense, a common experience.

Second, I wanted to demonstrate, through a close reading of the text, how these human passions, sentiments, behaviours and expectations are, through the lens of the criminal law, viewed as problems capable of legal resolution. The messiness, inconclusiveness and complexity of lived experience is rendered, though law, into a set of discrete resolvable questions to which answers may (and must) be given. At the same time, as the previous section has, I think, demonstrated, law is only able to ensure effective resolution (the reaching of a verdict) by constructing questions which necessarily deny that messiness, inconclusiveness and complexity. The problem is that those questions cannot (as the note from the jury demonstrates well) eradicate what they seek to deny. Life leaks in. To deal with this unfortunate reality there is resort to the hypothetical and the analogy. Sexual relationships become frozen ponds, boxing matches, rugby scrums, salmonella-ridden eggs, and foot and mouth infected countryside. Sexual partners become ice skaters, full backs, omelette eaters and ramblers. The intuitive sense that knowledge is critical to determining the presence or absence of consent is both *affirmed* (through the suggestion that a person who was aware of a partner's HIV positive status might be thought to have consented) and *denied* (because there is no legal obligation to disclose such status). And all this can apparently be reduced in the final analysis to a fictitious talking bird on the shoulder of somebody contemplating unprotected sex surreptitiously chirruping information that was not, in fact, provided to them at the time. These observations are not intended as a criticism of what the criminal law is and what the criminal law does, rather they are intended as an explanation of what criminal law inevitably is, and what it must inevitably do in contested cases such as this. As I suggest in the final chapter, it is precisely because there is no way of avoiding the kind of reductivism that criminal law employs, or rather must employ, in the adjudiciation of cases concerning the reckless transmission of HIV – one that inevitably produces over-simplified accounts of responsibility and irresponsibility, of guilt and innocence – that the case for decriminalising the reckless transmission of HIV is a defensible one.

My third aim in this chapter was to use the transcript of Mr Konzani's trial to identify some of the core themes which are taken up in the remaining parts of the book. In particular I wanted to show, using as far as possible the words of the participants themselves, the way in which HIV transmission is represented as a particular kind of harm (formally and legally equivalent to a broken leg, but so obviously understood as something far more serious – as nothing less than a signifier of mortality and a harbinger of death), and – through extracts concerned with harm, knowledge, disclosure, trust, risk and consent – the way in which the blameworthy defendant is constructed. These themes are pursued in detail in the following chapters. Here I would simply observe that the trial of Feston Konzani provides us with a valuable insight into the ways in which concepts and categories, typically articulated and explored merely as legal principles open to intellectual analysis and clarification within the comparatively sterile surroundings of the criminal appeal courts, have a vibrant and contested life, meaning and application in the real world of trial courts. If we ignore this, any criticism of the law in this area will be partial and, in my view, profoundly inadequate.

Chapter 3

Harm, causation and HIV infection

Since the onset of the AIDS epidemic, the HIV has become the center of an electrifying biomedical and cultural imagination, full of grave implications. Technoscience has made it possible to visualize and speak about this new truth. Yet, as the narrative indicates, it is, at best, an ambiguous truth: HIV is both lifeless and actively alive. It is a graspable, seeable, and somewhat innocent reality (as common as a rock or a stone) but simultaneously an unfamiliar object, a concept that exists only in the eyes of technology, a life-threatening entity beyond our control.

(Erni, 1994: 34–5)

Introduction

For those working in the criminal justice system – whether police, prosecutors, lawyers or judges – the concept of harm is unproblematic. Every criminal offence contains within it an *actus reus*, sometimes referred to (inaccurately) as 'guilty act', part of which comprises the conduct or consequence (or both) that must be established if the defendant is to be convicted of the offence in question. Whether or not the *actus reus* is established is a question of fact for determination by the jury or magistrates hearing the case. Thus, in the crime of theft, the prosecution must satisfy the tribunal of fact that the defendant appropriated property belonging to another, in murder that he unlawfully killed a human being, in rape that he unlawfully penetrated with his penis the vagina or anus of another person who at the time was not consenting to the penetration. The same is true in the context with which we are concerned, although HIV infection exists not as a specified harm in the criminal law but instead is treated as an example of a more general kind. In order to establish criminal liability for the transmission of HIV (whether intentionally or recklessly), the prosecution must prove that the defendant unlawfully caused another person to suffer grievous bodily harm.

The purpose of this chapter is, first, to engage critically with the way in which HIV infection is understood as a harm with which the criminal law should be concerned, and, second, at the difficulties involved in proving that a particular defendant has in fact caused the harm alleged. As to the first of these, some readers may, instinctively, consider this to be a pointless exercise (or at least one that need only be very brief). Surely, they may think, there is little to be gained from exploring the meaning of something that is so *self-evidently* harmful. What, they may ask (and I accept fully that it is a legitimate question) is there to be said about the harm that infection with an ineradicable virus that causes AIDS and leads to death? What could be more harmful than that? Well, I think there is much to be said. My intention is not to deny the gravity of HIV infection, nor to argue that its effects are not physically injurious. Rather, my purpose is to try and understand the precise ways in which HIV is understood as a harm, why it is a harm with which the criminal law has come to concern itself in recent years, and what the criminalisation of people for causing this particular kind of harm tells us about the ways in which criminal law reflects contemporary anxieties about our bodies, our relationships, and the society in which we live. In a criminal law textbook these questions would no doubt be thought irrelevant; but this is not a criminal law textbook. Understanding the harm that HIV infection represents, and the way in which it is proven, provides us with an important and fascinating insight into how the 'objective' scientific knowledge is translated into law and legal reasoning, and through that into the ways in which we conceptualise ourselves and our identities; it gives us the opportunity to think critically about the ways in which criminal law deploys categories of harm in its attempt to impose a particular kind of social and corporeal order (an attempt that, though successful in its own terms, inevitably fails to capture the messy and disordered complexity of experience); and it enables us to reflect on one of the ways in which the anxiety and fear produced by life in 'risk society' is translated through the criminal law into a proxy for the physical and ontological security that we crave, but which is inevitably denied us.

The structure of the chapter is as follows. First, I provide a brief account of the biology of HIV infection. I then explore the legal construction of harm in the context of non-fatal offences against the person. Here I emphasise the ways in which the criminal law has moved towards a model of harm that is increasingly focused on personal security and protection from those who would interfere with or undermine it, and explain how it is that it was not until 2003 that the English courts were able to convict someone for disease transmission (despite the fact that the relevant legislation is more than 140 years old). Third, I look at the peculiar difficulties that HIV transmission cases raise when it comes to proving causation (an issue that arises when a defendant denies that he was the author of the complainant's infection). The chapter concludes by addressing some more general questions about the implications of criminal law's reductivist construction of HIV as a corporeal harm, arguing that this (necessarily) entails an impoverished translation that cannot adequately reflect the lived experience of infection, and reinforces a politically conservative, regressive and stigmatising approach to those who are living with HIV and AIDS. My overall purpose is to suggest that the criminalisation of people for causing the 'harm' of HIV infection, as it is legally interpreted, is a culturally significant and symbolic moment in the contemporary history of criminal law – something that tells us far more about the law, and about the society in which we live, than the specifics of the offence would immediately suggest.

The biology of HIV infection [1]

HIV (human immunodeficiency virus) is a retrovirus. Identified in 1983, HIV is the causative agent of AIDS. As a retrovirus, HIV contains only RNA (Ribonucleic Acid). Because it lacks DNA (Deoxyribonucleic Acid) it cannot replicate outside living host cells. Mature HIV has a bar-shaped core that contains the viral genome. This genome is made up of two strands of RNA containing three principal genes (gag, pol and env), along with a number of enzymes (reverse transcriptase, protease, ribonuclease and integrase). These are all contained within a lipid envelope, or coating. This envelope has 72 surface projections that contain an antigen which helps bind HIV to host cells containing what are known as CD4 receptors. The gag, pol and env genes 'code' the various structural elements of the virus. It is the proteins that make up these elements (for example the envelope and the core) that are immunogenic (i.e. provoke an immune response in the host); and it is the antibodies produced in response to the presence of these proteins that enables testing for host infection with the virus. HIV is not stable, and – as a result largely of the error rate in the reverse transcriptase enzyme – mutates easily and often. This mutation has the effect of producing HIV variants in the host which are more toxic to cells, and more resistant to available anti-retroviral drug therapies. Although there are a number of variants of HIV, HIV-1 is the one responsible for the vast majority of infections. HIV-2, which is less easily transmitted and rarer, is more closely related genetically to simian immunodeficiency virus (SIV) than it is to HIV-1. HIV-1 itself has a number of subtypes, or clades. These sub-types are identified, through a process called phylogenetic testing, by shared genetic similarities in the virus's env genes. The different sub-types have varying properties, so that the effects of HIV infection can vary from person to person (or, because one person may be infected by more than one sub-type, within the same person).

---

1 The science of HIV and AIDS is extremely complex. This simplified exposition is based on a number of sources, principally the information provided by the University of Utah's AIDS tutorial: http://library.med.utah.edu/WebPath/TUTORIAL/AIDS/HIV.html, and on the information available via http://www.aidsmap.com (where further references and detailed discussion can be found). For a more detailed account, see Hutchinson, 2003.

In order to survive and replicate, HIV needs to enter host cells. The cells it primarily infects are those which have CD4 receptor molecules on their surface (although this is not essential). The cells which constitute the principal targets of HIV infection are, therefore, those of the mononuclear phagocyte system, T, B and NK (natural killer) lymphocytes, dendritic cells, endothelial and gastro-intestinal epithelial cells, the microgial cells of the brain and hematopoetic stem cells. Many of these cells are those that exist within the host to fight infection and sustain immunity. Having entered the body, the viral particles (virions) attach themselves through fusion to the membranes of cells that have the requisite CD4 receptor molecules, or by endocytosis (in which the host cell is encased in the viral envelope), and subsequently enter the cell. The virion then releases its RNA which, through a process known as reverse transcription (enabled by the reverse transcriptase enzyme coded by the pol gene), is transcribed to proviral DNA which in turn, using the integrase enzyme, is inserted into the host cell's genomic DNA. Once embedded in the host cell the proviral DNA cannot be destroyed without also destroying the cell itself. The HIV provirus (which is what the proviral DNA becomes) is then in a position to replicate itself, which it does either by 'budding' from the cell's surface or through lysis. The virions that are thereby produced are then able to infect new cells, in a continuing process of replication within the host organism. This replication occurs both at the initial site of infection, and – quickly afterwards – in lymphoid tissues (lymph nodes, spleen, liver and bone marrow). Soon after primary infection, the virus is readily detectable in the blood's mononuclear cells and plasma; there then follows a latency phase in which the virus is less detectable in peripheral blood, but replication is nevertheless continuing in lymphoid tissue. Also happening during this latency phase is the gradual and progressive destruction of the body's CD4 lymphocytes – which are critical to the body's immune defence. For as long as there remains enough immune system response, most infections will be prevented. However, once a critical number of CD4 lymphocytes have been destroyed, the body is unable to maintain its systemic immunity and this is what results in the clinically defined syndrome known as AIDS.

The transmission of HIV may be understood as a function of where the virus is located in the body of the host and how it is passed from that host to another. HIV is present in many bodily fluids, but its presence in genital secretions, blood and (to a lesser extent) in breast milk is the most significant factor in explaining onward transmission – which may occur as the result of sexual intercourse, the sharing of drug injecting equipment or other exposure to infected blood, infection transplacentally *in utero*, during childbirth or through breastfeeding. HIV may be transmitted during sex from male to male, male to female, female to male or female to female. Unprotected receptive anal intercourse has the highest probability of transmission in any one incident of sexual contact, and the probability of transmission is increased where a person has a high viral load (as the result of being newly infected or because they are in the latter stages of diagnosed AIDS-related illness), where an infected man is uncircumcised, where a woman is pregnant, or where there are open lesions as the result of other untreated STIs. Despite this, the probability of being infected with HIV during unprotected sexual intercourse with an HIV positive person is low compared with the risk of being infected with other STIs. The most efficient mode of transmission is parenterally (i.e. through the introduction of HIV directly into the bloodstream of the previously uninfected person). Although haemophiliacs who received blood and blood products in the earlier years of the epidemic were often infected this way, screening has all but eliminated this now. Needle exchange programmes, where they exist, provide a means of reducing the risk of parenteral exposure and infection as the result of contamination with infected blood.

A person who has been infected with HIV may respond with symptoms ranging from acute to mild/unnoticeable illness which then subsides into a latent period which may last years. During this period HIV replication is limited in the mononuclear cells of peripheral blood, and the person's CD4 count is a little lower. At the same time, however, the body's immune response is inadequate to prevent viral replication in lymphoid tissue. During this period a person may have no reason to suspect that they are infected, and it is not possible to identify those who are infected by their outward appearance. There is no evidence to suggest that those who have tested HIV positive will not eventually develop 'clinical AIDS', although there is significant variation among people in the time that this will take. Some 10 per cent of people with HIV infection are what are what are known as 'long survivors', which is to say that despite their infection they manifest no obvious decline in immune function. For the majority, however, such decline does inexorably occur. A concentration, or count, of CD4 below 500 per microlitre of blood signifies a movement towards clinical AIDS, and a count of below 200 per microlitre defines the condition. Once a person has clinical AIDS the probability of opportunistic infections which would otherwise not be serious or fatal (such as pneumonia) and of neoplasms (such as Kaposi's sarcoma, a kind of skin cancer) increases.

Prior to 1995 treatment for HIV infection, and for the opportunistic infections and other AIDS-defining illnesses, was far less successful than it is today. The drugs that currently exist, and which are under development, operate in a number of ways – although all focus on the enzymes that HIV uses to multiply in the infected person. Some target the process by which HIV binds to CD4 T-Cells and/or fuse with host DNA, while others – known as reverse transcriptase and protease inhibitors – prevent the virus from replicating and making copies of itself. Because HIV has a high mutation rate during the process of replication, the virus has the capacity to produce versions of itself that are resistant to one particular form of treatment. Because of this, the most effective form of treatment against disease progression is 'combination therapy', by which different drugs are used to disrupt the same enzyme or different enzymes concurrently. The best combinations are, usually, those that contain both protease and reverse transcriptase inhibitors. Those with access to such drug therapy (HAART), who begin treatment before their CD4 count falls below 200, and who adhere to that treatment, can remain well for many years despite the presence of HIV in their bodies. People with HIV undergoing treatment may still transmit HIV to others, although the probability of doing so is lower where, as a consequence, their viral load is substantially reduced.

The harm of HIV infection

Although I agree fully with leading commentators and scholars such as Paula Treichler (1988; 1999), Catherine Waldby (1996), Cindy Patton (1985; 1990), Douglas Crimp (1988; 2002) and others who argue that HIV and AIDS have no *essential* meaning, and that they can only be understood as social phenomena whose meaning is the product of their discursive formation, it is important in this context to be precise about the physical aspects of HIV and its transmission. It is important because the criminal law has adopted the biomedical model of HIV infection set out above, translated this to its own ends, and integrated it within its own formal and semantic categories. The criminal law is not interested in whether HIV and AIDS are best understood as the site of ideological contestation about heteronormativity, racism, patriarchy or sexuality. It is not (nor, as I shall argue later) concerned with the identity politics of people living with HIV and AIDS, with their experience of infection or illness, or with the ways in which they manage intimate relationships. Rather, it is simply interested in whether HIV – comprehended as a virus, an objective fact, a thing 'out there' – constitutes a physical harm that justifies the punishment of those who cause it to be present in the body of another.

Or at least this is the account the criminal law in some sense tells itself. For, as I hope to show here, it is an account that is implausible, hypocritical and (if I may be excused an arche-positivist term) false. The need for the criminal law to construct and re-construct, through the cases on transmission that have come before the courts, a narrative that affirms its disinterest in the meaning and significance of HIV infection (other than for the blighted victim of a convicted defendant's inestimable wrong) is explicable within a liberal, positivist, theory of law in which the legitimacy of censure depends on the observance in adjudication of the principles of neutrality, objectivity and generality. But try as it might, and try it does, this pretence at objectivity and exclusion of the value-laden, subjective and the specific, is only superficial. To be sure, as I argue in the final chapter, the criminal law must tell this particular story about itself, and have us believe it; for unless it does tell that story and unless we do believe it, governance through law (as we conceive it) would simply be impossible. But close analysis of the way in which the law has constructed the harm HIV infection shows, I think, how tenuous and contingent that story's claims really are.

The legal construction of physical harm

Before considering the harm that HIV represents for the criminal law, it is first necessary to provide some historical context. The root of the criminal law's approach to human physical harm lies in the idea of assault. This, contrary to lay perceptions of the term, is any act which causes the victim to apprehend immediate and unlawful physical violence. In other words, there need be no touching – no physical contact – between the offender and victim for the *actus reus* of the offence to be made out.[2] This, it will be obvious, is a very low threshold and is a concrete manifestation of the value which has traditionally, and still is, placed by the law on personal and physical autonomy. As Blackstone, England's leading jurist of the Enlightenment put it:

> ... the law cannot draw the line between different degrees of violence, and therefore prohibits the first and lowest stage of it; every man's person being sacred, and no other having a right to meddle with it, in any the slightest manner.
>
> (Blackstone, 1830 (1979))

It was not, of course, the case that everyone in the eighteenth and nineteenth centuries had bodies over which others could not 'meddle' – married women, slaves and children were certainly not legally protected from all unwanted touchings; but the lawfulness of 'assaults' upon them was a result of their status as objects of property. The general principle – that a man's body was inviolate and inviolable – was observed in the law then, and continues to be observed to this day. The merest perceived threat to our bodies is enough to satisfy the conduct element of the offence, a minimal infringement that appears to express an underlying belief that our bodies comprise not only what is bounded by our skin, but also by the sensed space that they occupy. This hypothesis is certainly borne out by a reading of the more modern case law.[3] For example, in *R v Lewis*[4] the defendant had threatened the victim, from whom he was separated by a locked door, with physical violence. As a result, the victim jumped out of a window, injuring herself. As the law stood at the time it was necessary, in order for a conviction under s 20 of the OAPA

---

2 The offence is not committed unless the defendant was at fault in so causing the apprehension – in the sense that he either intentionally or recklessly caused it. I am concerned here with the *actus reus* of offences against the person, and so do not deal with the *mens rea* element. For further discussion of *mens rea* see Ch 4.
3 For a thorough review see Horder, 1994; 1998.
4 [1970] Crim LR 647.

1861 to be made out, that the harm suffered was the result of an assault in the technical sense. In other words, the victim had to have apprehended the immediate infliction of unlawful violence upon her body (something that the locked door meant was extremely unlikely). Nevertheless, the Court of Appeal held that the fact of an assault could be implied.[5] Similarly, in *Smith v Superintendent of Woking Police Station*,[6] the Divisional Court was prepared to hold that an assault had been committed where the defendant had looked in through the closed windows of the elderly female victim's ground floor flat, causing her to become so frightened that she had to spend the night with a friend and subsequently had difficulty sleeping. In the words of Kerr LJ:

> . . . there is no need for a finding that what she was frightened of, which she probably could not analyse at that moment, was some innominate terror of some potential violence. It was clearly a situation where the basis of the fear which was instilled in her was that she did not know what the defendant was going to do next, but that, whatever he might be going to do next, and sufficiently immediately for the purposes of the offence, was something of a violent nature.[7]

More recently, the logic of this trajectory was extended to its fullest extent so that silent telephone calls that had the effect of causing an apprehension of immediate physical violence were held to constitute an assault.[8] In *R v Ireland; R v Burstow*,[9] Lord Steyn was categoric in his identification of the social ill with which the House of Lords had been called upon to deal:

> . . . it is easy to understand the terrifying effect of a campaign of telephone calls at night by a silent caller to a woman living on her own. It would be natural for the victim to regard the calls as menacing. What may heighten her fear is that she will not know what the caller may do

5 Though see now *R v Wilson* [1984] AC 242.
6 (1983) Cr App Rep 234.
7 Ibid at 238.
8 It used to be thought that words alone could not amount to an assault, and needed – if the offence was to be made out – an accompanying gesture that manifested the intent to harm. Thus in *Tuberville v Savage* (1669) 1 Mod Rep 3 there was no assault where the defendant indicated verbally while at the same time touching his sword that, were the judges not in town, he would not take 'such language' from the victim. Horder (1998) suggests that the judges in this case concluded there was no assault because they treated the defendant's statement as if it were a 'defeating condition' (i.e. there was no immediate threat of violence). However, consistent with his view that the essence of psychic assault is the experience of fear produced by confrontation, Horder suggests that it is possible to think of the statement as merely 'suspensory' (i.e. that the threat might be carried out once the judges left), and that if decided today the case would (and should) be decided differently.
9 [1998] 1 Cr App R 177.

next. The spectre of the caller arriving at her doorstep bent on inflicting personal violence on her may come to dominate her thinking. After all, as a matter of common sense, what else would she be terrified about? The victim may suffer psychiatric illness such as anxiety neurosis or acute depression. Harassment of women by repeated silent telephone calls, accompanied on occasions by heavy breathing, is apparently a significant social problem. That the criminal law should be able to deal with this problem, and so far as is practicable, afford effective protection to victims is self evident.[10]

His Lordship's answer to the problem was to hold that there was nothing in principle that should preclude the conviction of a defendant for an offence in which assault had to be proven, despite the fact that no words had been uttered, no physical contact had been made and he was – at the relevant time – distant from the victim:

> That brings me to the critical question whether a silent caller may be guilty of an assault. The answer to this question seems to me to be 'yes, depending on the facts'. It involves questions of fact within the province of the jury. After all, there is no reason why a telephone caller who says to a woman in a menacing way 'I will be at your door in a minute or two' may not be guilty of an assault if he causes his victim to apprehend immediate personal violence. Take now the case of the silent caller. He intends by his silence to cause fear and he is so understood. The victim is assailed by uncertainty about his intentions. Fear may dominate her emotions, and it may be the fear that the caller's arrival at her door may be imminent. She may fear the *possibility* of immediate personal violence. As a matter of law the caller may be guilty of an assault: whether he is or not will depend on the circumstance and in particular on the impact of the caller's potentially menacing call or calls on the victim.[11]

This language – of 'innominate terror', menace, deferred but anticipated violence, and spectres at the doorstep – testifies to a very particular kind of threat, that of the unknown, which could at any moment be realised; and in each of these cases the criminal and appeal courts were confronted by a real experience of fear on the part of the victims, and had to find ways of using the law to acknowledge the harm that this experience represented. There are, as Jeremy Horder has persuasively argued, real problems with attempts to squeeze the facts of these psychic assault cases into the (now all but theoretical) requirement of 'imminence'. None of them disclosed 'imminence' as

10 Ibid.
11 Ibid at 181.

that term is commonly understood, and this, as Horder also rightly points out, is in any event not the point. Rather, these cases may be seen as ones in which the essential wrong, the harm, is the illegitimate causing of fear, produced by confrontation and it is this which justifies the imposition of liability (Horder, 1998).

This extension of imminence to permit convictions in psychic assault cases has been mirrored in other areas of interpretive relaxation in the field of offences against the person. It has already been noted that the requirement for a conviction under s 20 of the OAPA 1861 (malicious wounding or inflicting grievous bodily harm) that there be an assault (whether psychic or in the more commonly understood sense of a battery) has been abandoned.[12] Although an assault in this sense was once conditional upon the direct application of force by the defendant to the body of another – for example, by a punch – it is now only necessary to prove that as a result of the assault, which may be of the psychic kind, force was directly applied to it (as where, in *Lewis*, the victim injured herself on coming into contact with the ground after being put in fear). Similarly, a person need 'do' nothing for the *actus reus* of assault to be established,[13] and both this offence (as well as those, like ss 47 and 20 of the OAPA 1861, in which assault is an included element) may be committed indirectly – where, for example, the defendant creates a trap or hazard[14] which subsequently results in injury to the victim, or where he sets a dog on him.[15] These judicial innovations – each of which has had the effect of making it easier successfully to prosecute those whose conduct evokes a sense of dread or fear in the victim, whether or not this results in injury to them (whether physical or psychological) – have been paralleled by legislative interventions, most notably in this context the various Acts concerned with abuse of telecommunications technology[16] and 'stalking'.[17]

---

12 This is of particular importance in the context of liability for the reckless transmission of HIV and is discussed further in more detail in Ch 4.

13 In *R v Santana-Bermudez* [2004] Crim LR 471 the defendant's appeal against conviction failed where he had assured the police officer who was searching him for drugs that he was not carrying 'sharps' (needles) and she stabbed her finger on a syringe in his pocket. This decision followed that of the House of Lords in *R v Miller* [1983] AC 161, where it was held that a person who creates a dangerous situation (in that case, falling asleep on a mattress with a lit cigarette that subsequently caused substantial damage by fire) will – if the requisite fault is established – be liable for those associated risks that materialise.

14 As in *DPP v K* [1990] 1 All ER 331 (DC) where the appellant was guilty of an assault as the result of having poured acid into an electric hand dryer with the result that the next user was injured. (This case was overruled on unrelated grounds in *R v Spratt* [1991] 2 All ER 210.)

15 *Murgatroyd v Chief Constable of West Yorkshire* [2000] All ER 1742.

16 See s 43 of the Telecommunications Act 1984 (as amended) and s 1 of the Malicious Communications Act 1988.

17 Protection from Harassment Act 1997. For critical commentary see Allen, 1996; Wells, 1997. Other contemporary examples of legislative and executive intervention that may be seen as responses to public safety and security anxieties include the Dangerous Dogs Act 1991,

All of these developments may, on one reading, be explicable on their own terms as evidence of an increased judicial and Parliamentary sensitivity to the contemporary limitations of applying legal rules whose doctrinal origins lay in the Middle Ages. On such a reading they manifest nothing other than the genius of the common law to adapt to changing social circumstances, and the principle of statutory interpretation that conceives of Acts of Parliament (such as the OAPA 1861) as 'living instruments' to be interpreted as context and mischief dictate. However, I believe this is too limited an explanation since it fails to locate the changes within the broader social, cultural and political environment in which they have taken place and which, explicitly or implicitly, they both mirror and reinforce. It seems to me no coincidence, for example, that the judicial interpretive approach in the substantive criminal law in this area (and – as we shall see in the following chapters – to reckless- ness and to consent) has run parallel with developments in institutionalised criminal justice responses to those who present, or are classified as represent- ing, risks, and (more latterly) with relaxations on the admissibility of evi- dence of defendants' previous offending, the re-invigoration of the victims' rights movement, heightened concern about paedophile sex offenders and the rights of householders to defend themselves against intruders. These judicial, legislative and political responses to those who threaten our physical, propri- etorial and – ultimately – ontological security are, far from being explicable discretely (as they are within much criminal law theorising in the moral- philosophical tradition) must, I think, be located within a more historically, politically and culturally attuned account. And such an account is certainly necessary if we are to understand the reasons why the sexual transmission of HIV, which for the first 20 years in the UK was conceived of as primarily a health issue, has come to be treated as a harm and, as such, a legitimate target for the coercive powers of the state through the medium of the criminal law.

Excursus: R v Clarence

I explained in the previous section how it is that cases in which the causing of 'harm at a distance' (as we might call it) came to be incorporated within the kind of injury that could be prosecuted under ss 18, 20 and 47 of the OAPA 1861. For the sake of completeness it is necessary to explain how it is that this development has been of particular relevance to the criminalisation of HIV transmission.

In 1888, 27 years after the OAPA 1861 was enacted, Charles Clarence was successfully prosecuted for having infected his wife, Selina, with gonorrhoea.

the Anti-Social Behaviour Order provisions of the Crime and Disorder Act 1998, and the extension of police powers and detention provisions to be found in recent anti-terrorism legislation.

He knew that he was infected, and she did not. The case was referred to the Queen's Bench for clarification, where 13 judges of the Court for Crown Cases Reserved considered what was acknowledged to be a question of fundamental importance – namely, whether a married woman could be the victim of an offence under these sections where that offence was committed during sexual intercourse to which she could not in law refuse her consent (at the time, a husband had a legal right to sex with his wife and could therefore not be liable for rape). The answer given by the majority of the court was no.[18] With respect to the conviction under s 20, which requires proof that the defendant *unlawfully* and intentionally or recklessly inflicted grievous bodily harm, Clarence's counsel had argued that the act which brought about the harm was sexual intercourse and that since this was not unlawful, there was no offence. And with respect to the conviction under s 47 (which has no unlawfulness requirement), he argued that an absence of consent was necessary for there to be an assault, and since there was consent to the act (of sexual intercourse), no assault was committed.

The reasons that the majority of the Court in this case gave when deciding to quash the convictions were complex and various. At one level, they manifest a commitment to a particular tradition of legal reasoning that has a tendency to justify conclusions based on the absurd or unfortunate consequences (as those are understood by those doing the judging) that would follow were an alternative more holistic, contextual approach taken. Thus, Wills J emphasises how, if the conviction were to be sustained, this would mean that any fraud perpetrated on a woman so as to induce her to agree to sexual intercourse would vitiate consent, render the intercourse an assault, and thus make the man a rapist. He worries that there is, in principle, no distinction between sexually transmitted infections and other contagious diseases, and that despite the prevalence of such diseases in the preceding centuries, and an established law of assault, no-one had previously been convicted of an offence relating to the transmission of disease. It was thus not conceivable that Parliament could have intended that ss 20 and 47 of the OAPA 1861 were meant to cover such a situation, especially when both either expressly or impliedly require an assault in the sense in which that term was then understood. The same concerns are expressed by Stephen J, who delivers the most comprehensive judgment. He too is exercised by the fact that to uphold the conviction, despite the harm that has been caused in this particular context, would establish a principle of unwelcome general application:

> It is also, I think, clear that, unless some distinction can be pointed out that does not occur to me, the sections must be held to apply, not only to

---

18 *R v Clarence* (1889) LR 22 QBD 23. For an excellent discussion of the case, emphasising the misogyny of Sir James Fitzjames Stephen and its effect on his reasoning, see Gleeson, 2005.

venereal diseases, but to infection of every kind which is in fact communicated by one person to another by an act likely to produce it. A man who knowing that he has scarlet fever or small-pox shakes hands with a friend and so infects him may be said to fall under s 20 or s 47 as much as the prisoner in this case. To seize a man's hand without his consent is an assault; but no one would consent to such a grasp if he knew that he risked small-pox by it, and if consent is rendered void by fraud, including suppression of the truth, such a gesture would be an assault occasioning actual bodily harm as much as the conduct of the prisoner in this case.[19]

For Stephen J there was no general principle of law that made the transmission of communicable disease a criminal act (although it might constitute a public nuisance under public health legislation) despite such transmission being, in his opinion, 'abominable'; and such limited authority as did exist was against criminalisation – since it would result in an unwelcome extension of criminal liability.[20] Aside from these general reasons, Stephen J focused on the specific language of the relevant sections and was not convinced that the transmission of disease could justifiably constitute an assault[21] (especially since there existed specific provisions of the OAPA 1861 dealing with poisoning (or 'administering a noxious thing')). For him, it was an abuse of the language of the Act to bring facts such as those in the case before the court within the ambit of assault, and he expressed the view that any extension of liability was properly a matter for Parliament.[22]

The emphasis of those in the majority in *Clarence* was, thus, on the 'proper' construction of the relevant sections, and on the undesirable and unintended effects that would arise if the conviction were quashed. No matter (as those in the minority, and especially Hawkins J, argued) that such a conclusion meant that a harmful consequence went unpunished. What mattered

---

19 *R v Clarence* (1889) LR 22 QBD 23 at 38–39.
20 Ibid at 40. Stephen J refers approvingly to Hale who, in his *Pleas of the Crown*, had stated:

> But what if such [an infected] person goes abroad to the intent to infect another, and another is thereby infected and dies? Whether this be not murder by the common law might be a question, but if no such intention evidently appears, though de facto by his conversation another be infected, it is no felony by the common law, though it be a great misdemeanour, and the reasons are: (1) because it is hard to discern whether the infection arise from the party or from contagion of the air. It is God's arrow, &c. (2) Nature commands every man in what condition soever to preserve himself, which cannot be well without mutual conversation. (3) Contagious diseases, as plague, pestilential fevers, small-pox &c., are common among mankind by the visitation of God, and the extension of capital punishments in cases of this nature would multiply severe punishments too far and give too great latitude and loose to punishments.

21 This is emphasised too by Coleridge LCJ (who in his judgment states that he agrees with 'all or almost all' of the views expressed by Wills and Stephen JJ).
22 Ibid at 46.

was that no harm was done to the law. For present purposes, what is important is that *Clarence* had the effect of establishing that where disease was recklessly transmitted it could not constitute a criminal offence because it lacked the quality of assault that was necessary for a conviction under either s 20 or s 47 of the OAPA 1861 and, furthermore, that these sections were inappropriately used even if it were accepted that disease could be said to constitute a bodily harm. It is no doubt the case, or there is at least a very strong argument to be made, that the decision in *Clarence* was as much the product of the misogyny of the majority (and especially of Stephen J) as it was the result of their commitment to logical formalism, and deference to authority and precedent (Gleeson, 2005). Certainly, the fact that the court was obliged to determine liability for the transmission of disease in the context of sexual relations between a husband and wife was – despite protestations to the contrary – significant, and it is difficult (given Stephen J's reasoning) to imagine that, had the defendant been a prostitute and the victim a middle class man, the emphasis on the undesirable consequences of upholding the conviction would have been as great, or indeed that the conclusion would have been the same. What matters here, though, is that the effect of *Clarence* was to prevent the reckless transmission of disease from being prosecuted until it was decided, in *R v Ireland; R v Burstow,* that there was no need to prove the application of physical force to the body of the victim for there to be a conviction under either s 47 or s 20.

Proving transmission

If *R v Ireland; R v Burstow* made it possible in principle to convict people for transmitting HIV (and, though there have been no reported cases on the point) other serious diseases, there remains the problem of proving that a defendant was the cause of a complainant's infection. And in HIV transmission cases, where there is the possibility that someone other than the defendant was the cause, this is critically important. Many criminal offences, usually referred to as 'result crimes', require proof of causation. Thus, for homicide offences (such as murder and manslaughter), the prosecution must prove to the criminal standard that the defendant caused the death of the victim; and for non-fatal offences against the person (such as the intentional or reckless infliction of actual or grievous bodily harm under ss 18 and 20 of the OAPA 1861) the prosecution must prove that the defendant caused the harm suffered. In the ordinary course of events, establishing causation is not problematic and is rarely disputed. A defendant will often admit that he was the cause of another's death or injury, because there is no question but that it was he who shot the gun or threw the punch. In cases like this, any challenge as to liability that the defendant wishes to make must relate instead to his mental state at the relevant time, or to the circumstances in which the death or injury occurred. So, on a charge of murder a defendant may deny that he intended to kill, or argue that he was provoked (and so is guilty of manslaughter), or that he was acting in self-defence (and that he should be acquitted on the basis that the killing was lawful). The same is true, in principle, for cases involving HIV transmission. A defendant may admit that he was the cause of the complainant's infection, but deny that he was reckless (on the basis that he was unaware of the risk of infecting his partner), or argue that the complainant consented to the risk of transmission and that no unlawful act has been committed.

There is, however, a significant difference between most run-of-the-mill cases involving non-fatal injury and those involving the transmission of HIV, or – indeed – other sexually transmitted diseases. That difference resides in the critical difficulty of establishing that the defendant was indeed the cause of the complainant's infection. Distinct from other offences against the person, where the consequence that comprises the *actus reus* is felt (a cut, a bruise), or felt (a fractured bone, an internal injury), and where the defendant's action is both objectively observable as the cause of that consequence and, more often than not, experienced by him as such, the transmission of HIV during sex is a silent, invisible, unfelt event outside and beyond his conscious knowledge or control. (It is important here to recognise the distinction between being aware of the risk that HIV may be being transmitted, and being aware that this has occurred; the former is, of course something that an HIV positive defendant who understands the risks associated with unsafe sex may be, but it does not follow that he is therefore aware of the fact that the risk of transmission has been realised in any particular incident of sexual intercourse.) Thus, whereas in 'ordinary' non-fatal offence cases, it is reasonable – barring any unforeseen or unforeseeable intervening events – that the defendant knows, or ought to know, that he is the cause of the harm that has occurred, in HIV transmission cases this simply is not possible. Confronted by a partner who has tested positive for HIV after starting a sexual relationship in which unsafe sex has taken place, a particular defendant may indeed *believe* that he is the cause of that partner's infection when he is not (either because believing otherwise means accepting the possibility of infidelity or because he feels morally responsible and therefore 'guilty'); or he may in fact be the cause. But he cannot *know* whether he is the cause of a partner's infection in the same way that someone who stabs another knows that he is the cause of that person's wound.

That said, this inconvenient truth about establishing causal responsibility for the transmission of HIV has not, as the cases prosecuted under s 20 have demonstrated, stopped people being convicted. Why is this? Why – when the prosecution must prove to the criminal standard that a defendant caused the complainant's infection – have people pleaded guilty when charged, or been found guilty after trial? The answers to these questions are three-fold. First, as we shall see in more detail below, the scientific evidence upon which the prosecution has relied has been misunderstood by prosecuting and defence lawyers. This has, in some cases, resulted in people accepting that they must be responsible for their partner's infection on the basis of misguided and misleading interpretations about the meaning of that evidence and, because they did not deny that they were reckless with respect to the risk of transmission, pleading guilty. As a consequence, the limitations of that scientific evidence in those cases was never subjected to thorough cross-examination nor evaluated by a jury. Second, even where cases have gone to trial, the scientific evidence has rarely been challenged (for the reasons just given) and convictions have resulted solely from jury determinations as to whether there was consent to the risk of transmission (and conclusions that there was not). Third, and lastly, it is important to recognise that scientific evidence of causation is only one element of the evidence that is brought against a defendant in a transmission case, and evidence of opinion at that. Thus, some defendants may indeed have caused the respective complainants' infections, and the broader evidential narrative against them may have been sufficiently compelling that they pleaded guilty, or were found so after trial, on that basis. This does not, however, preclude the possibility of wrongful convictions; nor does it make questions about the reliability of scientific evidence any less important. Given that we have a criminal law which allows for the convictions of people guilty of recklessly transmitting HIV we need, if those convictions are to have legitimacy, to be satisfied that the evidence upon which proof of transmission is based is sufficiently robust, and that even if such evidence is not by its very nature capable of establishing the truth of the matter, it is not used against defendants in a way that prejudices their right to a fair trial or results in unsafe verdicts.

Causation, HIV and phylogenetic analysis[23]

Given that it is not possible for the defendant to know, as I have been using that term, that he was the cause of the infection which forms the *actus reus* of the offence under s 20 of the OAPA 1861, resort must be had to scientific evidence that tends towards proving that he was. The evidence that has been used in criminal trials, both in England and other jurisdictions where liability depends upon proof of transmission, is based on what is known as phylogenetic analysis. Simply stated, phylogenetic analysis is a way of determining the relationship between two samples of HIV from different sources, by establishing their genetic distance from each other.[24] Using complex computational

---

23 See, generally, Bernard, 2007; Bernard *et al*, 2007.
24 Bernard *et al*, 2007: 10 explain that:

> Types, groups, subtypes, recombinants, and quasispecies are scientific terms used to classify different strains of HIV, from the global, regional and country level (types, groups, subtypes/recombinants) to the individual level (quasispecies). There are two types of HIV that infect humans – HIV-1 and HIV-2. Both HIV-1 and HIV-2 are

methods, it identifies differences between the genetic material in these sources and is thus able to give an idea of the likelihood, or probability, that the two sources are genetically related, and – if so – how close that relationship is. Because HIV, unlike DNA, is not unique to an individual, and because HIV undergoes genetic mutation inside its human host, phylogenetic analysis can only provide an estimate of the relatedness of the samples rather than a definitive match. It does not, and cannot (as we shall see below) provide a certain answer to the critical question in an HIV transmission case: 'Is the virus in the complainant the same as that in the defendant?'

Despite these difficulties, phylogenetic analysis has been admitted as evidence in a number of criminal cases, both in the UK and elsewhere, and used by the prosecution to argue that the defendant caused the complainant's infection.[25] The first occasion was in 1992, when defence counsel for a man who had been convicted of the rape of a female complainant and for deliberately infecting her with HIV, requested a virological report on the relatedness of the strains in each party. The conviction was upheld on appeal on the basis of the virological and other evidence. In his account of the way phylogenetic analysis was used, the virologist commented on its limitations:

> It is important to stress that even though our investigation showed that the strains carried by the male and the female were epidemiologically linked, we could not determine the direction of transmission, nor could we formally rule out the possibility that both the male and the female were infected by a third party. Thus, it was essential that the results from our sequence investigation be used in conjunction with other epidemiological information in the case.
>
> (Albert *et al*, 1994)

descendants of SIV (simian immunodeficiency virus) found in wild chimpanzees in Cameroon, in western Africa. HIV-1 is the type of HIV that is seen globally, whereas HIV-2 is limited predominantly to the areas around Cameroon. HIV-1 is further classified into three main groups called M, N and O. Again, it is group M that is seen globally, whereas groups O and N are limited predominantly to the areas around Cameroon. group M viruses are again further classified into subtypes (represented by letters of the alphabet, e.g. A, B, C) and recombinants, which are a combination of two subtypes. Recombinants are officially known as circulating recombinant forms (CRF) and represented by a number followed by the two combined subtypes (e.g. CRF01_AE, is a combination of subtypes A and E).

25 Before its first successful use in a criminal trial, phylogenetic analysis had been used in the US to determine the relatedness between samples of virus from two dentists and their respective patients. See (case 1) Center for Disease Control (CDC),1990; Cieselski *et al*, 1992; Ou *et al*, 1992; (case 2) Jaffe *et al*, 1994; Myers, 1994. In case 1 a CDC review determined that the dentist, who along with some of his patients subsequently died of AIDS-related illnesses, may have been the source of infection (though criminal charges were never brought). In case 2 it was determined that the dentist was definitely not the source.

The first time that phylogenetic analysis was used at trial, rather than as the basis for an appeal, was in the US in 1997. In the case of *State of Louisiana v Richard J. Schmidt*,[26] the defendant – a doctor – was accused of attempting to murder his former mistress by injecting her with blood taken from his patients and which was infected with HIV and hepatitis C. At a preliminary hearing phylogenetic analysis was ruled admissible in evidence, a decision that was confirmed by the Louisiana Court of Appeal.[27] Dr Schmidt was convicted of attempted second-degree murder, and his appeals to both the Louisiana Supreme Court and the US Supreme Court were both unsuccessful.[28] Since the Schmidt case, phylogenetic analysis has been used in a number of other jurisdictions (including England and Wales) as evidence tending towards supporting the prosecution's case in charges relating to the transmission of HIV.[29]

The limitations of phylogenetic analysis

Although the identification of specific transmission events with high statistical confidence through phylogenetics will always be subject to significant caveats (e.g., cannot exclude a common, unknown source of 2 similar infections, cannot identify direction of transmission, and ignores the potential of superinfection), as well as ethical concerns (consent for use to identify potential sources of infection), the potential to provide insights into transmission dynamics within communities is now being realized.

(Pillay and Fisher, 2007: 924)

It was explained earlier that, because of the nature of HIV and its genetic structure, phylogenetic analysis cannot establish definitive proof that HIV positive person X was the source of the infection in HIV positive person Y. All it can do is provide evidence of the degree of relatedness of the viral samples taken from each. This is done by building what is known as a phylogenetic tree – a visual representation of the results derived from phylogenetic analysis. A phylogenetic analysis tree diagram provides a way of demonstrating the

---

26 15th Judicial District Court, Lafayette Parish, LA, Criminal Docket No 73313, Reasons For Ruling of Louisiana State 15th Judicial District Court, Judge Durwood Conque (1997).

27 *State of Louisiana v Richard J. Schmidt*, 699 So. 2d 488, K97–249 LA Court of Appeal, 3rd Circuit (1997); writ denied 706 So. 2d 451, 97–2220 LA (1997).

28 For the virologist's account of the use of phylogenetic analysis in this case, see Metzker *et al*, 2002.

29 These include an Australian case where the defendant was charged with 'knowingly and recklessly' transmitting HIV during the rape of an intellectually disabled man (Birch *et al*, 2000); a man sentenced to six years' imprisonment in Denmark for sexually abusing and infecting a 12-year-old boy (Machuca *et al*, 2001); and a man prosecuted for raping and transmitting HIV to six women in Belgium (Lemey *et al*, 2005).

relatedness of independently sourced viral strains by representing the extent to which the samples under investigation share common ancestry. Take, for example, the simplified tree shown in Figure 3.1.[30]

Here, viruses B, C, D and E are all descended from virus A, but viruses C and D are more closely related to each other than B and E. All this means is that there is a higher probability that C and D are infected with the same virus than would be a defendant and complainant who were infected with, respectively, viruses B and E (or B and D, or B and C). This raises two further problems, as regards proof of causation in a criminal case, even if we accept the higher probability value of the relatedness of viruses C and D. The first is that even if we have a defendant and complainant who are, respectively, infected with viruses C and D, the relatedness of the viruses does not mean that D was infected by C or vice versa (in addition to not being able to provide definitive determination of the source a complainant's infection, phylogenetic analysis is not able to provide proof of the route of transmission, or an accurate estimation of the timing of its occurrence, either). The difficulty here is fairly self-evident, and can be illustrated by the following, not entirely unrealistic, hypothetical situation. Suppose C and D start a sexual relationship at T^1. Six months later, C tests positive for HIV, but does not disclose this to D. Some time later, at T^2, D also tests positive for HIV. D confronts C, and demands to know whether, prior to T^2, he knew he was HIV positive. C admits that he did. D goes to the police and recounts the narrative from his perspective, alleging that C was the cause of his HIV infection. The police interview C and draw the inference that C was indeed the cause of D's infection. He is arrested, charged, and phylogenetic analysis is undertaken which shows that the strain of HIV that they each have is closely related. C, on the basis of the chronology of events as I have set them out here, pleads guilty – because he believes the source of his infection is a relationship that happened prior to meeting D, and is sentenced to an immediate term of imprisonment. The problem with this, and the potential for a miscarriage of justice, is easy to see. Why? Because it is perfectly possible that it was D who

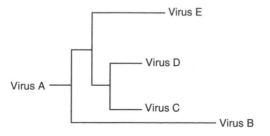

Figure 3.1 Phylogenetic analysis tree.

30 This is taken from Bernard *et al*, 2007.

infected C. The fact that it was C who discovered his HIV positive status first, has nothing to do with – is logically unrelated to – who infected whom. The fact that D identifies himself as the victim, understandably given the moral dimensions of the narrative, establishes a criminal justice logic that is, unless the limitations of phylogenetic analysis evidence are properly understood by all parties, difficult to dislodge. D becomes a viable and credible complainant and is treated as such by the police and the courts, and C becomes a viable defendant against whom it is easy to build a case. If, however, C had suspected that D was the source of his infection, he would have been able to confront D with that possibility, and D might then have established his (hitherto unknown) HIV positive status. On these alternative facts, it is unlikely – I would suggest – that D would go to the police. Furthermore, it should be noted that C would not have the option of bringing a charge against D even if he wanted to because, assuming that D did infect him, D had no knowledge of his HIV positive status at the relevant time and so is arguably not reckless within the legal meaning of that term.

A second problem, related to the one just set out, is that there is the possibility that either or both C and D were infected by an independent third party, or by third parties. Where C and D are in a non-monogamous relationship (or where one of them is non-monogamous) it is possible that neither is the source of the other's infection, although the narrative as related above might tend towards creating the impression that this is so (either subjectively from C's and D's perspective, or objectively as viewed by a jury charged with determining causation). The problem is compounded by the fact that where C and D share a geographically limited pool of sexual partners with HIV, the probability of them being infected independently by the same strain is higher than would otherwise be the case. Phylogenetic analysis is insufficiently accurate to be able to establish whether two people who share the same strain are the source of each other's infection, or whether both or either have been infected independently by a person, or by persons, also infected with that strain. Of course, it is possible that where there is compelling evidence that D has been sexually faithful to D, and where there is no evidence that D had symptoms associated with HIV infection prior to starting a sexual relationship with C, the fact that phylogenetic analysis cannot by itself establish that C was the source of D's infection will be less problematic. As explained above, phylogenetic analysis operates within a broader and more complex evidential narrative. However, where C and D are non-monogamous it will, it is suggested, be extremely difficult, for the prosecution to establish guilt on C's part; and any judge called upon to direct a jury on the weight to which they should give phylogenetic analysis evidence should, it is submitted, be extremely careful both in explaining its limitations and in pointing out the ways in which the chronology of testing and (non)-disclosure in a particular relationship might lead them to draw false inferences about the route and source of transmission. (There is a wide range of possible reasons for C and

D being infected with closely related strains of HIV, each of which poses potential difficulties in establishing causation: see Figure 3.2.)

The use of phylogenetic analysis in English HIV transmission cases, and best practice guidance

Given the limitations associated with phylogenetic analysis evidence, it is perhaps somewhat surprising that its use and interpretation has not been more widely challenged in the prosecutions that have been brought before the

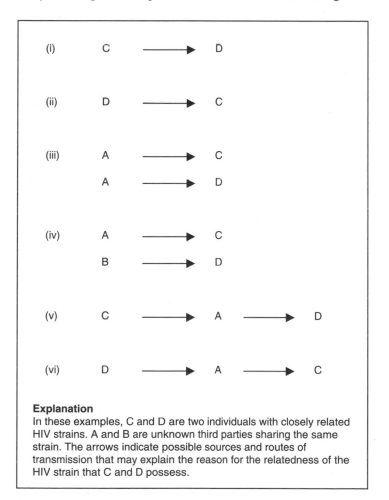

(i)   C ⟶ D

(ii)   D ⟶ C

(iii)   A ⟶ C
         A ⟶ D

(iv)   A ⟶ C
         B ⟶ D

(v)   C ⟶ A ⟶ D

(vi)   D ⟶ A ⟶ C

Explanation
In these examples, C and D are two individuals with closely related HIV strains. A and B are unknown third parties sharing the same strain. The arrows indicate possible sources and routes of transmission that may explain the reason for the relatedness of the HIV strain that C and D possess.

Figure 3.2 Possible sources and routes of transmission.[31]

31 This is adapted from Bernard *et al*, 2007.

courts. In all but one of the cases in England and Wales, defendants have either pleaded guilty or, where there has been a trial on a not guilty plea, their defence has been that their partner(s) consented to the risk of transmission. In each of these cases, therefore, the defendants accepted the phylogenetic analysis evidence that they were the cause of the complainant's infection. It was not until the summer of 2006 that a defence team sought to challenge the prosecution evidence on this point. At a trial in Kingston upon Thames Crown Court, Matthew Collins had been charged with recklessly transmitting HIV to his partner and pleaded not guilty. There was evidence before the court that his partner had been sexually active with other men, some of whom were HIV positive. The prosecution used phylogenetic analysis evidence to support its contention that he was the source of his partner's infection but, after initially directing the jury to retire to consider its verdict, the judge directed an acquittal on the basis that they could not, on the evidence presented, be sure that this was so. Commenting on the case afterwards, the expert virologist in the case – Anna-Maria Geretti, who was brought in by the defence to challenge the prosecution case[32] – stated:

> Virological evidence should be seen in the context of other facts. You should not build a case around this type of evidence alone. There could be a chain of transmission, where four or five people are infected with a similar virus, so it is impossible to tell whether transmission has occurred between two people with a related virus.[33]

The acquittal in the Kingston case is significant for two distinct reasons. Firstly, it has highlighted the importance of ensuring that where phylogenetic analysis evidence is used, both the evidence gathering process and its presentation/interpretation must be done with the utmost care so as not to mislead the jury as to its significance. There are certain measures that can be taken to ensure that this is so, and it is important that they are understood:[34]

1   It must be acknowledged by all participants in a criminal trial that HIV is a virus that exists and migrates within communities, rather than one that infects disconnected individuals. Everyone infected with HIV has been infected by someone else with HIV. Phylogenetic analysis alone (because of its inherent approximations and error rate) cannot prove that X infected Y, though it is able to exclude this possibility.

2   The phylognetic analysis used in criminal cases is, or to date has been,

---

32 Dr Geretti is one of the authors of Bernard *et al*, 2007.

33 For further commentary on this case, see O'Connor, 2006.

34 These points are developed from Bernard *et al*, 2007. For another discussion of the limitations of phylogenetic analysis in a forensic context see Budowle and Harmon, 2005.

undertaken in research rather than forensic laboratories. This is because very few of the latter have the equipment necessary to undertake it. Where a request for phylogenetic analysis is made to a research laboratory, it is critical that the samples are properly tracked (to eliminate the risk of cross-contamination, and that double-blind testing is carried out (to eliminate bias). (For example, the person undertaking the testing should not know in advance which sample is suspected of being the source of infection.) The samples also need to be blindly tested at two different time points, ideally in different laboratories, and the results should be consistent as between those times.

3   In order to establish the relatedness of the samples, the viral gene sequences that they contain need to be compared to gene sequences in independent control samples. There is a risk, if these controls are taken from populations that are temporally and spacially distant from the test samples (for example in relation to two samples from London in 2006 using controls from Australia in 2003), that the test samples will appear to be, and can be represented as, more closely related to each other than they are to the controls. In order to minimise the inference that this means that the defendant (sample A) is likely to be the source of the infection in the complainant (sample B), the controls ought ideally to be taken from a setting that is socially, geographically and temporally relevant to the case under consideration. Thus, if the defendant and complainant share a similar socio-sexual network, the controls should be drawn from that network. This will ensure greater confidence in the relatedness of the test samples where this is apparent, although it does raise complex consent and data protection questions relating to the use of control samples. Where it is not possible to derive controls as indicated, the risk of over-interpreting the relatedness of the test samples as compared with the control samples should be made clear.

4   The choice of phylogenetic tree model constructed for the purpose of demonstrating the relatedness of the samples being tested should be based on its reliability and fitness for purpose and for no other reason (for example ease of explanation to a lay jury).

5   If phylogenetic analysis suggests a genetic relatedness between the samples from two individuals, analysis of multiple genetic clones from each can strengthen evidence of that relationship.

6   It is important that phylogenetic analysis involves the sequencing of reasonable length ($\ddagger$ 500 nucleotides (sub-units of RNA), depending on the particular gene being investigated) of two or more genetic regions. The choice ought to target genes with different biological functions, different evolution rates, and different selective pressures (i.e. genes that are subject to different environmental factors). If using the *pol* region, it should be recognised that similar anti-retroviral treatment being taken by the individuals whose samples are being analysed can lead to similar

mutations in the virus and so give the impression for that reason alone of being closely related.

If these are the practical measures necessary to minimise the risk of injustice in cases where there is the possibility that the defendant was not the cause of the complainant's infection, and which were highlighted as the result of the Kingston case, the second potential lesson of that trial, and of this science, is of a different kind. It is that it will be far easier to dispute the prosecution's assertion that the defendant is guilty, all other things being equal, where there is evidence that the complainant was, or could have been HIV positive before starting a sexual relationship with him or her (such evidence including, for example, a history of other sexually transmitted infections), or where the complainant has been non-monogamous during the currency of the instant relationship. Raising evidence of each of these will inevitably be distressing for those complainants who wish to bring a case against a partner (although one might reasonably characterise them as a necessary cost). The more problematic, and politically divisive, issue is the effect of non-monogamy. If, as seems clear from the Kingston case (and from one other, the details of which are less clear[35]), sex with others potentially sharing the same HIV strain is a fact that makes it harder to assert with anything like certainty that the defendant is the cause of a complainant's infection, then it is possible that the CPS will be more likely to prosecute those whose partners have been sexually faithful, and/or who have a clean STI history. The requirement that public prosecutions are only brought where there is a reasonable prospect of conviction means that any credible challenge to the phylogenetic analysis evidence (which a defendant whose partner has been non-monogamous will be able to do) will tend towards non-prosecution. We are therefore confronted by a crime whose effective prosecution in the courts will be influenced not simply by the availability of strong evidence – that is common to all offences and is unremarkable – but, as it has been in rape, by the sexual promiscuity or otherwise of the complainant. But whereas in rape a woman's sexual history has typically been used as a way of undermining her credibility as regards non-consent, in the HIV transmission context its effect is rather different. A man may traditionally have found it easy to adduce evidence that his partner's sexual promiscuity cast doubt on her evidence of non-consent in an act of sexual intercourse with him, but this was not an argument that could be won without the evidence being admitted and explored in cross-examination at trial. It was an argument about the credibility of the complainant's version

---

35 The case occurred in early 2007 in Preston Crown Court. It would appear that after establishing that the complainant had a sexual partner other than the defendant, who was unwilling to provide a sample of blood for testing, the judge threw the case out on the basis that the forensic evidence presented by the prosecution was wholly inadequate (source: personal correspondence).

of events – not about her biological status, about something amenable to objective independent verification, and is in any event less easy to do now than it once was.[36] In contrast, phylogenetic analysis evidence is precisely about the biological 'truth' of the complainant, or something approximating it, and is something that can more readily be evaluated by prosecutors in advance of any trial 'on the papers'. Although it remains the case that other evidence about the complainant, his or her shared history with the defendant, and the nature of their sexual relationship will be important where the relatedness of the samples they give is close, any possibility that the complainant's infection may have come from a third party is likely to undermine the chance of a conviction and result in the abandonment of the prosecution.

Thinking differently about the harm of HIV infection

The difficulties of proving causation would not, of course, be an issue if the way in which the criminal law approached the 'harm' of HIV was one that focused on exposure to the risk of transmission, or on the context and circumstances in which transmission occurred rather than the fact of transmission itself – on the physiological difference that the virus effects in the body of the person whom the defendant infects. As for exposure, we saw (in Chapter 1) how an emphasis on the taking of risks *per se* is one that informs public health legislation, since the understandable (if problematic) logic of the policy behind such legislation is prophylactic. And it would be perfectly possible to construct a framework of liability, as many other jurisdictions have done, in which exposing someone to the risk of HIV, or to serious disease more generally, existed as a distinct criminal offence – even if the limited empirical evidence suggests that there would be little or no beneficial impact from doing so (Burris *et al*, 2007).[37] If the concern and function of the criminal

36 The position in England and Wales is somewhat different now. A person charged with rape under s 1 of the Sexual Offences Act 2003 is one charged with a sexual offence within the meaning of the Youth Justice and Criminal Evidence Act 1999. Ss 41–43 of this latter legislation place restrictions on the admissibility of, or cross-examination on, evidence of previous sexual history. Unless there is leave of the court, no evidence may be adduced or questions asked in cross-examination by or on behalf of the accused about any sexual behaviour of the complainant. Furthermore, such evidence will only be permitted provided statutory criteria are met and the court considers that it may reach an unsafe conclusion on an issue to be decided in the case if such evidence were not to be heard. Defence counsel are not permitted to engage in 'fishing expeditions' or ask general, character-related questions. Any questions asked or evidence that the defence wish to adduce must relate to a particular event or instance of behaviour on the part of the complainant.

37 In Europe, the following countries have exposure liability: Armenia, Azerbaijan, Denmark, France, Georgia, Germany, Iceland, Liechtenstein, Moldova, the Netherlands, Norway, Poland, Russia, Slovakia, Sweden and Ukraine (see Nyambe, 2006). Many states in the United States have similar laws: see, for particular discussions, Closen, 1993; Markus, 1999; McGuire; 1999; Shriver, 2001.

law were simply to mark the moral wrong in exposing someone to the potential for harm, then an argument could be made to legitimate such liability, but not otherwise.

As for the context and circumstances in which transmission took place, an emphasis on these rather than on the fact of infection would demand a rather different kind of justification. In the next chapter I suggest that imposing liability for the *reckless* transmission of HIV makes sense for societies in which risk is a dominant discourse, in which there is an increased concern with, and fear for, physical and ontological security, and in which the HIV positive person personifies this anxiety; and earlier in this chapter I suggested that this could go some way towards explaining why assault liability has been expanded in the way that it has been. Both the fault (of the HIV positive person) and the harm (of HIV) are powerful signifiers because we construct ourselves as *immune*. Our bodies are understood as having some kind of innate integrity at a descriptive level, and ought to be respected as such at a normative one.[38] Because physical integrity and/or immunity are so profoundly bound up with our understanding of selfhood, of what makes me 'me', and you 'you'; because these establish the distinction between us, and our respective distinctiveness, it is hardly surprising that the transmission of a virus which – literally – breaks down our immunity should be comprehended within criminal law as a serious offence, second only to the deprivation of life itself. This is a perfectly defensible position; but it is not one that I think can, or should, be defended without more. Put more strongly, I think we should interrogate the value of integrity, and more specifically 'bodily integrity' as concepts which those committed to critical legal scholarship should continue to use without reflection. My argument, such as it is, is that they are concepts that – despite their political value and intellectual appeal – lack descriptive truth and that their use can therefore result in theory (and hence justifications for criminalisation) that rests on an inadequate foundation.

It has become commonplace in critical, and especially critical feminist, legal scholarship to reject autonomy as a useful or appropriate analytical premise for framing discussions of responsibility and of harm. This stems, essentially, from a recognition that the liberal emphasis on autonomous personhood fails to capture the relational, embodied and affective dimensions of what human life comprises and entails. To start from a premise of autonomy is to make a claim about what it is to be a person – a claim that prioritises the mental over the physical, the individual over the social, the goal of self-realisation over that of shared and collective benefit, men over women.

In the context of law – and especially criminal law – it is a claim that

---

38 For a fascinating and extended discussion of the ways in which our sense of self is defined immunologically, and the inter-relationship between immunological models of immunity and philosophical approaches to self and identity, see Tauber, 1994.

underpins what is termed 'orthodox subjectivism' – the idea that the legal subject is one whose cognitive capacity, will, and freedom to choose justifies the imposition of state punishment when that capacity, will and choice are consciously and culpably misdirected, and where the interests of others (understood ultimately as the interests they have in their own autonomy, whether personal or proprietorial) are adversely affected. Because the law treats us *as if* we are autonomous (in this sense at least), and that these are the only interests that need or merit protection, it necessarily and inevitably neglects and denies the relevance of other interests and contexts that may be significant or meaningful to us. So, for example, a person's felt experience of unwanted physical contact, unwanted because it does not fully express her desire or understanding of intimacy, or because it occurs within an oppressive relationship, does not attract state censure. It does not attract censure because her apparent willingness to engage in such contact, and the other person's perception of context, are interpreted within a narrowly construed framework of voluntary action in which bodies are nothing more than the vehicles through which mentally formulated choices by people of full capacity are realised. In this example *she* is constructed as responsible for allowing the contact – to have 'consented', and *he* has inflicted no harm because her 'choice' is a manifestation of her 'autonomy'.

It is largely because the value of autonomy has failed to deliver justice for women, especially – though not exclusively – in the context of sexual offences and domestic or partner violence, that the concepts of integrity and bodily integrity have come to be preferred. They capture something about what it is to be human that autonomy cannot. They extend, in some sense, the range of interests that human beings have and which the disembodied 'person' of legal subjectivity lacks. And they extend – by implication – the legitimate reach and scope of measures that the state may deploy to protect those interests, or they may result in more or less subtle changes of emphasis in existing measures. The extension of what constitutes a harm necessarily extends the range of what is harmful. Thus, it is possible to interpret the changes in prosecution policy for domestic and homophobic violence in the UK as ones that reflect the reality of abused women's and gay men's experience, and the abolition of the honest belief defence in rape as an attempt (albeit a problematic one) to counter the privileged perspective of the man that the previous test affirmed. To this extent, and in these ways, the emphasis on integrity generally, and bodily integrity in particular, has had beneficial legal and political effects.

There is, however, a problem, and that problem resides – I think – in the use of a concept that is based on a fundamental misapprehension about what being a human being involves, and what the reality of embodied human experience consists in. For while it may be politically and theoretically astute to shift the emphasis from autonomy, with all its liberal baggage, to integrity, with all its radical possibilities, such a shift ignores, or discounts, the fact that human beings lack the very bodily integrity which is justification for that shift.[39] By this I mean simply that the bodily integrity of human beings is not *a priori*, but rather contingent, transient, fractured, discontinuous – always and ever dependent on the effective management and regulation of its porosity, accessibility and fragility. Just as our immune system serves to maintain normal physiological functioning by identifying the difference between self and non-self (a function that by its very necessity makes the case at an organismal level), so our caution, risk-aversion, and learned skills of self-protection serve to prevent or regulate those physical encounters with other humans that we wish to avoid or to experience on our own terms. And so just as it makes no sense descriptively to claim that we are autonomous, so it makes no sense descriptively to claim that our bodily integrity is a 'given'. Both claims may, to be sure, serve valuable political ends and produce beneficial effects; and they may each, I accept, be useful claims for human beings, at particular times, in particular contexts and for particular reasons, to make about themselves, because each provides us with the sense of entitlement and/or security that we crave. But to argue that a focus on bodily integrity solves the problems that personal autonomy poses, or that it somehow captures something 'truer' about human beings is wrong and leads necessarily, I think, to conservative thinking about wrongs, harms and responsibility, albeit conservative in a different way.

Nowhere, I think, are these general observations truer than in the context of HIV transmission, and the way in which the 'harm' of HIV is constructed and reproduced through law: it is no different from being beaten or poisoned.[40] And yet is this the experience of infection? Is it so at the moment transmission occurs, or afterwards when one learns that one is HIV positive, or later still if and when one develops AIDS? Is HIV, which though transmitted in an instant, silently and beneath the skin, felt, as one feels a knife or a bullet? And is the knowledge that one is HIV positive felt as one feels the physical pain of being stabbed, punched or shot? Is the medical diagnosis that one now has AIDS felt in this way? Of course it is not possible to generalise about how those who have been infected experience the knowledge of infection, or the illness which it leads to. It is perfectly possible to object to this way of thinking about HIV infection, as having to do essentially with individual experience, rather than as a harm that can be objectively defined as such by analogy with other offences against the person. It is as much a violation of bodily integrity, so many would argue, as a wound, a fracture, or an assault. But there is, I think, a case for putting the other view; that where transmission occurs in the context of sex, we should reflect on other ways of thinking about what the harm might be – not to accept uncritically the traditional

---

39   The position I adopt here is one that has parallels in the feminist legal focus on the concept of 'gendered harm' (see, West, 1997: Ch 2; Conaghan, 1996, 2002).
40   The following discussion is taken from Weait, 2001.

analysis, which in my view fails to capture the various and complex meanings of HIV infection. Put generally, the approach advocated here is one which resists the criminal legal imperative of taking conduct and dissecting it into various technical elements (such as *actus reus, mens rea* and causation) and, if each is present, concluding that the conduct satisfies the conditions of a crime. Such a technical and decontextualised approach fosters the idea that crimes are simply the sum of their parts. Rather, I think that we should undertake a more critical dissection, one which involves an exploration of the broader concepts these elements represent – concepts such as harm, blame and responsibility. If, and only if, it is possible to establish that these are present, are manifest in the conduct, should we begin to think in terms of possible criminal liability and all that this entails.

So let us reflect a little on the harm which transmission represents. Viral transmission occurs between bodies, and so the body provides an obvious focus for thinking about the wrong. It is something that happens to a body, through the agency of another body. One body leaks, the other absorbs and becomes a different body – an infected body; and the fact of that infection, which is conceived as the infliction of a corporeal harm, is what the criminal law and those who would apply it take as their starting point. Something has been done to the body of the 'victim', something but for which that body would have remained essentially the same. But it is not the enduring difference which infection produces, nor its meaning, with which the criminal law concerns itself, at least not formally. What matters, at the level of criminal conduct, is the fact of infection, the fact of transmission. The criminal law isolates the wrongful conduct, the moment of infection, constitutes that as its centre of attention, and draws all subsequent attention to that moment. For law, time stops. The legally relevant moment is the moment of differentiation, not the consequences or experience of differentiation (nor indeed, in any socially meaningful sense, the cause). There is the time before transmission – the time during which the imagined future is one free of infection (where mortality is immanent, but denied), and the time after, when the fact of infection delimits the future (where the immanence and imminence of mortality elide). And there is the present and instant moment of infection: an unfelt, unacknowledged moment, which marks the boundary between the two.

This legally relevant moment is, of course, the least relevant in terms of the experience of infection. It may be years, if ever, before the harm, as defined by law, becomes known to the person infected, during which time there is no experience of having been physically injured. Even when that knowledge is gained, through testing HIV positive, it will not be everyone who experiences the moment of revelation as injury of a corporeal kind.[41] There will be fear

41 The reactions of some of those infected by people against whom cases have been brought certainly bear this out (see Ch 4 below).

and anxiety, certainly – but these are responses and feelings, which are essentially forward-looking, not retrospective. There may also be feelings of betrayal, that the trust one had in a lover has been broken. In this sense, there will surely be hurt. But these incorporeal feelings – of time stolen, of a future damaged, of intimacy soured – which may more adequately reflect the harm experienced, are irrelevant in establishing whether an offence has been committed under the law as it stands. That amounts to nothing other than a technical question turning on when and how transmission occurred, and on who was responsible (in the sense of its cause). In rendering liability a technical question of this kind, the law forces us to imagine any wrong that may have been committed as essentially momentary, physical and complete.

Why does this matter? Why ought it concern us that the law should ignore, occlude or deny the felt experience actually experienced as being relevant to liability? After all the theft of property with sentimental associations is no more and no less theft than that of property to which the owner has no such attachment. And just as these differences of context and meaning may be reflected in sentencing, why should a person's feelings of anxiety, fear and betrayal, which flow from the knowledge that a lover has infected her with HIV, not be acknowledged at the stage of determining appropriate punishment? My answer is that in the case of HIV transmission, the 'harm' is not (as s 20 requires it to be) the fact of infection as such. Criminalising those who have transmitted the virus on the basis that they have caused grievous bodily harm means that the context in which transmission happens and its meaning for the person infected are rendered irrelevant. This matters, because (as I shall later suggest) it is precisely the context of transmission and the meaning of infection, which determine whether it is legitimate and appropriate to treat all those who recklessly infect others as having committed a public wrong deserving of moral and legal censure. We might, as a society, wish to judge, and find wanting, those who breach trust in intimate relationships, those whose failure to communicate does nothing to assist others in making informed choices about the kinds of relationship they want to have. But if we accept a legal framework that with every conviction affirms the idea that HIV infection as something that is in and of itself harmful – and, by implication, that those people who are HIV positive are somehow 'damaged', 'abnormal' and 'lacking' – we risk reinforcing the stigma, shame and prejudice that those who are infected may feel and experience.

Concluding observations

The bio-medical account of the nature of HIV, its transmission and the consequences of infection might be thought to provide a complete explanation of, and justification for, the treatment of HIV infection in criminal law as a bodily harm and, thus, as an offence against the person: to wit, put simply, HIV is harmful to bodies. Just as do those who break legs, fracture skulls, bruise kidneys, cut faces and stab torsos, the person who transmits HIV has, by his conduct, effected an adverse change in the physical function-ing of the person who is thereby infected. And because it is a particularly serious adverse change, in the sense that it results in the (presently) irreparable impairment of the newly infected person's immune function, it is appropri-ately treated as serious bodily harm, to be dealt with as any other such harm would be under the relevant aggravated assault provisions of the OAPA 1861.

This is, certainly, one way of looking at it – a perfectly simple explanation that has the apparent merit of treating HIV infection no differently from any other kind of physical harm. And by conceiving of HIV infection as merely a species (of serious bodily harm) within a genus (of bodily harms), the crim-inal law may, additionally, be thought to have avoided the charge of 'HIV/ AIDS exceptionalism' that many commentators and HIV/AIDS organisa-tions have counselled against (see, for example, UNAIDS, 1998).[42] But while this 'way of seeing' the harm of HIV infection may be superficially plausible, it bears little, if any, scrutiny. Leaving to one side the critical scientific difficul-ties involved in establishing causation, especially where one or both parties have been involved in a non-monagamous relationship, and ignoring the very special role that expert witnesses have in cases where causation is challenged, is it really possible to argue that cases involving HIV transmission are no different from those involving other kinds of serious physical harm? To be sure, within the confines of abstract legal reasoning this may be true; but when was the last time a judge imposed a reporting restriction preventing the identification of someone whose leg had been broken?[43] When was the last time a judge questioned the identity of observers sitting (quite legitimately) in the public gallery of the Crown Court during the trial of a defendant charged with an offence under s 20 of the OAPA 1861?[44] When was the last time a police investigation into an alleged offence under s 20 resulted in a trawl through all the people with whom the defendant had had physical contact to see whether they too might have been injured by that person in the past?[45] When was the last time a regional Crown Prosecution Service annual report carried a photograph of a defendant convicted under s 20, taken from the

---

42 See above, Ch 1.
43 Such restrictions are common in cases brought under sexual offences legislation, though exceptional in other contexts. In all the cases that have so far come before the UK courts, whether on guilty or not guilty pleas, the identity of the complainants has been subject to a publishing ban.
44 I personally have had my 'credentials' questioned (when observing the third of Mohammed Dica's trials), and the same is true of others I know who have observed HIV transmission cases.
45 This is what happened in Sarah Porter's case (see the brief account in Ch 1, and the extended discussion in Ch 4).

front page of a tabloid newspaper?[46] When was the last time the tabloids and broadsheets dedicated – time and time again – lurid front page coverage and extended editorial comment to convictions under this section? And why, if it is just like any other crime under s 20, have the punishments imposed on those convicted *all* been custodial, and uniformly longer than those imposed on others convicted of this offence?[47] I do not pretend to know the answers to all these questions, but they are not – as I hope is clear – simply asked for rhetorical effect. The fact is that cases involving the transmission of HIV, despite their formal legal equivalence to any other case involving the reckless causing of serious bodily harm, are different in every way and at every stage.

46 See the Crown Prosecution Service for Cleveland's Annual Report for its coverage of Feston Konzani's conviction (CPS Cleveland, 2003–4: 6).

47 A conviction under s 20 of the OAPA 1861 for the reckless transmission of HIV has, in all cases, been treated as a serious offence justifying a long term of immediate imprisonment (see above, Ch 1). This is particularly noteworthy since (a) only 55 per cent of those over 18 sentenced for a s 20 offence in 2003 (N: 3,811) received an immediate custodial sentence; and (b) of that 55 per cent (N: 2,078) only 4 per cent received sentences of more than 36 months (see Sentencing Guidelines Council, 2005: Annex A). Furthermore, in *Konzani* the trial judge was not impressed by a written plea for leniency by one of the complainants (who, as we saw in Ch 3, was herself a reluctant witness for the prosecution). The interests of victims may be increasingly taken into account, but only – it would seem in this context – if they are willing to play the part that has been assigned them.

Chapter 4

Risk, recklessness and HIV

A concept like recklessness, when used properly, can unite the individual
and the social in a moral judgment of what risks are and are not permissible, and how people should or should not address themselves to them.
Without homogeneity, however, a society based upon fundamental social
conflicts must seek ways of making its judgments on individuals while
cutting out the element of moral and political evaluation of conduct. The
latter can only lead to political contestation within the law itself.

(Norrie, 2001: 80)

'Risk' like 'health' is a concept which contributes to how we think about
modern life. These concepts are tied up with the values of a culture and the
moral rights and responsibilities of members of that culture, and as such are
implicated in how people understand themselves as reflexive, ethical subjects. Because these conceptions are contingent, the subjectivities which are
created around risk, health and work are also relative: if this means that we
are constrained by cultural conceptions of subjectivity, it also means we
can resist.

(Fox, 1999: 30)

Justice as security is both goal and legitimation for governance in modern
liberal democracies so its negative counterpart, risk, is both target and
legitimation of criminal justice.

(Hudson, 2003: 43)

Introduction

All those sentenced and imprisoned in England and Wales for having infected
their sexual partners with HIV have been convicted under s 20 of the Offences
Against the Person Act 1861. For a conviction under this section, the prosecution must prove that the defendant did in fact cause serious bodily harm
to another person and that, at the relevant time, he was aware of the risk of
causing some degree of bodily harm.[1] In legal language, the prosecution must

---

1 *R v Savage; R v Parmenter* [1992] 1 AC 699.

prove that the defendant was *reckless* with respect to the causing of such harm. In this chapter I set out to explore the ways in which the concept of recklessness is deployed and articulated in cases involving the sexual trans-mission of HIV. My argument is that we cannot fully understand the criminal law's response to the reckless transmission of HIV unless we locate the concept of recklessness, and the fault which it represents, within a broader understanding of the concept and significance of risk in contemporary political, social and penological discourse. Similarly, we cannot fully under-stand the implications of treating and holding people responsible in law for risk-taking unless we understand the extent to, and ways in which, risk-taking is constitutive of individual subjectivity, both legal and otherwise. The chapter thus begins with a brief account of the way in which English law approaches and structures the fault requirement of criminal offences, fol-lowed by a lengthier discussion of the significance of risk in contemporary society. It then considers the ways in which the body is understood as a site of risk, with particular emphasis on the HIV-infected body and its represen-tation. The chapter concludes with a more detailed discussion of recklessness in criminal law and suggests that the fault of recklessness, far from being a less culpable form of fault (as it is conventionally understood to be, especially when compared to intention), may be understood as *the* paradigm fault of modernity.

Criminal fault[2]

Criminal law texts typically draw an analytical distinction between those offences which require proof of fault, and those which do not. Offences in the former category (including, for example, murder, rape and theft) are ones that may be said to articulate certain fundamental cultural, political and eco-nomic values (here, those associated with life, bodily autonomy and private property), while those in the latter are ones that serve what is sometimes referred to as a 'regulatory' purpose. Whereas offences that require proof of fault manifest, in their very definition, both a moral and cognitive dimension – in the sense that they are made out if, and only if, there exists a particular state of mind with respect to circumstance, conduct or consequence, those that do not are established merely if a person (irrespective of his state of mind at the time) acts in a proscribed manner, or through his actions causes a proscribed consequence. Within the category of offences that do require proof of fault there exists, with minor variation across common law legal systems, a further distinction between the kinds of fault that are considered sufficiently blameworthy to justify a criminal justice response. Broadly speaking, that distinction consists in a differentiation between intention, recklessness and

2 See generally Ormerod, 2005: 90–157.

(more unusually) negligence. Of these, proof of intention is typically reserved for those offences that are viewed as the most serious. An intention to act in a proscribed way, or to bring about a proscribed consequence is conventionally understood as the most heinous state of mind because it indicates (at least in the popular imagination) that it was a person's desire, or purpose to engage in unlawful conduct, or to bring about an unlawful result.[3] Intentional action manifests a person's consciously willed determination to behave in a way proscribed by law, and as such justifies either conviction for the most egregious of offences (such as murder) or, where an offence may be committed either intentionally or recklessly, being sentenced more severely than would otherwise have been the case.

Proof of recklessness, on the other hand, does not require such a direct or focused relationship between the consciousness of a person and their conduct at the time the offence was committed. Where, for example, an offence requires the prosecution to prove that a person was reckless with respect to a consequence, all that needs to be established (assuming that the person did indeed cause that consequence) is that he was aware of the risk of that consequence occurring,[4] and that the risk-taking conduct was unjustified in the circumstances.[5] So, although proof of recklessness still requires the prosecution to establish that a person consciously adverted to the possibility of the proscribed consequence occurring as the result of his actions, there is no need to establish that his mind was directed towards accomplishing it. It is because there lacks such a direct connection between the person's will and the outcome of their actions that offences which can be committed recklessly are, conventionally, not viewed as being as serious as those that require proof of intention, and where the same offence may also be committed intentionally its reckless commission typically results in the imposition of a less severe penalty.

The broad distinction between intention and recklessness in criminal law is one that has intuitive appeal. Most people would, I suspect, draw a clear moral distinction between the person whose purpose when he acts is to cause the death of another, and the person who was merely aware of the risk that death

3 Criminal law typically draws a distinction between direct, or purposive, and indirect, or oblique, intention. The latter may be found to exist where, although it was not the defendant's purpose to bring about a proscribed consequence, that consequence was virtually certain to occur and the defendant himself foresaw it as virtually certain. In such cases a jury is, in English law, entitled to infer, or find, that an intention to cause that consequence existed. See *R v Nedrick* [1986] 1 WLR 1025, *R v Woollin* [1999] AC 82. For commentary see, e.g., Norrie, 1999.

4 One of the anomalies of the case law that has developed under OAPA 1861 is that a person charged under s 20 (which requires proof of serious bodily harm) need only foresee that some bodily harm (i.e. not necessarily serious harm) might result.

5 Thus, a person who is aware of the risk of further injuring someone whose life he is trying to save would not be criminally liable for recklessly causing any additional bodily harm.

might occur as the result of his conduct. The former is more morally blame-worthy and may legitimately be convicted of murder, whereas the latter lacks this degree of culpability and, despite killing unlawfully, ought therefore to avoid the social censure and level of punishment associated with that crime. The distinction is also one that, in addition to its intuitive appeal, is firmly embedded in the moral-philosophical values and assumptions that inform both criminal law doctrine and penal theory. In a criminal justice system whose roots lie in the early modern era, it is no accident that the person who directs his will towards achieving an outcome is identified as the paradigmatic criminal. Such deployment of the will not only demonstrates the cognitive faculty which identifies a person as having mental capacity – a pre-condition for the legitimacy of punishment in the liberal tradition; it also manifests his rationality (understood in the neutral sense of the capacity to make reasoned choices), and his failure to ensure that the exercise of such rationality is constrained by the values, principles and *mores* of the wider society in which he lives. In short, the person who acts intentionally, whether or not with respect to a proscribed consequence, is – in a very real sense – the ideal subject of criminal law, clearly responsible in thought and deed. And, because deed is so closely identified with thought, he is justifiably punished for both to the fullest permissible extent. In contrast, the person who acts recklessly – whether with respect to his actions, or to their possible consequences – may still be characterised as responsible, but for different reasons and to a lesser degree. He is still properly understood as responsible, in the sense that he has capacity to make reasoned choices and has made a choice, and culpable, in the sense that the choice made is one that manifests a lack of due regard to the interests of others; but because his fault lies in a failure to have regard to those interests and in an absence of foresight, rather than in a desire to harm, his fault is best characterised as culpable *ir*responsibility and punished less severely than would otherwise have been the case.

This is, at least, is the conventional rationale for the moral and legal distinction between intentional and reckless wrongdoing; but it is – I would suggest – one that fails to express the complex relationship between risk and fault.

The risk society

The contention that we live in a 'risk society' has, over a relatively short period of time, attained the status of political, economic and social orthodoxy (see, generally, Lupton, 1999). Although the variety of theoretical perspectives and epistemological traditions within which this claim is made are such that it is impossible to summarise neatly what it means, it has at its core the idea that our individual, collective and social lives are organised around, informed and, to some extent, determined by the concept of risk. This concept, like the 'risk society' of which it is constitutive, is no less easy to explain simply. Although its historical roots are murky, most scholars accept that in its pre-modern usage it signified those events in the future which were beyond human control – natural and other disasters that manifested the hand of God and against whose occurrence no precautions could therefore be taken (Ewald, 1991; 1993. See also Luhmann, 1993). This meaning, which still has marked lay resonance, altered perceptibly from the seventeenth century onwards. From the beginnings of what is commonly referred to in Europe as modernity, comprising the Enlightenment and the later development of industrialised capitalist society, risk became something that had to be managed if humans were to achieve the mastery of nature and populations necessary for efficient and effective governance – and which could be managed through the application of rational analysis grounded in objective scientific knowledge of the world and the mathematics of probability (Hacking, 1990). Unless the laws of nature (which came to include the behaviour of people) could be discerned, calculated and predicted – or, rather, understood as capable of discernment, calculation and prediction – such governance would simply not be possible (Giddens, 1990; Castel, 1991; Reddy, 1996; O'Malley, 2004).

One of the consequences of this way of seeing the world, one which intensified in the twentieth century, was that risk came to be seen as belonging to the province of experts. Only those who were able to undertake the necessary calculations and make the relevant predictions had access to what risk was and how it could and should be managed. Economists, mathematicians, actuaries, insurers, regulators – these were the people who, by virtue of their privileged knowledge, education and status, could tell the lay person how to organise their lives, and politicians how to develop and implement policies, so as to minimise adverse individual and collective consequences. This expert/lay distinction – intensified by the development of ever more 'risky' technologies (such as nuclear power and internet communication), by ever more sophisticated methods of evaluating their associated risks, and by increasing public concern about their effects (on health, on the environment and so on) – is a critical component of what Beck, Giddens and others have identified as the 'risk society' (Beck, 1992a; 1992b; 1996; Giddens, 1990; 1991; 1998). This is a society in which the possibility of governance through effective risk management, pursued for the amelioration of humankind, is realisable despite global technological and environmental uncertainty. And it is a society that is, increasingly, wary and sceptical of that claim (Rose, 1993). For Beck, Giddens and others risk is, ultimately, ideological – a discourse that is deployed for the legitimation of socio-economic policies and that pretends to certainty when such certainty does not, and cannot, exist. The extravagant promises of modernity – of health, wealth and security – are ones that not only cannot be delivered, but are ones that, paradoxically but inevitably, modernity itself has rendered undeliverable. The reflexivity that is central to modernity, the questioning of the modernising project itself, lays open to criticism and critique any claim to expert knowledge about the natural world, about populations, and about people and their behaviours. The belief that everything has an identifiable cause and predictable effects has been replaced by an awareness that events in the world are the product of multiple, complex and contradictory factors that are not readily amenable, or amenable at all, to identification and assessment. Society is becoming more fragmented, changing more quickly than ever before, and traditional mechanisms of cohesion (religion, the nuclear family, stable careers) can no longer be relied upon to provide that cohesion. Furthermore, this distrust of expertise and these social changes are complemented, in modernity's emphasis on responsibility for the self and its liberal pre-occupation with individual autonomy and self-realisation, by a distrust of others more generally (Rose, 1989; 1996a; 1996b). Rather than being a source of strength and solidarity, our fellow human beings represent potential threats to our own physical, economic and psychic security (Hudson, 2003: 44). In sum, modernity has been replaced by a post-modernity characterised by scepticism and anxiety (Giddens, 1990; Massumi, 1993) in which we are fearful for ourselves and distrustful of others, and in which the desire for personal and social security is matched only by their unattainability.

The risk society thesis, of which this is merely a brief snapshot, is one that has been subjected to a number of forceful critiques. These critiques, from as wide a variety of theoretical perspectives as the thesis itself, while acknowledging the centrality of risk in modern and post-modern society take issue with a number of its presuppositions. For the purposes of this chapter, which is intended to provide a theoretical basis for an understanding of the relationship between HIV, risk and criminal law, particular attention will be paid to those aspects of the thesis and their critique which centre on the lay/expert divide in knowledge about risk (especially in matters of health), the role of trust (and the consequences of its loss) in relations between people, and the place of risk in governance through law. It will also be necessary to elaborate further on the relationship between modernity, post-modernity and the liberal political values that underpin criminal law itself.

Risk and the socio-cultural construction of HIV

Those who transmit HIV to others or, in some jurisdictions, who merely expose – or who have the potential to expose – others to the risk of transmission, may and do find themselves subject to the coercive powers of the state. Those coercive powers may take the form of quarantine, isolation and detention measures under public health legislation;[6] or they may involve

6 See Ch 1, pp 11–21.

prosecution, conviction and imprisonment under the criminal law. Although we are principally concerned with the latter mode of coercion in this book, the exercise of public health powers and the criminalisation of transmission are each responses to the risk that HIV represents, whether potential or realised, to individual bodies or to the population at large.

In the context of criminal law, we have seen that HIV is constructed as a physical injury that constitutes a harm with which the criminal law is legitimately concerned. The essence of that harm is the fundamental and irreversible compromising of the immunity of the person to whom HIV is transmitted, an immunity which is constitutive of the physical and psychic identity of that person (and of all people) as healthy and 'normal'. HIV transmission in this reading entails permanent disruption of prior physiological integrity, and – which is more abhorrent – the inevitable and irreversible relocation of the newly infected individual into the category of the unhealthy and abnormal'. Infecting someone with HIV thus harms them both in the sense of adversely interfering with their physical self, and in the more symbolic sense of reconfiguring their personal and social identity – making them Other – and forcing upon them a new legal subjectivity; for, as a result of becoming HIV positive they too are rendered potential criminals – a person whose physiological status marks him out as someone with the potential to harm others, as someone who by virtue of their HIV status now legitimately falls under the watchful gaze of the state, and who, unless he conforms to the law's prescriptions, may find himself in the role of culpable perpetrator rather than innocent victim.

But not all incidents of transmission constitute harms that legitimate a criminal justice response. It is only if the causing of the physical injury through transmission is accompanied by a relevant kind and degree of fault on the part of the infector that it will be characterised as a harm for the purposes of criminal legal intervention. In English law, as was explained earlier, that fault must either be an intention to cause serious bodily harm, or recklessness with respect to the causing of bodily harm. Central to the latter mode of establishing liability is the concept of risk, because proving recklessness with respect to a consequence (i.e. transmission) requires proving that the defendant consciously took an unjustifiable, or unreasonable, risk with respect to transmission. It is the taking of that risk, aware of the possible consequences, that justifies the imposition of liability and legitimates the characterisation of the defendant as responsible – both for the risk-taking conduct itself, and for the consequences that are attributable to that conduct.

Understanding the meaning and significance of risk and risk-taking is, therefore, critical to an understanding of criminal liability for the reckless transmission of HIV. Unless we fully understand the fault and associated conduct that recklessness represents we will not fully understand the legal, and broader social justifications for punishing those who recklessly infect others. While it is possible, and necessary, to provide an account of recklessness in this context in the law's own terms – one grounded in the moral-philosophical and liberal political theories that are conventionally understood to underpin the law's reasoning – it is also, I believe, necessary to adopt a more expansive approach, one that accommodates the broader significance of risk, risk-taking and those who take risks in modern, and post-modern, society.

HIV, risk and identity

A 'person with HIV' is, by definition, a person with diagnosed HIV infection. Unless and until a person has tested positive for the antibodies produced in response to infection by the virus, and unless and until that positive test result is communicated to her, she may be infected but will be unaware and ignorant of her status. If she is unaware and ignorant because she never takes the test, then so will everybody else be. If she is unaware and ignorant because she decides not to discover the result of a test that has proved positive, only those with access to the results of the test will know. The person with diagnosed HIV is, therefore, someone who has – prior to, and independently of, their own knowledge of the fact – been identified and categorised as such, through routine screening or voluntary testing, by others. Those others – the laboratory scientists, clinicians, general practitioners, health advisers – have already determined that this person is now a specific kind of person, a person defined for their purposes as HIV positive. The person with HIV is, consequently, already and necessarily, implicated in the range of interventions that are (where these are available) triggered by a positive test result. She has become a member of a class, a person to be counselled, treated and monitored. Quite apart from her own response to diagnosis, she has been defined by, and become the object of, those with scientific and professional expertise – of virologists, pathologists, pharmacologists, epidemiologists and the broader concerns of those working in the field of HIV and AIDS healthcare. As a person with HIV, her subject position in relation to these experts has shifted irreversibly.

The same is true of her subject position and identity in relation to non-expert others, though this is not dependent on actually having and being aware of an HIV positive diagnosis. All those with HIV, diagnosed and otherwise, or who are thought to be infected with HIV, or who belong to groups with a high prevalence of HIV, occupy a particular place in the popular imaginary. For the HIV scientist and professional a person is either infected or not, 'at risk' of infection or not, or – if infected – diagnosed or not. A person is thus someone whose HIV status produces a binarised response, and with respect to whom different but complementary logics apply, depending on that status. From the lay perspective the response is far more complex. The person with real or imagined HIV infection, irrespective of that person's own knowledge of status, serves not to justify particular modes of expert intervention – that is necessarily for the experts themselves. Instead, she represents a threat both to the physical integrity and health that we assume is ours as of right, and a threat to our ontological security – to the security that is central to our sense of self and our intimate relationships with others. Because the threat to security that such a person poses is not dependent on it ever being realised, or on the actual status of that person, the person with (real or imagined) HIV may be both hazard and risk. If she is infected, there is the possibility (however remote) that she may be the source of another's infection. It is the fact that there is a probability value (however small) that can be attached to the hazard she represents that she may be classified as a risk (Fox, 1999). If she is not infected, she may also be classified as a risk *if others believe her to be*, because her imagined status (whether the result of her association with a particular risk group or otherwise) serves as a category of their understanding. She, and others, are imagined to be infected – in other words the entire class of people who are believed to be infected with HIV – are, in this sense, a risk. It may not be one that will, or can, materialise; but this is essentially irrelevant to the way in which those who are, or believe themselves to be, uninfected set up and oppose their identity against those whom they place in that class. And this, make no mistake, is a privileged identity – privileged because it is 'normal' by virtue of its freedom from infection (or because it is believed to be so). It is the nature of this privilege, in both a physical and cultural sense, that must be understood if we are to make sense of the risk that people with HIV are seen to pose and, thereafter, to make sense of the response of the criminal justice system to that risk.

Safe bodies/unsafe bodies

The secular Cartesian inheritance, as much as its Christian counterpart, is one which places the mind against the body and in which the latter is, and must be, subordinate. The body, which bleeds, breaks, fucks, sweats, farts, vomits, ejaculates, cries, shits, gives birth, urinates, gets high, gets diseased, transmits disease, and dies, comprises processes and passions that the mind must – so far as this is possible – overcome, regulate and control. Just as modernity involved the attempt to master the natural world through science and the application of logic and reason, so the ideal person of modernity was one who could only play his part in that project if he rendered his body subject to the dictates of rational action. To be weak-willed, to fail in this endeavour, was to fail at being human – to be no better than the animals. In Judaeo-Christian theology, the venal and carnal has similarly been set against the soul, flesh against the spirit, immortal against the immortal. In the Old Testament, plagues and pestilence were sent by a wrathful God to punish disobedience and immorality (a belief that still informs some religious fundamentalist responses to AIDS); in New Testament teaching, to suffer from affliction and disease (or passion and pleasure), is to experience what it is to be human – and something to be remedied through the infliction of corporal punishment so as to restore spiritual balance and a refocusing of the soul.

As Elizabeth Grosz has explained so eloquently, it is our Cartesian inheritance that has served to inform conceptions of the relationship between body
and mind in the science and philosophy of modernity (Grosz, 1994: 8–10).
One dimension of this inheritance is to conceptualise the body as an object
– a 'thing' to be analysed, whether in psychology's engagement with the
aesthetic dimension of human experience, in philosophy's interest in the
ontological and epistemological status of the body, or in ethnography's concern with its cultural variability and social transformation. Whether in the
context of biomedical science (where the human body is 'merely a more
complex version of other kinds of organic ensembles' (ibid: 8)), or the
humanities (which 'reduce the body to a fundmantal continuity with brute,
inorganic matter' (ibid)), the body is without unique specificity. Such lines of
investigation:

> . . . share a common refusal to acknowledge the distinctive complexities
> of organic bodies, the fact that bodies construct, and are in turn
> constructed by an interior, a psychical and a signifying view-point, a
> consciousness or perspective.
>
> (Ibid)

A second line of investigation, exemplified in liberal political philosophy
from Locke onwards, the body is seen as the property of a subject and at the
service of the subject's will. This conception forms the basis both of the
patriarchal tradition of philosophy that informs contemporary criminal law
(where actions are understood as the product of volition, and culpability for
conduct and consequences is located in the mind), and of much feminist
theory, in which the body (a site of contests for control) is placed at the centre
of emancipatory politics (ibid: 9). In this line of investigation:

> Whatever agency or will [the body] has is the direct consequence of ani-
> mating, psychical intentions. Its inertia means that it is being capable of
> being acted on, coerced, or constrained by external forces.
>
> (Ibid)

Lastly, the body is understood as a 'signifying medium' that serves both to
experience, translate and respond to external information through the senses
and to express the subject's interior, psychic, domain. In this conception too,
the body is a functional mechanism, and for it to operate efficiently the messy
fleshliness and specificity of the body has to be subdued:

> If the subject is to gain knowledge about the external world, have any
> chance of making itself understood by others, to be effective in the world
> on such a model, the body must be seen as an unresistant pliability which
> minimally distorts information, or at least distorts it in a systematic and

comprehensible fashion, so that its effects can be taken into account and information can be correctly retrieved. Its corporeality must be reduced to a predictable, knowable transparency; its constitutive role in forming thoughts, feelings, emotions, and psychic representations must be ignored, as must its threshold between the social and the natural.

(Ibid: 9–10)

Each of these three lines of investigation, which Grosz argues constitute some of the 'pervasive, unspoken assumptions' about the body in the science and philosophy of modernity, are ones which in some sense devalue the body. Her particular concern is to rescue the body for feminism, which she suggests can only avoid complicity in women's oppression if it takes on board the importance of restoring the body within feminist theory. But her analysis is also a useful starting point for understanding the ways in which the body (both our own, and that of others) has come to represent a risk, may be deployed in risky ways, and how law responds to those whose bodies do pose risks that do, in fact, materialise.

One element, associated with both the risk society thesis and its correlate, reflexive modernisation, is the argument that the lack of certainty which risk produces renders each of us responsible for creating our own biographies. In societies marked by a breakdown in traditional mores and conventions, in which socio-economic structures and roles are no longer 'givens', we have become responsible for negotiating and determining our own life-courses (Beck, 1992a; 1994; Beck and Beck-Gernsheim, 1995). That negotiation and determination takes place in collaboration, or in conflict, with others – whether in the world of work or within social and intimate relationships. The Enlightenment ideal of autonomous self-realisation, along with the modern-ist imperative to master one's environment – and through this to establish the security we crave as individuals – creates further anxieties. Each choice we make, each relationship we enter into, each person in whom we place our trust, may be either the route to that security, or a path to emotional, finan-cial or physical ruin (see, for example, Giddens, 1992). Whereas the person in pre-modern societies was absolved of responsibility for poverty, failure and loss – this was the consequence of one's socio-economic position, or of fate, or of God – the person of modernity has only himself to blame.

In such a world, there is self-evidently a substantial investment in getting things right, in making the correct choices. Those choices frequently centre on bodies – how we comport or deploy our own, how we interact with those with whom we come into contact, and how we respond to the advice of others (whether lay or expert) with respect to each of these. Here, as Grosz suggests, our bodies are understood as mechanisms through which we are able to implement our will – and the bodies of others mechanisms through which we experience theirs. But that will is never, and can never, be 'free floating', entirely abstract (except in the minds of the most reductionist of analytical philosophers). It is a will whose expression in choices and decisions is formed through, and informed by, exposure to culture. Those choices and decisions we believe to be rational (and judged by others to be so), are rational because there is a particular set of social and cultural expectations of what 'rationality' entails in any given situation. Those choices and decisions we believe will further our security interests will be informed by what security means to us. Those choices and decisions we believe will serve to minimise or avoid exposure to risks that may undermine that security will depend on how we understand, estimate and respond to risk.

Clearly, then, it is either false or at best overly simplistic to contend, as Beck has done, that the globalised and supranational nature of risk in late modernity has the effect of erasing and levelling individual difference – of universalising and democratising risk, so that each of us is equal in its face (Beck, 1992a: 109). While this may hold if the 'risk society' is understood only in terms of environmental change (such as global warming) and technological developments (such as nuclear power and mass communication), it does not apply if risk society also comprises – which it surely must – the more immediate choices, decisions and encounters that we confront, reach and negotiate in our personal lives on a routine basis. To understand the ways in which risk plays out in the mundane but critical world of the everyday, and to understand how important the construction of self and Other as embodied subjects is in this context, it is necessary to locate the discussion at the level of the body and its cultural significance.

As Lupton has explained, the European pre-modern, or medieval, body was 'an open world which embraced forces that gushed forth through the orifices of the lower body' (Lupton, 1999: 124–5). It was thus corruptible, and open to invasion just as much as it was 'uncontrolled, sensuous and volatile' (ibid: 125). Such protection as was available against the sinister forces that threatened the body was provided by rites, rituals and taboos aimed at eliminating evil and restoring purity. There was no sense in which such a body was, or could be, the property of an independent mind, or subject to an independent will; no sense it which these natural, or supernatural, hazards could be avoided through conscious decision-making; no sense in which the diseases communicated by other bodies were preventable through the exercise of informed, rational, choices; no sense in which these could be conceived of as risks that could be identified, predicted and avoided. One's own body was not at risk, nor could the bodies of others pose a risk to oneself, because risk was simply not a category of understanding within which thought and action could be organised.

With the advent of modernity this changed (see, generally, Elias, 1939 (1994)). The body that had been open to the elements, subject to fate's vicissitudes, was gradually shorn up and closed off from its environment, the division between mind and body firmly established. The mind, as the seat of reason, came to be seen as the means of, and thus responsible for, corporeal regulation. In philosophy and science, as explained above by Grosz, the body became an object, separate from (if intimately connected with) the mind – something that could, and should, be analysed, reflected upon, directed. This, along with the fact that it was also a body which was conceived of as distinct, separate and individuated, meant that there was an increased investment in maintaining its boundedness. To 'open up', to revel in the physicality of the body, was to lose the control critical for self-regulation and the realisation of autonomy:

> The progressive change from the open 'grotesque' body to the closed or 'civilised' body . . . resulted in the intensification of anxieties about the orifices of the body and what flows in and out of it. When the body was conceptualized as open to the world, as inevitably porous and only weakly subject to the control of the individual, pleasure as well as fear accompanied the flow of forces in and out of the body. The increasing emphasis on self-regulation, the closing off of the body as much as possible, resulted in greater anxiety about the possibility of the loss of self-control and the blurring of boundaries between inside and outside, and self and Other.
>
> (Lupton, 1999: 26)

To take risks with the body, wilfully to expose it to anything that might damage or impair it, was the height of irresponsibility. The value associated with physical integrity, and the concomitant wrong of physical violation, assumed enormous significance – one which, as we saw in the last chapter, was reflected in the law relating to offences against the person and the very low threshold for assault – an offence established by the merest of non-consensual touches.

But of course no body is, or can be, an island. The very construction of the body as bounded establishes and confirms the notion of its limits, its edges, its surfaces. And the reality of the physical body is that its boundedness is necessarily confounded by its need to eat, drink, defecate, urinate and reproduce. These functions, along with the more sensuous desires and passions whose realisation demands – for most, at least – connection with other bodies, creates a body that is always and inevitably compromised, or open to compromise. It is here, in this imperative of self-control and vigilance that is the sign of the civilised body, and its impossibility in the face of what being human involves, that the anxiety about the body has its source; it is here that the cultural meanings and significance associated with different kinds of body and different modes of human connection are generated and reinforced; and it is here that the bodies of others and the ways in which we connect with them are accommodated and embraced or rejected and despised, where they become identified and classified as either threatening or affirming our physical and ontological security.

Nowhere is this anxiety about the body and the need for vigilance more intense, and the cultural demarcation between self and Other more clearly delineated, than in relation to health and sex. The good, safe and civilised body of modernity is the healthy body – one that is 'normal' in its functioning, behaves predictably and regularly, has demonstrated both interior control and stability and resistance to external contagion, has maintained its boundedness and self-regulation. The bad, risky and uncivilised body of modernity is, it goes without saying, the converse – one that is 'abnormal' in its functioning, behaves erratically and irregularly, is out of control and unstable and opened itself up to the outside, has become unbounded and ceased to regulate itself. The good, safe body is one that is *of itself*, free from destabilising and compromising contaminants. The good, safe and civilised body – insofar as it must acknowledge its physicality – does not fart or burp in public, seeks privacy to urinate, defecate, copulate, masturbate and breast-feed, uses deodorant, brushes its teeth, washes regularly, cuts its hair and trims its nails;[7] in contrast, the bad, risky and uncivilised body does not care about the offence, distaste or revulsion that the failure to conform to such norms of comportment and behaviour may cause. The good, safe and civilised body nurtures itself, polices its margins, regulates the access of others and maintains its distance; the bad, risky and uncivilised one lets itself go, fails to conceive of itself as having margins, allows others unlimited access and ignores spatial conventions. For the good, safe and civilised body – the normal archetype – its obverse serves as a self-legitimating reference point: I am not *that*. More than this, any manifestation of the obverse – of its qualities or behaviours – provokes a physical response, whether of anxiety or repulsion, whose cause cannot simply be understood aesthetically but rather in terms of a threat to self-identity and security, and to the socio-cultural values and norms in which these are grounded (see, for example, Lupton, 1999: 127–9).

The HIV negative and HIV positive person occupy these relative positions in contemporary western society.[8] In the previous chapter I set out the ways in which HIV infection is constructed as harm, both socio-culturally and in law. Here I am concerned instead to focus on the related, but distinct, question of how HIV, and more particularly its embodied manifestation, is constructed as a threat, hazard and risk to the physical and ontological security of others. I will also be concerned to explore the reasons why, when HIV has such ontological significance, people (whatever their HIV status may be, and

7 An excellent study of the various ways in which the law contributes to the construction of the civilised body is provided by Hyde (1997).
8 I use these terms for the sake of brevity. There are, of course, those who believe themselves to be HIV negative when they are in fact HIV positive, and people who are HIV negative who others believe to be HIV positive, or to have AIDS. Because it is what HIV, and the HIV infected person, represent in the popular imaginary that actual status is – for the purposes of the present discussion at least – irrelevant.

whether diagnosed or otherwise) are prepared to take risks with their own health and that of their sexual partner(s). We will then be in a position to consider both the significance of, and reasons for, the criminalisation of reckless HIV transmission – in terms of the fault that recklessness represents, how it is framed within legal discourse, and the response of the criminal justice system to those who, with that kind and degree of fault, in fact transmit HIV to others.

HIV, risk and embodiment

The HIV positive person is, arguably, the paradigm Other of the risk society and late (or post-) modernity. An immanently de-stabilised subject, whose shifting and mutable identity is the product of biomedical, legal, political, economic, cultural and other discourses, such a person not only represents the embodiment of a globalised threat to humanity itself – and, because HIV is only ever embodied, is understood *as* the threat – but challenges every presupposition and assumption we have about our bodies and how to regulate and defend them, our ability to control our natural environment, and our capacity to determine our own destinies (see, generally, Treichler, 1998; Crimp, 2002). The ways in which this identity has been constructed, the form it takes, and the modes of its representation are complex and multidimensional. Here I want to focus on a number of key aspects of that identity and its formation (or, rather, production and reproduction – for it is one of the singularly remarkable features of HIV positivity that its meaning has been determined and colonised by those with certain self-serving investments). Those aspects upon which I will concentrate are: the socio-cultural framing and significance of the HIV positive body, and how we come to conceptualise that body through its popular representation. I will be particularly concerned to explore the sexualised and gendered construction of HIV positive bodies and to identify the ways in which they have come to be understood as 'risky'.

Elaborating on Grosz's account of our Cartesian inheritance in matters corporeal, and on the discussion of the ideal modern body set out above, we may best understand the HIV infected body as one that is seen to confound, confront and unsettle. It provokes these reactions, amounting to a threat to security and self-identity, because it is one that challenges the account of the body as closed, impermeable and bounded. This quality of the HIV positive body is one of liminality and hybridity (Lupton, 1999: 131–6). Social order and the security it promises is established by creating and sustaining boundaries. This is as true at the level of the organic body as it is at the level of the body politic. The idea of an inside and an outside, of a within and a beyond, of what belongs and what does not is important to our sense of self. The HIV positive body confounds the binary logic that sustains these oppositions. It attests to the permeability and fragility of the body – to the impossibility of maintaining absolute corporeal security, to the immanence of mortality, and to the contingency of these oppositions and the security they serve to provide. The HIV positive body is thus liminal and hybrid, an anomaly that occupies the self/Other borderland and constantly threatens to disrupt that functionally symbolic distinction.

The HIV positive body is liminal because it occupies a space between the healthy body and the sick one. It is hybrid because its identity is contingent and compromised. It is, as result of the impossibility of ridding the body of the virus once infected, one that is already and forever inscribed with its mortality; but, at the level of observation, it is no different from any other body. The interior processes occurring at the level of the cellular and the genetic provide – unless and until it succumbs to an AIDS-related illness – no outward or visible sign of sickness, and so preclude the allocation of 'this body' to 'that class of bodies'. The HIV positive body is, in one sense at least, ineffective as a 'signifying medium' for these purposes because it resists the imperative of reduction to a 'predictable, knowable transparency' (Grosz, 1994: 10). On the other hand, its cultural significance is amplified for this very reason – a significance that does not depend on the virological and patho-logical 'truth' of any particular body but rather on the assumptions and presuppositions that circulate and are continuously reproduced about the threats that This Body contains and – critically – occludes. The HIV positive body is, thus, always an imagined body, whose significance depends not on HIV infection itself but on its omnipresence and unknowability.

The insecurity that such liminality and hybridity creates is reinforced fur-ther by the transmissibility of HIV and, in particular, the contexts and modes of its transmission. Its transmissibility identifies the HIV positive body as a source of pollution, a dirty body, where dirt is understood as what is not in its proper place and which has the capacity to pollute:

> Dirt offends against order. Eliminating it is not a negative movement, but a positive effort to organise the environment.
>
> (Douglas, 1966 (2002): 2)

The elimination of 'dirt' at a political level finds expression, at its most extreme, in the slaughter of the Jews by the Nazis, in the apartheid regime of South Africa, in eugenic science and rules relating to miscegenation. It is evident in any attempt by a society to maintain its 'purity' by imposing bor-der controls that require would-be immigrants to undergo tests that filter out the sick and unhealthy. At an individual level, the elimination or exclusion of dirt – or rather the practices, attitudes and response mechanisms that attempt to achieve this – mirror the political project:

> The body can/does function to represent, to symbolize, social and collect-ive fantasies and obsessions: its orifices and surfaces can represent the

sites of cultural marginality, places of social entry and exit, regions of confrontation or compromises.

(Grosz, 1994: 193)[9]

The HIV positive body is a paradigm site for such obsessive fantasy because of its capacity to reproduce itself in the body of those for whom it represents a threat to physical and ontological security, and because that reproduction occurs – and can only occur – through the merging of bodies via the co-mingling of their 'inside':

> Body fluids attest to the permeability of the body, its necessary dependence on an outside, its liability to collapse into this outside (this is what death implies), to the perilous divisions between the body's inside and its outside. They affront a subject's aspiration toward autonomy and self-identity. They attest to a certain irreducible 'dirt' or 'disgust', a horror of the unknown or the unspecifiable that permeates, lingers, and at times leaks out of the body, a testimony to the fraudulence or impossibility of the 'clean' and 'proper'.

(Grosz, 1994: 193–4)

That this threat of pollution and the death it implies may take place at the very moment we seek union with others through sexual intimacy, in contexts of sensual pleasure, at times when we trust enough to yield and give up our boundedness renders the HIV positive body yet more of a threat. As William Haver explains:

> . . . etiological constructions of AIDS situate the origins of HIV infection, and therefore the essential fatality of the body, in material erotic relations: in IV drug use and in the incorporation of alien blood, semen, vaginal fluids, and breast milk . . . An entire semiology has been constructed here: the fatally erotic relation is construed in terms of taking what belongs least of all to the property and propriety of one's own body into the innermost recesses of the privacy of the clean and proper body. The incorporation of the radically other becomes the very identity of the self: the other is my finitude. It is the transgression of a proper identity . . . that not only brings but incarnates death. The price of disrupting the opposition of outside to inside is death. Further, these transgressions occur at particular sites, the body's lamellae – the puncture wounds of

---

9 Grosz's analysis is, in large part, a response to Julia Kristeva's psycholanalytic theory of abjection – the process by which, as infants, we come to understand the boundaries of our bodies through the expulsion of waste (Kristeva, 1982). For a clear introduction to Kristeva's work see Oliver, 1993. For a legally inspired critique see Hyde, 1997: 205–221.

the needle, the mouth, the vagina, the tip of the penis, and above all, the anus. In all cases we are dealing with surfaces that are both inside and outside, and therefore neither 'inside' or 'outside', sites at which the putative corporeal integrity of the so-called self is always already ambiguous, sites that are always already wounds and therefore susceptible to infection by the other; indeed by otherness 'itself'.

(Haver, 1997: 11–12)

First excursus: women, HIV and risk

It is not, of course, the case that the HIV positive body has entered discourse as a free-floating signifier. Although in itself it comprises a specific and irreducible threat, it is already and inevitably located in, and thus identified with, those bodies, identities, sexualities and relations that threaten our heteronormative and patriarchal social order. In this way it achieves even greater cultural significance and symbolic power, is even more confounding, confrontational and unsettling. For Grosz, it is women's bodies, their unstable and destabilising corporeality, that serve both to affirm men's belief in their own inviolability and, thus, the bounded body (i.e. male bodies) as the normal, universal and legitimate form of subjectivity. The seminal flows that emit from male bodies, reduced to a by-product of sexual pleasure rather than conceived as a manifestation of immanent materiality, and as something that is directed, linear and non-reciprocal, enables men to sustain the fantasy of the closed body and of the possibility of control over it. The socio-cultural and psychological dimension of Mackinnon's (in)famous assertion about the power necessarily instantiated in heterosexual relations ('Man fucks woman: subject verb object' (Mackinnon, 1982: 541)), this fantasy is a prerequisite for the maintenance of masculinity, and of the mastery – over women, over nature – that masculinity enables, or which is its prerogative. To receive flow, or to be in position where there is a risk of flow in the other direction, is to be identified with the feminine (whether as woman, or as passive homosexual) and to lose the phallic advantage; to acknowledge the essential materiality of the body, that its flows are not merely by-products of the body but constitutive of it (and this is what acceptance of certain claims by some feminists entails), is an admission that strikes at the heart of masculinity, at the security which is its privilege, and at the legitimacy of the hierarchised and gendered socio-economic order upon which its privileged status depends. Understood in these terms, it is unsurprising that it is women's bodies (despite the relatively low risk of female to male sexual transmission) that are – within the discourse that frames the heterosexual HIV pandemic – characterised as the source of infection. As Grosz explains, this discourse is one that makes:

... women, in line with the conventions and practices associated with contraceptive procedures, the guardians of the sexual fluids of both men and women. Men seem to refuse to believe that *their* body fluids are the 'contaminants'. It must be women who are the contaminants. Yet, para-doxically, the distinction between a 'clean' woman and an 'unclean' one does not come from any presumption about the inherent polluting prop-erties of the self-enclosure of female sexuality, as one might presume, but is a function of the quantity, and to a lesser extent the quality, of the men she has already been with. So she is in fact regarded as a kind of sponge or conduit of *other men's* 'dirt'.

(Grosz, 1994: 197)

This (and indeed others of Grosz's theoretical observation) is one that finds concrete expression in the coverage of the criminal conviction of Sarah Porter at Inner London Crown Court in June 2006. In addition to its racial-ised dimensions (see below, pp 136–40), the case was one in which Porter was represented in the media (especially the print media) as an 'evil' woman who had destroyed the life of the man she pleaded guilty to infecting. Demonstrating the extent to which the abstract analysis of corporeality and its immanent finitude presented above finds its way almost unmediated into the lay discourse of the person who discovers himself to be infected, this man (identified as Mr C):

> . . . said that he felt 'numb', was in 'absolute shock' and knew that there was a 'timebomb' living inside him.
> He said: 'Before being infected with the HIV virus I led a happy care-free life. I had a happy childhood and was studying for a career that I was passionate about and had good friendships and what I thought to be a good relationship.
> On the whole I considered myself to be baggage-free. Now everything has changed and will never be the same again.
> Besides the pain already suffered by me and family and partner I am petrified about what is to come. I know my health will deteriorate and I know how devastating this will be for her to watch.'

(Fresco, 2006a: 7)

And, in the on-line version of the same account (excluded from the print version) Mr C is reported to have said:

> 'I know that I have this thing inside me and I know it shouldn't be there. It is in my head all the time and feels like a physical scar, but there is nothing I can do to hide it from myself.'

(Fresco, 2006b)

Without wishing in any way to diminish the felt experience of Mr C, his willingness to engage in unprotected sex with Porter resulted in infection that produced desensitisation and disbelief, and a body whose altered state would eventually reveal itself catastrophically. The identity of which he was the author unravelled. His 'baggage-free' life was irreversibly changed, his intimate, social and economic future rendered more uncertain than it would otherwise have been. The virus is omnipresent, embedded eternally in Mr C's psyche and his flesh. The virus is alien, does not belong, but cannot be denied. Such was the effect on Mr C, that exposing himself to the gaze of others, maintaining the semblance of control, and sustaining himself became impossible. Annihilation of the self he had become was, in light of what that self entailed and what it signified, a viable alternative:

> His long cherished ambition to study graphic design at university was ruined as he became clinically depressed and found it difficult to leave the house.
>
> 'I was having what I believed to be a breakdown and at this stage I could not cope with life', he said. 'I did not care for myself and stopped washing and cleaning my clothes.
>
> At times even making dinner was too difficult. On one occasion I took some paracetamol and washed them down with alcohol intending to kill myself.
>
> I stopped myself before I took too many, but did consider suicide at several other points during this time. I hated myself and felt worthless.
>
> I tried to convince myself that HIV was just another virus but really I knew it wasn't. I knew how much hatred some people had for those infected with HIV and that it would eventually kill me.'
>
> (Fresco, 2006b)

It is irrelevant whether it is in fact HIV infection that will be the cause of Mr C's death, because the specificity, meaning and significance of HIV are such that it has, in a sense, already killed him. It does not matter that implicit in his narrative of others' hatred is his own, because he now occupies the subject position to which he imagined himself immune. The time to come, the time over which he (and we) need to conceive as ours for the taking, no longer belongs to him. It is marked by anticipation and uncertainty:

> Mr C has to go to hospital every three months to have a blood sample taken, but then has to face an 'anxious' week-long wait for the results.
>
> 'I am not on medication yet but I know that this day will arrive and I am terrified.' Mr C added: 'I feel as though there is a ticking time bomb inside me, just waiting to go off.
>
> The doctors have not told me how long I can expect to live and I have not asked.
>
> It is so variable there seems little point.'
>
> (Fresco, 2006b)

What is interesting about the coverage in *The Times*, the newspaper of record from which this account is drawn, is its focus almost entirely on Mr C – the person upon whom Sarah Porter acted. He is the effect, she the cause. To the extent that Sarah Porter has an identity in the story it is as a mugshot, as the object of vilification (cruel, dishonest and 'pure evil'), and as the source of an unknown but potentially enormous number of other infections (the report states that police 'believe she may have slept with dozens of men'). The fact that of the four men who came forward for testing only Mr C was in fact HIV positive is, it is implied, only a matter of luck. The lead police investigator, whose opinion takes on the status of fact, is reported as saying 'I feel this is might be the tip of the iceberg', and the account from which this quotation is drawn makes a thinly veiled criticism of her character, stating that Porter 'had unprotected sex with four men, including her boyfriend, in six months' (Fresco, 2006b). The local press coverage of the story is, if anything, even more 'victim'-centred. One of Porter's other lovers, 'Paul', interviewed after her conviction, explained:

> 'Sarah is very, very attractive, the sort of woman any guy would love to be with. But make no mistake; she is a very dangerous woman. She's sick in the head.
> She has had an awful lot of counselling over the HIV but it doesn't seem to have worked.
> Her thinking seems to be, "Why should I be the only one to suffer? Why shouldn't they suffer as well?" '
>
> (Ashford, 2006)

Paul's analysis, which serves to absolve him of any responsibility, is supplemented by an 'explanation' of why he had a sexual relationship in which HIV could be transmitted with someone about whose status he was ignorant (and whose possible HIV positive status never crossed his mind):

> 'Sarah is a very, very good dancer. She has a real presence and doesn't have to work hard to attract men. She's the sort of woman you dream of ending up with.
> We hooked up, went to a few clubs. She was older than me, she was clean-living, she had her head together.
> I really felt I had met the girl of my dreams. We took things slow at first but when we finally had sex it was intense.
> She was aggressive and full-on. Sometimes we used condoms but she didn't seem bothered if they broke.
> When one of her friends warned me she had "issues", I thought to myself, Who doesn't? The thought she might be HIV positive never entered my head.'
>
> (Ashford, 2006)

After being told by another mutual friend that Porter was HIV positive, Paul confronted her and she disclosed. His immediate response was to go to the police 'because there was no way she could get away with this'. He added, 'I was really freaking out. I was suicidal. I was so angry I actually wanted to kill her.' Despite testing negative for HIV infection, it was Paul's complaint that initiated the police investigation into Porter's sexual history and which resulted in the conviction for infecting Mr C. The report concludes by explaining that, following Porter's sentencing

> . . . Paul urged anyone who has had sex with this siren to come forward immediately, adding: 'Don't be shy, you must come forward and be tested.
>
> Sarah has been around for a long time, she had been on the clubbing scene since the soul days and knows an awful lot of people.
>
> If you've slept with her you could be HIV positive, you could be passing the virus to your wife, your girlfriend or boyfriend.
>
> Come forward and stop this thing from spreading and spreading.'
>
> (Ashford, 2006).

In this account, Porter is the seductress against whom everyone must be protected and yet to whom everyone is (fatally) attracted. Both Medusa and siren, she is a woman who precludes the exercise of men's agency, whose maturity and sexual energy confounds the feminine archetype and is thus as alluring as it is dangerous, who by her looks and movements enchants, disables and ensnares. She is a long-time reservoir of infection, who is single-handedly driving the epidemic, placing at risk everyone who has ever had sex with her, and who has, in turn ever had (or might have) sex with them. In terms of both quantity (of men) and the quality of the relationships she has had, she epitomises Grosz's assertion that women are indeed regarded as 'the sponge or conduit of *other men's* dirt'.[10] The fact that (one assumes) Sarah Porter was herself infected by a man is something that is never even mentioned, or worth mentioning; or – it may be suggested – something that is (if the story is to conform to, and reinforce, the discourse of HIV and AIDS into which it so effortlessly insinuates itself) simply unmentionable.

Excursus: race, HIV and risk

If the body of Sarah Porter, and the bodies of women 'like her' (the promiscuous body, the body that charges money for sex), are understood as

---

10 My commentary here is in similar terms to that of Paula Treichler in her analysis of hepatitis transmission by 'Maggie', a nurse in Colin Douglas' novel *The Intern's Tale* (Treichler, 1988: 190–192).

reservoirs and as a potent source of HIV infection, and therefore as the cause of the heterosexual pandemic, it is no less so for the black body. Whereas the white heterosexual woman has (until relatively recently) occupied a marginal, exceptional and therefore – paradoxically – more threatening position in both HIV epidemiology and popular representations, the converse is true for the black man. Porter's partners, Mr C, Paul and the others, were Afro-Caribbean. Her child, insofar as it was possible to tell from the pixellated images that were meant to ensure his anonymity, is mixed race (and as such further evidence of her unwillingness to conform to the norm of non-miscegenation). Although in her narrative they were the victims, black men, especially (in the UK) those from sub-Saharan Africa, are more often than not identified as the source, the threat and (as a class) a risk.

The racialisation (and, more particularly the 'Africanisation') of HIV and AIDS is coterminous with the pandemic. It continues a long tradition of western-European representations, in politics and culture, of Africa as an immanently unstable, primitive, dangerous, uneducated and hyper-eroticised continent and – more recently – of Africa as being the source of HIV and therefore the 'cause' of AIDS. Simon Watney, whose 1989 piece *Missionary Positions* is concerned to explore the media representation of African AIDS, provides one of the most comprehensive and insightful accounts of how AIDS (rather than HIV itself) has come to be identified – through feature articles and news reports – as 'a disease of "African-ness" ' (Watney, 1989 (1994): 112) and as an apocalyptic image of, and premonitory warning about, our (i.e. European and North American) future. In these representations, emaciated children with hollow eye-sockets and prostitutes luring truck drivers into fatal copulation vie with monkeys and stagnant water to create a sense of immanent and irredeemable (in both the religious and secular sense) contagion and hopelessness. The 'primitivism' of Africans – a category without distinction – resists all well-intentioned Western efforts to promote the logic of safer sex. This, given the 'airborne' transmission of HIV – airborne in the sense of being borne by those who travel by air from that continent to the civilised West, whether as returning tourists who have taken advantage of the pleasures it provides, or as asylum-seekers fleeing its many repressive and violent regimes – renders Africa, and Africans (or, I suspect, anyone who is assumed to be African, or to have African blood), a threat without parallel in the white Western imaginary.[11]

These representations of, and elisions between, Africa(ns) and HIV are (and I do not wish to labour the point here) ones that fit squarely into the more general analysis of the risky, uncivilised body that was presented above.

---

11 The cultural construction and representation of 'African AIDS' has also been expertly ana-lysed by Treichler (Treichler, 1999: 205–234). For a critical account of the ways in which Haiti (and Haitians) have functioned in similar ways for Americans see Treichler, 1999: 99–126.

Within a predominantly white culture (as the UK is), the black body is different and thus framed within dominant discourses as Other. The qualities and character of its Otherness, ones which overlap depending on the discursive or ideological purpose to which the black body is being put, are, variously sexual potency, desirability and promiscuity, laziness, economic unproductiveness, stupidity, and (especially for young black males) criminality. These qualities, when combined with fears about HIV and about the impact of immigration and asylum from Africa on the UK's economy, culture and mores, serve to create a heady and dangerous climate of fear and mistrust, and to increase already present racist hostility.

Nowhere have these elisions found more extreme expression in England and Wales than in cases involving the reckless transmission of HIV. These cases, against Mohammed Dica, Feston Konzani and Kouassi Adaye especially, each received substantial media coverage and – whether through photographic images, the way in which the story was framed, or a combination of both – this coverage made much of their ethnic origins and immigration status. Here, for example, are excerpted extracts from the local Liverpool press's online coverage of Adaye's conviction:

> A bogus asylum-seeker has been successfully prosecuted for infecting a Liverpool woman with the deadly HIV virus.
>
> African Kouassi Adaye, 40, pleaded guilty at Liverpool crown court to causing grievous bodily harm to the 48-year-old woman.
>
> Adaye, of Wynnstay Street, Toxteth, but originally from the Ivory Coast, had sex with the victim eight days after being told he was HIV positive.
>
> The news had been broken to him by his wife who was still living in South Africa.
>
> . . .
>
> Adaye also pleaded guilty to a string of other offences including bigamy.
>
> The court heard that he married a 57-year-old woman on January 10 last year when he was still married to a woman in South Africa.
>
> He also pleaded guilty to 20 charges of fraud.
>
> The court heard that Adaye came to the UK in 1999 and falsely claimed asylum and state [benefits].
>
> (Chapman, 2004a)

In this account, 'African' Adaye is 'of' a local street, but 'from' the Ivory Coast. He infects a 'local' woman with a 'deadly virus'. The clear implication is that his HIV infection is one that he has brought with him from Africa, to a country where he falsely represents both his entitlement to support and his marital status. As is the way with stories such as these, the details get mixed up in the accounts that are presented so that *who* Adaye is, and *what* precisely he has done, are uncertain. Here for example is an excerpt from another report published at the same time.

A MAN who knowingly infected a Liverpool woman with the HIV virus has been jailed for six years.

Liverpool crown court Judge David Lynch called South African Kouassi Adaye 'a danger to women', after he pleaded guilty at to inflicting grievous bodily harm on a 48-year-old woman.

John McDermott QC, prosecuting, told the court Adaye, an asylum-seeker who was originally from the Ivory Coast, had unprotected sex with the woman last April, just eight days after he was informed he may be HIV positive.

Adaye, 37, of Wynnstay Street, Toxteth, also had sex with two other women, one of whom he had married bigamously, but it was not alleged that he had infected them.

Mr McDermott said Adaye left his South African wife and daughter in 1999 and made his way to the UK, claiming asylum on the grounds of religious persecution.

His claim was refused, but following an administrative error, Adaye's claim was held in abeyance and was still being considered by the Home Office when he was arrested in May last year.

Adaye, who has a qualification in law from the Ivory Coast, obtained a French passport, identity card and driving licence so he could obtain a National Insurance number.

Calling himself Jean Michel Adaye, the asylum-seeker got a job at the Kingdom of Leather furniture store in Edge Lane, then as a meter reader for Scottish Power, where he earned £11,000 a year.

Mr McDermott said it was while he worked at the shop when he met his 48-year-old victim, who was described as a married professional woman.

He told her he was a French solicitor and that he had been working in Chester until he had an accident.

The court heard their relationship became a sexual one and he had unprotected sex with her after being told it was probable he had the HIV virus.

(Chapman 2004b)

Here, Adaye's civil status is less clear, but we are treated to the further details that unlike Adaye (who worked in blue collar jobs and was in any event on the take) the complainant was of a different class altogether – someone who would (we are led to assume) only have a relationship with a respectable professional, from one of Liverpool's most affluent dormitory neighbours – and how could such a man possibly pose a risk of any kind to anyone?

A serial liar, infected and African, Adaye's predicament (and I make no

value judgment here, merely the observation that he was in a predicament –
especially as regards the difficulties associated with disclosure of HIV status
so soon after apparently learning it) is not averred to. While this absence of
context may be thought reasonable in news reports, rather than feature stories,
what is not reasonable is the failure to report on any of the legal complexities
of Adaye's story. For it appears to be the case that Adaye did not have an HIV
positive test result prior to being arrested, nor is it clear that there was any
scientific evidence in the possession of the prosecution that demonstrated that
the HIV sub-type of the complainant was the same as his (i.e. no scientific
evidence that would tend towards establishing the route of transmission or the
source of infection). The statement in the news report that Adaye had been
told of his infection by his wife in South Africa (which is peculiar in itself,
given half a moment's thought) was elsewhere reported as a call in which she
had simply told him of her own positive diagnosis (by which, one assumes, we
are invited to conclude that he must be positive too and to know that). This
latter version was false and ordered to be corrected by the trial judge, but it is
unclear whether such correction ever occurred. In any event, because there
was no trial, such evidence of Adaye's 'knowledge' of his HIV positive status,
and of him being the cause of the complainant's infection (a pre-condition
for a finding that he inflicted the harm on her), was never tested. At the
sentencing hearing it has been reported that a doctor had been willing to give
evidence that she had *recommended* that Adaye have an HIV test (a recommendation he appears not to have followed) because he was, in her opinion, at
'high risk'. It was this that seems to have provided the judge with the
justification for claiming that Adaye should have been aware of the risk and
for characterising his subsequent behaviour as 'despicable' (Dodds *et al*,
2005: 26–7).

Whatever the 'truth' surrounding Kouassi Adaye and his conviction, none
of the background information is relevant to a story that serves to affirm the
threat which he, as a member of a class (or classes – black, infected, deceitful,
untrustworthy), represents. In this he is no different from Mohammed Dica,
variously portrayed as from Somalia or Kenya (Africa is, after all, just one
undifferentiated mass for these purposes), who was sentenced after being
found guilty of infecting one woman at his third trial, or Feston Konzani
(whose trial was analysed in detail in Chapter 2) (Dodds, 2005: 25–6, 27–8).
Unlike Sarah Porter, the 'siren' temptress, these black men are assassins and
predators who, with their black counterparts in other (predominantly non-
black) parts of the world figure as insatiable and archetypical threats to innocent, white and 'native' femininity.[12]

---

12 Philip Alcabes, for example, has noted that in America, Nushawn Williams was variously
   described as an 'AIDS predator', a 'monster', a 'dirtbag', a 'maggot', the 'bogeyman incar-
   nate'. He had 'hundreds of partners' who 'preyed on schoolgirls'. He was a 'guy who . . . shot

Excursus: homosexuality, HIV and risk

> . . . Aids [*sic*] is not only a medical crisis on an unparalleled scale, it involves a crisis of representation itself, a crisis over the framing of knowledge about the human body and its capacities for sexual pleasure.
>
> (Watney, 1987: 9)

The third risky body of HIV is that of the (male) homosexual. If woman pollutes, and is a risk to men, and black man pollutes, and is a risk to women, the homosexual man (black[13] or white) constitutes one of the most profound threats, because he strikes at the heart of heteronormative sexuality itself, and at the institutions through which it is reproduced. Male homosexuality has been implicated in the HIV/AIDS pandemic since its earliest manifestation in the US in the early 1980s, and its implication has had a profound effect on the way society, or at least Western industrialised societies, have understood and responded to it (Crimp, 2002 (1987); Treichler, 1988; Watney, 1994). There is a number of explanations for this, and each explanation has had different effects – some positive, some catastrophic. The first explanation is that the syndrome we now refer to as AIDS was first identified in the US among sexually active gay men. Indeed, its first incarnation was as GRID (Gay-Related Immune Deficiency).[14] In deploying this acronym, clinicians, public health functionaries and epidemiologists, both reflected contemporary understanding within the biomedical establishment of what it was they were dealing with – the nature of the disease – and served to crystallise in the public imagination its source. That the syndrome – then simply a range of unusual presenting symptoms manifested in the bodies of people (young gay men) who would normally be expected to enjoy good health – preceded the

---

a number of people with a different kind of bullet' (Alcabes, 2006: 5). James Miller, writing about the Canadian case of Charles Ssenyonga has written that 'What the media detected in Ssenyonga can only have been the ideological symptoms of African AIDS, the imaginary strain made especially virulent by its association with murderously uncontrollable Black male lust' (Miller, 2005).

13 The particular and specific issues surrounding the inter-relationship between the black homosexual body, HIV and AIDS are not addressed here. For an excellent discussion see King, 2004.

14 In New York hospitals in the early 1980s it was referred to informally as WOGS (Wrath Of God Syndrome), which neatly encapsulates the kind of sick humour used by physicians and clinicians to deal with tragedy as well as the view of the condition shared by many among the 'moral majority' (Treichler, 1988: 53). No doubt Freud would have had a field day with the way in which both this acronym, and others, have played their part in enabling people both to define the Other of AIDS and so affirm their own immunity (Watney, for example, explains how the French acronym SIDA was appropriated and taken to mean *Syndrome Imaginaire pour Decourager les Amoureux* (Watney, 1989 (1994): 109). Elsewhere AIDS has – more radically, and more accurately – been used to stand for African Immigrant Damnation Syndrome (Miller, 2005).

identification of its cause was inevitable;[15] but the consequence of this was profound. Most importantly, it elided gay political identity – for which many homosexuals had fought so hard in the preceding decades – with the sexual practices and lifestyles commonly associated in the public imagination with (male) homosexuality. These practices and lifestyles (drug use, anal intercourse, bath-house and group sex, multiple sexual partners, exotic foreign travel) not only framed and informed much biomedical research of the period (Kulstad, 1986; Fettner, 1988; Wellings, 1988), but were looked on with opprobrium and suspicion by the dominant conservative heterosexual establishment.[16] It was therefore only to be expected that AIDS should be seen as a 'gay disease' to be judged and treated accordingly. The establishment of a politically meaningful, liberatory, gay identity – of being gay, rather than being defined by reference to sexual conduct – thus gave rise to a grisly paradox. In the words of Dennis Altman, writing in the early years of the epidemic:

> As the definition of homosexuality have [sic] moved from a form of sexual behaviour ... to the character and lifestyle of a minority, it becomes possible to conceive of it as even having its own particular diseases. Thus the spread of AIDS becomes linked in the public imagination to the very presence of homosexuals (including lesbians), and the gay visibility and affirmation of the past decade becomes the basis for some very nasty scapegoating.
>
> (Altman, 1984: 95)

There was then, a complex but easily assimilated, socially acceptable, explanation of AIDS which identified its *causes* with the *practices* that defined an *identity* that constituted a *risk*. This in turn served to (re)associate the identity with the practices with the causes in a retrograde causal chain that allowed AIDS to be understood as self-inflicted (and therefore no one's responsibility but that of the person affected), served to reinforce the idea that AIDS was a punishment for morally wrong conduct, and meant that, for several crucial

15 The official history of AIDS could be said to have begun on June 5, 1981 when the US Center for Disease Control (CDC) published an editorial in its *Morbidity and Mortality Weekly Report* which discussed the cases of five young, otherwise healthy, gay men who had contracted *pneumocystis carinii* pneumonia and speculated as to the association between the presenting illness and their lifestyle and/or sexual practices (CDC, 1981). See also Gottlieb *et al*, 1981. An overview of theories about the etiology of AIDS during the early years of the epidemic is provided in Lederer, 1987; 1988.

16 It would be wrong to ignore the fact that there were gay men at this time who also pursued a conservative moralising agenda. The exemplar of this is perhaps Randy Shilts, whose bestselling book *And the Band Played On* was excoriating in its criticism of the gay community's mores and practices (Shilts, 1987). For an excellent criticism of the book see Crimp, 2002 (1987): 45–54.

years to come, AIDS was seen as something to which heterosexuals, by virtue of *their* (privileged) identity – their differentiation from a biomedically defined 'risk group'[17] – were immune. Even where there have been 'sympathetic' portrayals of gay men with AIDS (frequently represented as men who could not have known the risks, and are thus 'innocents' to be pitied rather than condemned), such portrayals also ratify and legitimate a (hetero)sexuality within and for which such suffering is distanced, alien and impossible to contemplate.[18]

Although it is true that the term GRID was dropped in 1982 as soon as the other 'three "H" identities (Haitians, haemophiliacs and heroin addicts) were diagnosed as presenting with the same symptoms as homosexuals, the 'gay plague' label endured.[19] It was taken up in the media, both in the US and the UK, with vile abandon and used, especially in the popular/populist tabloid press,[20] to set apart those who deserved to be punished, to die, or even to be shot,[21] rather than supported, treated and empathised with. The fact that AIDS was identified during a period when conservative, family-oriented administrations were in power on both sides of the Atlantic[22] no doubt contributed to moralising public discourse, and to the sense of 'moral panic' that suffused those administrations' respective electorates.

The demonisation of the 'other', the different or the 'unnatural' to make

17 The concept of a 'risk group' – a category of persons defined by reference to the positive correlation between the prevalence of a particular condition and range of objectively determined and observable shared characteristics – has been central in the history of HIV/AIDS. Being a member of a 'risk group' marks one out, whatever one's actual HIV status or personal risk.

18 There is a yet more insidious mode of moralising, exemplified in the media treatment of Rock Hudson's death from an AIDS-related illness in 1985. Hudson's crime was to have lived a double life, one in which he exemplified the all-American heterosexual on-screen (and was thus both role model and object of desire) but was in 'real life' a perverted homosexual. His betrayal of the fantasy was doubly condemnable because the security he provided in his performance of the masculine archetype was revealed to be precisely that – a performance. His falsehood, one that was gloatingly illustrated in the British press *via* numerous 'before and after' photographs (and here we may read 'before and after' as preceding AIDS, where 'AIDS' stands in for just deserts) captured the imagination of a public that was both enthralled and appalled (Watney, 1987 (1997): 87–90).

19 This was, in part, because the US Center for Disease Control continued to place gay men with AIDS in the category 'homosexual', irrespective of whether they were also members of the other three categories (Fettner, 1985: 43).

20 One of the more sensationalist interventions, recounted by Simon Watney, was a *News of the World* survey which reported that 56.8% of its readers were in favour of giving sexual appetite suppressants to, and the sterilisation of, 'AIDS carriers' and 51% were in favour of the recriminalisation of homosexuality (Watney, 1987: 138).

21 *The Sun* newspaper published a now infamous story about a vicar who was reported to have said that he would shoot his son if he had AIDS (see Bersani, 1988: 200–201).

22 Ronald Reagan was President of the US between 1981 and 1989, and Margaret Thatcher was Prime Minister of the UK between 1979 and 1990.

sense of novel social phenomena that threaten the interests of the majority has – as we have seen – a long and ignoble history, and where that phenomenon invokes fears around sexuality, illness and death it is especially powerful. In Gayle Rubin's words:

> Sexual activities often function as signifiers for personal and social apprehensions to which they have no intrinsic connection. During a moral panic, such fears attach to some unfortunate sexual activity or population. The media become ablaze with indignation, the public behaves like a rabid mob, the police are activated, and the state enacts new laws and regulations. When the furore has passed, some innocent erotic group has been decimated, and the state has extended its power into new areas of erotic behaviour. Moral panics rarely alleviate any real problem, because they are aimed at chimeras and signifiers. They draw on the pre-existing discursive structure which invents victims in order to justify treating 'vices' as crimes.
>
> (Rubin, 1984: 297)

While Rubin's analysis may be persuasive and intuitively attractive, and may indeed provide an adequate account of the nature, and source, of reactions to AIDS when the public were first alerted to it, its use as an explanatory or critical resource is limited. The 'moral panic' model is one characterised both by its temporal specificity and transience, and by the isolation of a conduct and/or identity from which those in the majority can distinguish and distance themselves.[23] In contrast, the social response to AIDS is one that, affects – and continues to affect – all of us, albeit in different ways and with varying degrees of intensity. Thus, as Simon Watney has said of the 'moral panic' analysis:

> Such a view makes it difficult to theorise representation as a site of *permanent* ideological struggle and contestation between rival pictures of the world. We do not watch the unfolding of discontinuous and discrete 'moral panics', but rather the mobility of ideological confrontations across the entire field of industrialised communications. This is most markedly the case in relation to those images which handle and evaluate the meanings of the human body, where rival and incompatible institutions and values are involved in ceaseless and remorseless struggle to discover and disclose its supposedly universal 'human' truth.
>
> (Watney, 1994: 9–10)

---

23 The most thorough exposition of the concept of 'moral panic' and its socio-cultural and political functions is to be found in Cohen, 1972. For a discussion of its deployment in the context of AIDS see Watney, 1987 (1997): 38–57.

It is, therefore, wrong to assert that the 'gay plague' metaphor was simply a means of enabling people to articulate their homophobia. Rather it had, and continues to have, a profound effect on discourses surrounding HIV and AIDS, because it facilitated the articulation of more fundamental concerns about morality and the value of culturally privileged social institutions and practices (especially monogamous, procreative, heterosexuality).[24] This has meant that whenever HIV or AIDS is discussed, the popular imagination is peopled with gay (and bisexual) men, and their supposed responsibility for the epidemic. Homosexuality (or more accurately the imagined, hedonistic, uncontrolled sexuality that AIDS has ensured it represents) has provided a justification both for its own condemnation, and operates as a social object-lesson in what can happen to you if you fail to observe social and sexual mores. As Simon Watney puts it, with typical passion and incisiveness:

> This 'truth' of AIDS . . . resolutely insists that the point of emergence of the virus should be identified as its *cause*. Epidemiology is thus replaced by a moral etiology of disease that can only conceive homosexual desire within a medicalised metaphor of contagion. Reading AIDS as the outward and visible sign of an imagined depravity of will, AIDS commentary deftly returns us to a pre-modern vision of the body, according to which heresy and sin are held to be scored in the features of their voluntary subjects by punitive and admonitory manifestations of disease. Moreover, this rhetoric of AIDS incites a violent siege mentality in the 'morally well', a mentality that locks only too easily into other rhetorics of 'preemptive defense'. Thus an essentially modern universalising discourse of 'family values', 'standards of decency', and so on, recruits subjects to an ever more disciplinary 'knowledge' of themselves and 'their' world.
>
> (Watney, 1988 (1994): 50–1)

Each of these three bodies of HIV and AIDS (the sexually active woman, the black African man and the male homosexual[25]) exist in the public consciousness not as *a priori* categories or identities, but as figures of, and (re)produced through, media representation. In the absence of personal knowledge of people with HIV or AIDS (given the size of the UK national population of approximately 60 million, while the number of people with diagnosed HIV

---

24 In his essay 'Is the Rectum a Grave?' Leo Bersani provides one of the most thorough and provocative analyses of the historico-cultural meaning of AIDS (Bersani, 1988). Sympathetic to, though not uncritical of, the radical feminism of Catherine Mackinnon and Andrea Dworkin he uses a Freudian psychoanalytic framework to argue that while it is possible to frame sex as violence, gay promiscuity and (in particular) anal sex should be celebrated rather than condemned; not because it offers a model pluralism and diversity, but because it reaffirms selfhood.
25 The injecting drug user is, no doubt, another.

is in the tens of thousands) this is likely to be the norm rather than the exception, especially if one accounts for the fact that not everyone with a positive diagnosis will disclose this fact. The media (both press and broadcast) thus serve as a critical conduit for the circulation of 'knowledge' and 'information' about HIV and AIDS, and about the bodies, identities, sexualities and practices that pose a risk to their audiences (who are, other than in publications aimed at and produced for HIV positive people, almost universally assumed to be HIV negative).

This 'knowledge' and 'information' is almost always framed (whether explicitly or implicitly) within a moralising discourse which ensures that it makes sense in a certain way, confirms rather than challenges certain popular – and populist – assumptions about HIV and AIDS, and can be guaranteed to produce certain effects (see, generally, Watney, 1997 (1987)). And when such 'knowledge' and 'information' is combined with crime, as it has been in the cases involving the reckless transmission of HIV, the assumptions and effects are magnified immeasurably. Although it is impossible to prove a causal relationship, it is – it seems to me – at the very least unsurprising that the first transmission cases in the UK were brought against, respectively, a convicted drug user, three black African male migrants, a Portuguese immigrant heroin addict, a white man who infected a woman in her eighties, a gay man, and two heterosexual women, one of whom had a history of sexual relationships with Afro-Caribbean men. The very categories that have been identified as the 'cause' of the HIV and AIDS pandemic, as Other and therefore a risk to hegemonic heteronormative white male sexuality, are those against whom prosecutions have been brought successfully. If the representations of the HIV infected body that populate the media have served to confirm in the popular imaginary that those who are – by virtue of their membership of the categories which the media sustains *through* their continued representation – already culpable, or (at the very least) 'fair game', then it should come as no shock that people who are infected by people in those categories should think of themselves as having been wronged and to turn to the criminal law for 'justice', or that the widespread reporting of one successful prosecution should lead to others being brought. As research has demonstrated in relation to other offences, the media has a significant influence:

> . . . in shaping the boundaries of deviance and criminality, by creating new categories of offence, or changing perceptions and sensitivities . . .
>
> (Reiner, 1997: 211)

Although it would be hyperbolic, and inappropriate, to compare the relatively few criminal cases involving HIV transmission as manifesting a 'moral panic' akin to the fear of being mugged (Hall *et al*, 1978), the intensity and nature of the coverage of those few cases that have been brought is – I think – significant. And just as the fear of muggings provoked an intensification of the policing of young Afro-Caribbean men, and so established and con-firmed the general public's view that all such men were legitimate suspects, so it is only to be expected that the police should, in a perverse but comprehensible reversal of logic, intensify their policing in this context by sending out the message that anyone who has slept with a convicted HIV transmitter (such as Sarah Porter) is a potential victim and, if so, has a legitimate claim to vengeance.

In saying this, I wish I could be as optimistic as Richard Sparks who, in a perceptive and thoughtful essay, takes issue with those who emphasise (as I have done) the ways in which media coverage of crime evokes 'regressive' emotions. In his view:

> our interest in and attention to the alarming, outrageous, unnerving and disgraceful happenings in crime news and crime stories are more than the tokens of our gullibility or indicators of our reactionary and punitive dispositions. Instead, those interests that we display . . . intelligibly summarize our sense of relations to the objects of our experience. We can engage, emote and evince sympathy with others only in such ways and on such occasions as are culturally produced for and made available to us. In this sense our engagement with crime and punishment is inherently ambiguous. It catches us much in and through our attempts to express our better (more moral, more sympathetic, more civically responsible) selves as through the hatreds, enmities, prejudices and distortions so much beloved of media scholars, radical criminologists and moral panic theorists.
>
> (Sparks, 2001: 210)

Perhaps there is ambiguity – and perhaps those who read the coverage of Dica, Adaye, Konzani, Porter *et al* have thereby been provided with the means of reflecting on the complexities of HIV transmission, living with AIDS, the nature of sexual responsibility and the justifications for imprisoning those who infect others. But I am sceptical whether such coverage will or can have this positive politicising effect. It seems to me far more likely, as Sparks himself recognises, following Douglas (1992), that risk, fear and blame are critically important in maintaining a particular moral and social order, that 'risk is irredeemably moral and unavoidably emotive and controversial' (Sparks, 2001: 206), and that – at least where the coverage of HIV/ AIDS and crime elide – ambiguity is, if not impossible, presently, if not permanently, deferred.

Risk and criminal justice

So far in this chapter I have suggested that we live in a society defined in large part by our exposure to risk, and that the quest for physical and ontological security is to a significant degree, and in a variety of ways, guided by attempts to identify and manage that risk. An important part of that identification and management is undertaken through establishing and maintaining a sense of self, one that is affirmed both by controlling (or attempting to control) one's own body (and privileging the body that is controlled, closed and thus 'civilised') and through maintaining distance from the Other (understood as any body, identity or practice that exhibits 'abnormality' of a kind that is experienced, and/or culturally constructed and represented through the media, as disruptive or threatening). The 'normal' body, understood as one that is autonomous, that has mastered its environment and is in control of its boundaries, orifices and destiny (or which functions as if this were the case), is conceived in European and North American cultures as one that is white, male, heterosexual and healthy. For such a body, and those who have internalised the ideal it represents, black, female, homosexual and diseased or sick bodies not only reinforce the values that it incorporates, but are each – in their own way – risks to the security for which it strives.

I have also suggested that the prosecutions for transmitting HIV to sexual partners may have been brought because of the cultural meaning of HIV and AIDS (at the level of both the real and physical, and the symbolic, cultural and ontological), the ways in which HIV and AIDS, and their embodiment in particular categories of people, have been portrayed in the media, and the sensational populist coverage that has been given to cases that have already been brought (coverage that has alerted people who have been infected to the possibility of securing 'justice' through criminal law, even if this operates as a proxy for the security their infection has denied them). Although these seem to me to be compelling social-structural explanations (albeit unproved, or indeed unproveable), they do not, of course, account fully for the bringing of the first prosecution in England and Wales (that of Mohammed Dica), nor, more importantly, do they take us beyond the motives people may have for turning to law. We may, however, gain some understanding of the reasons why and how (given the motivation of individuals to prosecute, and whatever the source of that motivation may be) it has been possible to contemplate prosecutions for the transmission of HIV in the first place. Put more generally, what is it about contemporary penality that comprehends, and legitimates, prosecutions and convictions for the reckless transmission of HIV and what, if anything do such prosecutions tell us about the nature, functions and ideological contours of criminal justice at the beginning of the twenty-first century?

The answer to that question lies, I believe, in the relationship and conflict between the security values that inform criminal law and its institutions, and the 'risk society' within which these values find their expression and those institutions operate.

Security

One of the central tenets of liberal political theory is that without security (of the person, of property) there can be no liberty. Security is:

> to everyone's feelings, the most vital of all interests. All other earthly benefits are needed by one person, not needed by another; and many of them can, if necessary, be cheerfully forgone, or replaced by something else; but security no human being can possibly do without; on it we depend for all our immunity from evil, and for the whole value of all and every good, beyond the passing moment, since nothing but the gratification of the instant could be of any worth to us, if we could be deprived of everything the next instant by whoever was momentarily stronger than ourselves.
>
> (Mill, 1972: 56)

In more senses than Mill can have imagined is security the thing we need for our continued immunity. What we crave and what we need in order to pursue the 'good' of individual happiness, security is the price we pay – the constraint we must accept – for liberty. It is a constraint, because security entails the curtailment of our own liberty (to act as we would in a state of nature, to pursue our own self-interest) in order to guarantee the liberty of others (Mill, 1972; Gray, 1983). For Mill's philosophical forefathers, contemporaries and successors, security was, and has been, no less critical. Locke, for example, understood natural rights (those positive freedoms that human beings would have in a state of nature) as being worthy of protection, and which could only be protected through government grounded in a social contract based on 'tacit consent'. Such consent comprised an agreement to forego unlimited freedom to pursue self-interest in exchange for the security that the state would provide through the enactment, implementation and enforcement of laws designed to guarantee the enjoyment of property (comprising in Locke's philosophy not only material possessions, but life and liberty as well) (Locke, 1988; for commentary see Gray, 1995). For Bentham too, security too was vital. Although the primary goal of legislation was the greatest happiness of the greatest number, among the subordinate goals of subsistence, abundance, equality and security, security was paramount because it was a necessary condition for guaranteeing the other three (Bentham, 1962; Dean, 1999: 117).[26] More recently, John Rawls – whose concern was to provide a coherent theory of justice, rather than to espouse the virtues of any particular vision of the 'good' – has argued that in order to ensure the fair distribution of rights and liberties:

26 Another (rather more cynical) view is that Bentham was concerned not so much with the principle of security as a means of securing liberty, but with the potential disruption to social order that might follow from the Enlightenment vision of individual intellectual and political self-realisation (Rosenblum, 1978).

each person is to have an equal right to the most extensive basic liberty compatible with a similar liberty for others.

(Rawls, 1999: 53)

This too may be interpreted as meaning that without security (understood as freedom from the exercise of liberty by others that is incompatible with one's own exercise of liberty) justice – at least as Rawls conceives it – is unattainable.

This need for security in states whose dominant political orientation is liberal, whether conceived of as a philosophy or a mode of governance (Dean, 1999), is most explicitly assured through criminal law and the institutions of criminal justice. In the next section we will be focusing on how the criminal law of recklessness reflects and reinforces liberal political values. For the moment I want instead to emphasise the ways in which those values are expressed in the institutions and processes through which that law is realised.

The criminal justice complex comprises the policing, prosecuting, judicial and penal organs of the state. The functions of a state's criminal justice system are, put simply, to 'deter crime and restrain criminals' (Hudson, 2003: 41). In liberal states the deterrence and restraint functions are, or have traditionally been, characterised by the balancing of the twin interests/values of liberty and security. Security is, as we have seen, understood as a precondition for the enjoyment of liberty, where security is conceptualised as a 'public good' (i.e. as a good that all are entitled to enjoy equally), in much the same way as education and health (see, for example, Walzer, 1983). As a public good, security is something that must be protected from those who would commandeer it in their own self-interest. Thus, economic security derived from the fruits of national insurance and taxation must be protected from free-riders (such as benefit cheats and 'health tourists'), national security must be protected through border controls and ID cards, and personal physical and proprietary security must be protected from those who threaten or violate it (such as muggers, rapists and burglars). At the same time, liberals are wary of the totalitarian consequences of unlimited state-sponsored security measures. As advocates of limited government, limited in such a way that it maximises individual autonomy, and allows human beings the opportunity for self-realisation and to pursue their own vision of happiness or the 'good', they recognise the importance of constraints on the exercise of state power. Thus, even though those who commit crimes that violate a person's (or a nation's) security interests are entitled to respect. They remain, despite their conduct and any harmful consequences they have caused, rights-bearers. Any interference with their right to liberty (through punishment or other coercive state sanctioned mechanisms[27]) must, therefore, be legitimate and justifiable,

---

27 Legislation intended to protect public health is an obvious example (see the Public Health (Control of Disease) Act 1984, and the discussion of this in Ch 1).

and there should be no more interference than is strictly necessary to restore security.[28] At a criminal procedural level this finds expression in the rules relating to the arrest, detention and charging of suspects, in the requirement that a prosecution can only be brought if there is sufficient evidence and the prosecution is in the public interest, in rules relating to the admissibility of evidence and in the right to challenge it, in a high criminal burden of proof, in rights of appeal, and so on. Such 'due process' values (Packer, 1969) are supplemented by the principle that punishment should be proportionate to the offence, and that only those rights which are necessarily suspended by virtue of imprisonment are denied those who are given a custodial sentence for their crime.

These rights, values and principles are, of course, liberal ideals which, in the day to day practice of criminal justice, risk being honoured as much in the breach as in the observance. They are also only one side of a coin, the other of which is concerned with the imperatives of crime control (Packer, 1969) (a goal that whose attainment depends (and has always depended) on the non-observance, curtailment, suspension or abrogation of due process 'rights' where interests of national security,[29] or of victims,[30] or – increasingly – of 'justice'[31] demand this) (see, for example, Sanders, 1997: 1051–4). There is, as the brief outline above sought to illustrate, no necessary hypocrisy in the liberal state's commitment to due process and the principle of personal liberty, and at the same time limiting these in pursuit of the greater good. As Alan Norrie has explained, the philosophically grounded Enlightenment vision of the individual sovereign subject was displaced with the coming of modernity and industrialisation by a jurisprudence (and this term is significant – we are no longer concerned merely with philosophical and metaphysical abstractions) of the aggregate (Norrie, 2005: 20–4). Not for nothing were Bentham and his utilitarian brothers concerned with the greatest good of the greatest number. Such a notion would have been unthinkable in an era where 'one' (both numeral, and impersonal 'I') was the only number/identity that really mattered. With the advent of the notion of populations, whose members' unrestrained egos – or whatever the pre-Freudian equivalent may

28 These principles find concrete expression in the jurisprudence of the European Court of Human Rights, where any interference with a qualified right (such as the right to respect for private life) must – if it is to be lawful – be proportionate (i.e. the interference must be in pursuit of a legitimate objective, be no more than is necessary to secure that objective, and – taken as a whole – be such that the ends justify the means).

29 The custody provisions of the anti-terrorism legislation enacted by the UK Parliament in response to the events of 9/11 are obvious examples (Prevention of Terrorism Act 2005), as are the provisions relating to the introduction of ID cards (Identity Cards Act 2006).

30 On the development of the victims' rights movement see, generally, Zedner, 1997: 595–607.

31 Here I have in mind the abolition of the rule against 'double jeopardy', and liberalisation of the rules relating to the admissibility of hearsay and similar fact evidence (see Criminal Justice Act 2003, Pt 10; Pt 11, c 2)

have been – could wreak havoc on the economic and social progress that was the modern liberal state's promise, social security through law became a paramount concern. So it was that it became conceivable, on utilitarian premises, that *if* an innocent person was punished *but* this deterred others from committing crimes, this was not necessarily unjust. The 'nonsense on stilts' of natural rights – to the extent that these were understood as inviolable – had no place in a political and legal order that was concerned with efficient and effective governance. Criminal law may have retained a core set of values that, as we shall see, continue to place emphasis on culpability understood in terms of individualised concepts of fault; but, as Norrie points out, this has led to immanent contradiction, or 'antinomy', in the law. On the one hand there have, since the early nineteenth century, been concerted attempts to 'demoralise' the law, attempts grounded in a vision of law as a de-politicised technical function,[32] and on the other there has remained a commitment to the idea of the autonomous subject of law whose responsibility (as both human being and legal subject) depends on her identification as a moral agent. She not only has volition and will (which thus enables her to make rational, prudential, choices); she has a moral sensibility, whether conceived of as innate or as learned through nurture and in society. As an object of governance she may be conceived of as, and held, responsible for failing to exercise her cognitive capacities in such a way that she restrains herself from violating the security interests of others; as a subject of law she may only justly be conceived of as, and held, responsible if (given those capacities) she is at fault in doing so.

But I am moving ahead of myself. Just as the history of the criminal law through the nineteenth and twentieth centuries is one of a system at war with itself, a war whose skirmishes and battles find occasional – but inevitable – expression in the contradictory pronouncements of appellate judges, so too is the history of the criminal justice system itself. At no time is this more apparent than in 'risk society'. As I sought to explain at the beginning of the chapter, this is a society conceived of in terms of a generalised anxiety produced by the failure of industrialisation to deliver the socio-economic security it promised – a failure that was (as Beck, Giddens *et al* have emphasised) an inevitable consequence of industrialisation itself. The modernist desire to master nature, the belief in the possibility of doing so, and the need to achieve this objective demanded – and was grounded in – a vision of autonomous, rational, self-realising human beings (or, more accurately, men). However, the desire of such human beings to succeed at the expense of others – a desire that

---

32 Attempts have been made not only by positivist legal theorists from Austin onwards, but – as Norrie rightly emphasises – by state functionaries (such as the Criminal Law Commissioners in the early to mid-nineteenth century) concerned to rationalise the legal system (Norrie, 2001: Ch 2).

might be expressed through illegitimate means, rather than through the legitimate route of capitalist enterprise – meant that a pre-condition of effective governance was a legal system oriented towards collective security even if its underlying philosophy was one informed by the values of individual freedom.

In the nineteenth century this immanent contradiction found expression in the identification of the 'dangerous classes' who at any time might rise up in revolution and who needed discipline to render them docile and obedient, and later (with the advent of the science of psychology) with a division of individuals into the 'mad and the bad', each of which required different modes of coercion and containment. In the twentieth century these categories were subject to further refinement and their members to the application of increasingly specified techniques whose legitimacy and justification was grounded both in prevailing political ideology and in changing visions of the role of the state. Thus, we witness a move from a belief in individual rehabilitation (which finds expression in – for example – indeterminate sentences, borstal, and the introduction of probation and parole) to a more 'justice' or 'just deserts'-based model in which a retributive response to the criminal act replaces the focus on the reform of the person who is its author (see, generally, Hudson, 2003). This transition is, though, one that is tempered by an increasing concern with risk. So it is, for example, that the Criminal Justice Act 1991 was informed by principles of proportionality but allowed, for the first time, judges both to impose a more severe sentence on the basis of the defendant's record of previous criminal convictions than the instant crime would have justified (s 1(2)), and to extend the length of custodial sentences for those violent and sexual offenders that were considered to be dangerous and from whom the public needed protection (s 2(2)) (see, for commentary, Ashworth, 1997: 1099, 1112–16). These innovations, which were paralleled by the later introduction of mandatory sentences for certain categories of repeat offenders,[33] by calls for the probation service to focus its attention on the safety of the public rather than the needs of the offender, and by the introduction of Anti-Social Behaviour Orders[34] and a Sex Offender's Register,[35] all testify to an increased anxiety about the risk that criminals (especially those who commit violent or sexual offences) pose to public security.

They are also innovations that testify to a more general trend that bears all the hallmarks of governance in 'risk society'. As Barbara Hudson has succinctly put it:

> they see a significant shift in the balances between crime control and due process; between inclusionary (keeping offenders in the community)

---

33 Crime (Sentences) Act 1997. For critical comment see Hood and Shute (1996).
34 S 1(1) Crime and Disorder Act 1998.
35 Sex Offenders Act 1997.

and exclusionary (banishing them, to other territories or to segregative institutions) penal techniques; between 'normalising' (making the deviant more like the normal citizen) and managing (not seeking to change the deviant, but restricting his/her possibilities of movement and action so as to minimise the threat to the normal population) strategies; between individualising (responding to the needs of the individual offender) and aggregating (controlling groups or categories of offenders and potential offenders) . . . These changes are all in the direction of identifying offenders according to the degree of risk of reoffending they pose rather than addressing them as rational moral agents.

(Hudson, 2003: 41–2)

Although I would take issue with Hudson's assertion that this shift need only be seen in terms of the risk of *reoffending*, she is undoubtedly correct in her general synopsis of institutional responses to criminal behaviour. We have moved from a criminal justice system oscillating between deterrence/rehabilitation and retribution/containment to one whose principal concern is the management and control of risk (Clear and Cadora, 2001). Such a system cannot (at least if one deploys its own reasoning system) be criticised for 'false positives' (the punishment of those who have not in fact committed a crime) or 'false negatives' (the failure to punish those who have) because the 'success' of the system lies in its ability to correctly identify risk factors – rather than whether the predictive assessments, for the purposes of determining mode of punishment or release from custody, are in fact correct (Hudson, 2003: 49). Nor can such a system be criticised (on its own terms) for a failure to accord priority to the individual and her liberty, since it is – *par excellence* – a system that is framed in terms of protecting precisely that. In any event, there is no necessary contradiction between the apparently value-neutral actuarial approach to criminal justice that this transition exemplifies and the underlying justifications for intervention (which remain liberal to the core). In the words of Stenson and Edwards (summarising Ericson and Haggerty, 1997):

Risks associated with crime are part of the burgeoning agenda of the grave risks, the 'bads' of civilization, that citizens expect modern state governments to manage, contain or redistribute.

(Stenson and Edwards, 2001: 70)

The state, and its techniques of governance (including criminal law), may be risk- and security-oriented, but they remain dependent – if order is to be maintained – upon 'obedience to a shared and superordinate morality' (O'Malley, 2001: 91). That morality, which is itself at risk if free rein is given to individuals' pursuit of their own self-interest 'and associated excesses of hedonism, irrationality and rampant individualism' (ibid), is what I turn to consider now.

Recklessness, risk and security

If the management and control functions of the criminal justice system at the turn of the millennium exemplify the political and institutional response to life in 'risk society', the fault captured by the notion of recklessness exemplifies the substantive criminal law's own particular contribution to securing social order and public safety. And just as the criminal justice system has over time mirrored, if imperfectly, the changing security concerns and conflicting values of the liberal state, so too has the criminal law's approach to the imposition of liability on those whose willingness to take risks manifests both a disregard for those concerns, and a failure of the individual self-control upon which social order in liberal society depends.

Pre-modern (i.e. pre-Enlightenment) criminal law was grounded in what Norrie has termed 'substantive morality', which means – as I understand it – that there was a necessary correspondence between criminal liability and the moral wrongfulness of the conduct of the accused. This wrongfulness was not based on fault as we understand this term. In the absence of a model of human action, or of volition, in which mind controlled body it was literally inconceivable that a person could be treated as culpable on the basis that they acted intentionally or recklessly, or that the consequences of their conduct were intentionally or recklessly caused. Nor, in the absence of such a model, could a person be thought of as, or held, responsible in a sense that corresponds with our contemporary understanding of the concept of responsibility. Instead, criminal fault was conditional on a finding that a person's actions manifested malice, or vice. Thus, a killing that occurred 'on the sudden' (as the result of a provocation, for example) was less culpable than one that was planned – which is why *malice prepense* (or 'malice aforethought') was a pre-requisite for a finding of murder. This fault requirement does not correspond with our modern notion of murder as an intentional killing, which is based on the idea that a person's mental state at the relevant time is an objective fact that can be determined on the basis of evidence, but was instead a requirement based on context and communal notions of right and wrong.

With the advent of modernity the correlation between 'substantive morality' and criminal law became both increasingly harder to sustain, and less important. The dualism of Cartesian philosophy had established a clear distinction between the mind and the body in which the latter was subject to the will of the former. Anything the body did, and any effect it caused, found authorship in the mind; and that mind, being the seat of reason, became co-extensive with subjectivity and with responsibility. A person with cognitive capacity (in other words anyone who was not an infant or a lunatic) was, by virtue of that fact alone, someone who could legitimately be held accountable for his actions before the law. Of course, this tells us nothing about the content of the law, or anything about the way, or context, in which it was applied. For present purposes it is sufficient to note that these developments were entirely at one with the Enlightenment vision of the self-realising, rational, autonomous person and with the liberal political project of which he was constitutive. That vision and project was one that could, as we have seen, only succeed if order was maintained. With industrialisation that order was put under substantial pressure. So it was that, in the early nineteenth century we witness the foundation of the first organised police force, the rise of the penitentiary and Bentham's vision for a panopticon that would – merely by virtue of its existence – deter potential offenders (Bentham, 1995). And so it was too that, in the context of the substantive criminal law, there was a move to rationalise – to eliminate, so far as this was possible, questions of value from questions of fault and thus render the law a technically efficient mechanism for ensuring the maintenance of the status quo.

This rationalising project had its roots in the penal philosophy of reformers such as Beccaria, who – in the latter half of the eighteenth century – had argued that deterrence would only work if people were treated fairly, in the sense that any punishment they received should be proportionate to the wrong that had been committed (Beccaria, 1966). The terror and mercy that had sustained Europe's *anciens régimes* had failed, and was no longer viable as a mode of governance in societies whose success depended on individual entrepreneurialism and whose thinkers – whether economists, philosophers or political theorists – were united in extolling the values and benefits of liberty, autonomy and limited government. A high point of the rationalising project in England came with the work of the Victorian Law Commissioners in the 1830s and 1840s (Norrie, 2005: 84–5). Among their concerns was the meaning that should be given to malice in the context of the law of implied malice (a form of fault that permitted a conviction for murder when a killing took place during the planned commission of another crime). Pre-modern criminal law had conceived malice as a form of wickedness, depravity or malignancy of spirit (Kenny, 1902: 196 (quoted in Norrie, 2005: 84)). The Commissioners were concerned that such an interpretation of malice (which is the term used in the Offences Against the Person Act 1861 to capture the fault we now describe as recklessness) led to inconsistency in the application of the law. To avoid this, they proposed that malice should, instead, be taken to mean wilfulness – in the sense of awareness of risk:

> It is the wilful exposure of life to peril that constitutes the crime . . . Where the offender does an act with manifest danger to life wilfully, that is with knowledge of the consequences, he may properly be said to have the *mens mala*, or heart bent upon mischief.
> (Criminal Law Commissioners, 1839, xxiv, quoted in Norrie, 2005: 84)

This approach, which subsequently found expression in the application of the law,[36] reduced the substantive morality of wickedness to a factual question of foresight of risk. Wilfulness, rather than expressing a 'malignant spirit', was instead to be proven if the defendant was aware of the risks associated with his actions – a purely factual, non-evaluative, question concerned with his cognition at the relevant time. As Norrie explains, the consequence and motivation of the Commissioners' work was that:

> there developed a concept of recklessness that was designed to secure the Enlightenment value of certainty, and in order to do so, the law had to be shorn of the elements of value-judgment. This was achieved by focusing on the factual question of awareness of risk, and abstracting that question from the broader contextual, moral and political question of evaluation of risk. The advertence/inadvertence dichotomy secured a subjective conception of recklessness in which the question to be asked of the accused was the purely factual one 'did he foresee the risk'?
>
> (Norrie, 2001: 77)

The subsequent history of recklessness is not, however, as simple as this question suggests it should have been. For Norrie, this may be explained by the antinomial, or immanently contradictory, nature of criminal law in modernity. On the one hand there is an attempt to exclude questions of moral judgement in order to ensure consistency, certainty and clarity (an ongoing project which reflects the inexorable rise of positivist legal theory in a liberal state whose principal legitimating feature is the rule of law); while on the other there is the inconvenient fact that criminal law is enacted, interpreted and applied not in a moral vacuum inhabited by value-free technocrats but by human beings who live in a pluralistic, morally informed, politically diverse community. And the same is true with respect to those who, as finders of fact (whether magistrates or jurors) will inevitably engage in an evaluation of the 'facts', however neutral and impartial they are asked to be. Let us recall, for example, the direction that the judge gave the jury at the close of Feston Konzani's trial:

> In drawing any inference be reasonable, be fair, be logical, use your common sense and your knowledge of the world. The subject matter of this case is a very human matter, isn't it? You will need to get to grips with people as they were behaving and as they were thinking – and that is an important element – some years ago now, so draw inferences that you think to be right and fair and proper but be fair in doing so . . .
>
> You twelve people come from different walks of life, different life experiences and most importantly in a case like this you can apply your

---

36 See, e.g., *R v Cunningham* [1957] 2 QB 396, CCA.

accumulated wisdom – if you will forgive the word, it is a bit of a pompous one – but do you see what I mean? You apply your experience of life to the questions that arise in this case. Do not shrink from drawing such inference as you might think right to draw but be careful not to jump to conclusions, illogical and unfair ones.

I have said, 'Use your common sense and your knowledge of the world and of people'. Make sure that emotion does not enter into your judgment in this exercise that you must embark upon. There is an old saying that, 'When emotion comes in, sense moves out'. Emotion has its place, of course, but it can mislead judgment.

I quote this at length again because it shows, I think, precisely the problem that Norrie is getting at. There is an admonition that in reaching conclusions on the facts the jurors must be fair, logical and proper (Enlightenment virtues if ever there were any). They must avoid emotional responses, because that distorts reason. At the same time, and inevitably, there is a recognition that in doing so they will use their 'common sense' and 'knowledge of the world'. They are human, and their evaluation of the facts, as established by evidence, cannot be divorced from the meaning that those 'facts' have for them.

This antinomialism, or conflict, in the law of recklessness found its most vivid articulation in the early 1980s with the decision of the House of Lords in *R v Caldwell*.[37] That case concerned a disgruntled employee who – as result of setting fire to his employer's premises – was charged under ss 1(1) and 1(2) of the Criminal Damage Act 1971. His defence to the charge under s 1(2)[38] was that, because he was drunk, he had not given any thought to the possibility that life might be endangered by the fire and that he was not therefore reckless. If the reasoning in *Cunningham*[39] had been followed, Caldwell would have been successful in his appeal against conviction because there was evidence that he was not, in fact, aware of the risk. However, Lord Diplock – who gave the leading judgment – used the case as an opportunity to revisit and modify the test for recklessness. This is not the place to go into great detail about the decision,[40] but in essence he held that a person could, for the purposes of the Act   and any other that specifically included the term 'recklessness' and its derivatives – be treated as reckless if:

---

37 [1981] 1 All ER 961.
38 S 1(2) is as follows: 'A person who without lawful excuse destroys or damages any property, whether belonging to himself or another – (a) intending to destroy or damage any property or being reckless as to whether any property would be destroyed or damaged; and (b) intending by the destruction or damage to endanger the life of another or being reckless as to whether the life of another would be thereby endangered shall be guilty of an offence.'
39 n 36 above.
40 For detailed discussions see Norrie, 2001: Ch 4; 2005: Ch 5; Halpin, 2004.

(1) he does an act which in fact creates an obvious risk that property will be destroyed or damaged and (2) when he does the act either he has not given any thought to the possibility of there being any such risk or has recognised that there was some risk involved and has none the less gone on to do it.[41]

It was the first part of the second limb of the test which caused consternation in an academic legal community which, by and large, was firmly committed to the principles of 'orthodox subjectivism' (see, for example, Williams, 1981; Syrota, 1982). For the first time, it seemed, a person could be found guilty of a criminal offence in which recklessness was sufficient to ground liability if he had not consciously averred to the potential consequences. To some the judgment demonstrated a wilful disregard for the principles of statutory interpretation, to others it was objectionable because it made convictions easier to obtain. Some commentators were concerned that it held those who lacked the capacity to form an awareness of risk to the standard of the reasonable person (who, by definition, could),[42] while others focused on the apparent elision between recklessness and negligence, and the fact the important moral distinction between the two had been lost. Lastly, there were those who criticised the fact that there were now two tests for recklessness: where the fault was described as 'malice' (as it was in offences against the person) a subjective test applied, while an objective test was to be applied where the term 'reckless' was used (see, generally, Norrie, 2001: 61–3).

What is important for our purposes is that the criticisms were grounded, essentially, in a liberal philosophy of law in which individual responsibility should be grounded in the fault of the offender, understood as fault that was a manifestation of their consciousness and will. To hold someone liable for what they were *not* aware of undermined the rationalising and positivising project of the previous 150 years because it brought politics and value judgement back in. In determining whether someone was reckless it was no longer simply a question of determining the 'factual' question of whether the defendant was aware of the relevant risk at the relevant time, but whether the reasonable person would have been so aware. And to determine this the tribunal of fact would, necessarily, have to draw on its 'common sense' and experience: in other words, to evaluate and judge on the basis of factors external to the mind of the defendant.

The decision in *Caldwell* has since been reversed, and the subjective approach restored.[43] This does not, however, render the debate that it

---

41 1 All ER 961 at 967.
42 See, for example, the decisions in *Elliot v C (a minor)* [1983] 2 All ER 1005; *R v R (Stephen Malcolm)* (1984) 79 Cr App Rep 334 (CA).
43 *R v G* [2003] 4 All ER 765.

generated irrelevant for that debate went to the heart of the way in which law should respond to those whose conduct poses a risk to others – whether to their property, life or limb. It provoked, most critically, a debate about the status of the subjective test which – for some – was too narrow. Anthony Duff, for example, has argued that by limiting liability to those who consciously aver to the risk of harm the law fails to censure those who are 'practically indifferent' to risk (Duff, 1990: Ch 7). Such people may, in his view, be legitimately censured and punished because by their actions they manifest a culpable indifference to the interests of others. The objective test for recklessness, in his view, is too broad because it fails to distinguish between those who fail to take account of those interests because of stupidity or ignorance and those whose failure may be characterised as 'callous', while the subjective test is too narrow because it excludes the latter from the ambit of liability. Duff's argument is important because it highlights a fundamental conflict in the way law responds, and should respond, to risk-taking behaviour in a society committed to liberal values but concerned also with the maintenance of social order and individual security. However, it too (like the objective test) would, as Norrie explains, have the effect of bringing moral and political considerations back in to determinations of liability:

> The practical indifference test disrupts [the positivising] historical project by asserting that to be reckless can involve more than a state of awareness of risk. One can be reckless by displaying in one's conduct a practical indifference or callousness that may not invoke awareness, but does involve a subjective attitude. This seems to be right, but it shows that the concept of recklessness is not just a mental state that can be anchored in the individual in abstraction from the broader social context in which he operates. To be reckless in this sense entails a socio-political value judgment about what constitutes callousness, and, for it to be properly subjective, an ex post facto agreement between audience and actor that his conduct did indeed reveal callousness and not just thoughtlessness, negligence or stupidity. Practical indifference brings politics back into law by showing that recklessness is, in each case, a matter of individual and socio-political judgment. Such judgments change over time and reflect developments in the society of which they are a part, particularly as these are influenced by dominant ideological currents which enjoy power in society. They are also inherently conflictual with regard to the subject matter of the criminal law.
>
> (Norrie, 2001: 78)

It is these 'dominant ideological currents' that interest me here. Norrie argues that the practical indifference test is problematic because we cannot pretend that those who sit in judgment share the same set of values, or that such judgment is, or can be, 'apolitical or universal' (ibid: 74). Consequently it would, without further refinement, result in inconsistency that the subjective test purportedly avoids. This is no doubt important, but not what concerns me. More critical, for present purposes, is the fact that (as Norrie himself acknowledges) the subjective test (the one that applies in cases involving the reckless transmission of HIV) is one that itself admits an objective, evaluative, dimension. For it is not the case that a person is reckless with respect to a consequence simply if he is aware of the risk that it may occur. He is reckless if he consciously takes an *unreasonable* or *unjustifiable* risk that it may occur. In other words, a person may avoid recklessness-based liability if, being aware of the relevant risk, it was one that the judging audience consider to have been one worth taking in the circumstances. Conversely, the person who takes the same risk will, irrespective of his own subjective evaluation of its reasonableness, be found to have been reckless if his evaluation is one that the audience does not share, and found guilty if he has no valid defence.

At a general level we may expect that this audience (jurors or magistrates) will – if Norrie is right – be affected in their evaluation of reasonableness and justifiability by the 'dominant ideological currents'. Furthermore, we may expect that if (as the 'risk society' thesis suggests, and as the discussion earlier in this chapter elaborated) one of the dominant ideological currents in post-industrial liberal society is concern about the risks that the Other and his behaviour represents to our physical and ontological security, then a restrictive, conservative approach to reasonableness will be adopted. In some cases the question will no doubt not even arise. There is, one assumes, a general consensus that throwing bricks over walls, or falling asleep with a lit cigarette, manifests unreasonable risk-taking. The run-of-the-mill recklessness cases that come before the criminal courts will not usually entail elaborate arguments about, or turn on, the reasonableness or otherwise of the conduct in question. However, in some cases – those which involve conduct about which there is dissensus, no obvious social consensus, or no prior deliberative reflection on what would be reasonable or justifiable in the particular situation – the question of reasonableness could arise and be critical in determining liability.

Consider, for example, a (hypothetical but not unimaginable) case in which the defendant is charged with recklessly transmitting HIV to his partner during sexual intercourse. His 'defence'[44] is that he was not reckless because – even though he is aware that HIV may be transmitted during sex – he wore a condom (which the prosecution accepts). Essentially, the defendant is inviting the jury to share with him his evaluation of the reasonableness of his preventive action. How are the members of the jury to determine whether it should? First, it is important to recognise that the fact of transmission is

---

44 I say 'defence' because technically the defendant is merely denying the presence of an element of the offence, rather than raising as defence as such.

not (in this hypothetical instance) in dispute. The defendant's evaluation of the risk (whether or not it was reasonable) was therefore misguided as a matter of fact, and this can only colour the juror's perception of events, and of him. But, second, even if this suggestion is not accepted, and we imagine that the jurors are not negatively disposed to the defendant by the fact that transmission occurred (or because he failed to disclose his status, or gain his partner's consent to the risk of transmission), they will have to draw on their 'common sense' and knowledge of the world in reaching their conclusion. And how, one may legitimately wonder, are they to do that? How, precisely, is a jury which is – statistically – unlikely to contain any HIV positive people to judge whether an HIV positive person's use of a condom constituted reasonable/justifiable risk-taking? There is – to my knowledge – no case law on what constitutes reasonableness/justifiability in the context of recklessness, and the 'the law' derives from authoritative jurists, such as Smith and Hogan:

> Whether is it is justifiable to take a risk depends on the social value of the activity involved relative to the probability and the gravity of the harm which might be caused.
>
> (Smith and Hogan, 1999: 61)

And what, were the prosecution to argue its case on this basis, is the 'social value' of the activity involved – indeed what (a logically prior question) is the relevant activity? Sex? Protected sex? Protected sex between sero-discordant partners? Protected sex between sero-discordant partners in which no disclosure has been made, nor consent to the risk of transmission been given? Whichever activity this principle applies to, one can – I think – be fairly sure that it is not going to be treated as being in the same league as injuring someone while rescuing them from a burning building. Nor, even if the most liberal, positive and enlightened interpretation of 'social activity' were adopted, is it clear how this would play out given the second and third limbs of Smith and Hogan's test. What is the probability of transmission occurring despite condom use? How low does the probability have to be before the 'gravity of the harm' outweighs it? And how are these two limbs to be applied: disjunctively? Conjunctively? The point is that, even if the judge were to provide a model direction, there are no easy or obvious answers to these questions, and any that are forthcoming will, and can, only reflect the jurors' own personal moral and political values and beliefs. To the extent that those values and beliefs are informed (as we have seen) by media representations of HIV positive people who infect others as dirty, deceitful, promiscuous scumbags, and – more generally – by fearfulness and ignorance about HIV and AIDS, it is not far-fetched to imagine that the defendant's invitation to share his evaluation that the risk he took was reasonable and/or justified may – more often than not – be declined.

Of course there are those who would argue that this does not matter, or that such evaluative determinations are inevitable. I would disagree with the first assertion and agree with the second. I disagree that restrictive determinations of reasonableness in the context of recklessness do not matter because (as the example I have provided shows) they have the potential to result in convictions reflecting the views of a society that are grounded not in fair-minded, informed deliberation and reflection but in prejudice, incomprehension, ignorance and fear. The 'subjective' test in a case such as this would, far from ensuring a fair or just outcome based on a finding of fact, instead allow those negative perceptions of HIV and AIDS to determine – or at least substantially influence – the verdict. As Norrie explains (albeit in more neutral terms):

> The process of social construction of what is dangerous, which excludes the political issues from the courtroom, is completed inside the courtroom by the objective test of justifiability of a risk. This leaves it impossible for the defendant to raise his subjective value position in the same way as *Caldwell* leaves it impossible for him to raise his subjective perception of the facts. There is a process of exclusion of politically contentious questions and arguments from the courtroom. It begins with the wider political and ideological environment, filters into the decisions of the personnel of the criminal justice system who bring cases to court, informs the perspectives of the adjudicators in the courts, and finally enters the very bones of the substantive criminal law.
>
> (Norrie, 2001: 79–80)

I argued earlier in this chapter that the response of the criminal justice system to those perceived to present a risk to the social order and to the security of individuals manifests the state's institutionalised attempts at governance in 'risk society'. Those attempts, which centre increasingly on the identification and management of those who, by virtue of the kinds of crimes they commit, or persist in committing, are – however – informed by residual but important liberal values. Determinations relating to, for example, the risk of reoffending, may be based on the extent to which the individual manifests risk factors derived from the observation and analysis of populations, but there is still a formal commitment to due process (whether at trial, in sentencing or in parole decision-making). Community sentences and probation may be increasingly oriented towards public protection than rehabilitation, but offence seriousness and the needs and character of individual offenders remain important. The prison population may be rising, but the legal and human rights of prisoners (largely as a result of the enactment of the Human Rights Act 1998) are acknowledged as important and protected through law.

This conflict, between risk, security and protection and the liberal commitment to individualism, fairness and certainty underpinned by rights, is

– I would argue – mirrored in the modern history of recklessness in criminal law and one that is exemplified in the criminalisation of those who recklessly transmit HIV. People living with HIV do not, by virtue of that fact, lose their status as legal subjects. And as people who are rendered peculiarly vulnerable by their status (no different, in this sense at least, from prisoners), they are precisely that kind of legal subject for whom rights-based protection is of particular and immediate importance. As legal subjects, and as responsible agents, they are no different from those who are uninfected, and consequently held to the same standards of conduct that apply to everyone within the jurisdiction. But this 'sameness', which legitimates state censure when the conduct of people living with HIV is found wanting, ignores – must ignore – their distinctive experience. While they may be entitled to respect for their human rights (freedom from discrimination, right to a fair trial, liberty and security etc), such respect does not, and cannot, extend to special treatment within a liberal legal system (such as that of England and Wales) under-pinned by the rule of law. People living with HIV are accorded the protec-tions of due process and are judged, when they transmit HIV to others, according to the principles that apply to all. If they are charged with reck-lessly transmitting HIV, the test of recklessness applied will (and can) be no different from that which is applied to everyone else. The problem is that the test, which elides subjective fault (conscious risk-taking) with an objective element (unjustifiability) is one that will, if I am correct, inevitably result in the precedence of security concerns. Because people living with HIV have been demonised and marginalised, because they represent the paradigm Other, because they exist both as representatives of a 'dangerous class' and as discrete individuals with whom intimate relationships can be formed, and because they have the capacity to reproduce themselves, within those rela-tionships, in people whose interest in bodily integrity is vital to their sense of self but at the same time fragile and contingent, it will be all but impossible for them to avoid the accusation (or the verdict) that an incident of onward transmission was *their* responsibility and no other's.

Chapter 5

Consent, knowledge and disclosure

Introduction

The concept of consent is of central importance to criminal liability for the sexual transmission of HIV. This is so because a defendant alleged to have transmitted HIV to a sexual partner may wish to argue in his or her defence (a) that the partner consented either to the transmission itself or to the risk of transmission, or (b) even if there was no such consent, that he believed this to be so. If either defence is successful it will result in an acquittal, even if the defendant admits that he was the cause of his partner's infection and that he was aware of the risk that transmission might take place. This is because a successful defence of consent serves to render what would otherwise be an unlawful act a lawful one. It is, in effect, a defence which negates the *actus reus* element of the offence.

Understanding the scope and applicability of, and justification(s) for, the defence of consent is thus vital if one is to understand the legal dynamics underpinning the criminalisation of HIV transmission. Later in this chapter I consider some of the political and theoretical difficulties associated with the concept of consent. Before doing that it is necessary to explain the way in which the law frames, defines and limits the defence. Although not directly relevant to the issue of criminal liability for HIV transmission itself, this explanation requires (for reasons that will become apparent) some discussion of the meaning of consent in the offence of rape.

Consent as an offence element – rape, and the relevance of HIV status

There are a number of important distinctions that need to be drawn when considering the defence of consent. First, there is a difference between (i) asserting the existence of consent when its absence is constitutive of the definition of an offence and (ii) where it operates as a defence to an offence. The offence of rape, for example, is defined in the Sexual Offences Act 2003 (SOA 2003) as follows:

1(1) A person (A) commits an offence if–

   (a) he intentionally penetrates the vagina, anus or mouth of another person (B) with his penis,
   (b) B does not consent to the penetration, and
   (c) A does not reasonably believe that B consents.[1]

It follows from this definition that if rape is to be proved, the prosecution must establish both that the complainant did not consent and that the defendant did not reasonably believe that there was such consent (if this is the nature of the defence he has raised). The reason for the burden falling on the prosecution in this way is that the essence of the offence of rape is non-consent. It is an offence which attempts to draw a clear distinction between conduct that is socially and culturally accepted and valued because it constitutes the expression of sexual intimacy between people – in particular the autonomy of the penetrated person – and conduct which constitutes the obverse of this – the violation of a person's right to choose how to express such intimacy and with whom. This idea is conveyed rather more prosaically in s 74 of the SOA 2003, which states:

a person consents if he agrees by choice, and has the freedom and capacity to make that choice.

The essence of consent in the context of rape (and other non-consensual sexual offences[2]) is thus defined in a way that emphasises choice, freedom and capacity – all of which are constitutive of a liberal understanding of what is meant by personal autonomy and its expression. The question remains, however, as to what these concepts mean in practice, i.e. what counts as, or amounts to, choice, agreement and capacity in the context of sex? The answer to this, so far as the SOA 2003 is concerned, is provided by allowing the jury to determine whether there was in fact no consent (deploying the definition provided in s 74) unless the facts fall into one of two categories. The first such category consists of circumstances which, if found, create an irrebuttable presumption of non-consent. In other words, if a jury are satisfied that these circumstances exist as a matter of fact they have no choice but to find that there was no legally relevant consent to penile penetration (whether vaginal, anal or oral). Those circumstances are set out in s 76(2) and are as follows:[3]

1 See, further, Temkin and Ashworth (2004).
2 Ss 1–4 SOA 2003. For an excellent commentary of the policy background to the legislation see Lacey, 2001c.
3 These conclusive presumptions also apply to those non-consensual sexual offences that do not require proof of penile penetration (e.g. sexual assault).

(a)   the defendant intentionally deceived the complainant as to the nature or purpose of the relevant act;[4]

(b)   the defendant intentionally induced the complainant to consent to the relevant act by impersonating a person known personally to the complainant.[5]

For present purposes, what is interesting is the conclusive presumption in s 76(2)(a). While it may appear, superficially at least, to be an uncontroversial provision (and one that captures, for example, doctors who take advantage of the ignorance of the sexually ignorant and uninitiated by falsely representing intercourse or intimate touchings as medically necessary procedures), it is by no means obvious what is meant by 'nature and purpose'. Under the pre-2003 law, the female sex worker promised payment for sexual intercourse was not raped where she agreed to being penetrated by a male client who subsequently refused to pay (because there was no fraud as to the nature and purpose of the act itself);[6] but the woman who agreed to having her breasts measured by a man whom she believed (wrongly) to be medically trained or qualified was sexually assaulted (because while there was consent to the nature of the act, there was no consent to its quality).[7]

It is extremely difficult satisfactorily to reconcile these cases, both of which remain persuasive authorities under the SOA 2003. For example, it is far from self-evident whether a man who intentionally deceives a sexual partner about the purpose of having intercourse (by representing that his intentions are procreative, when they are in fact purely for his own sexual pleasure), or a man who says he will use a condom when asked to do so but does not, have intentionally deceived their respective partners as to, respectively, the purpose and quality of the act. More critically for present purposes, it is far from obvious whether a person who lies or is silent about his HIV positive status, or about his infection with another serious STI, has deceived his partner about the act's quality. If a restrictive, narrow, interpretation to s 76(2)(a) were adopted – one that affirmed the reasoning in *Linekar*,[8] then the answer would be that such defendants have not engaged in a relevant deception, and that the conclusive presumption does not apply. If, on the other hand, a more

---

4   This provision effectively mirrors a similar provision in the Sexual Offences Act 1956 (itself consolidating earlier legislation) under which fraudulent misrepresentation by the defendant as to the nature of the act he was in fact engaged in (penetrative vaginal intercourse) vitiated the consent of the complainant: *R v Flattery* (1877) 2 QBD 410; *R v Williams* [1923] 1 KB 340. For the best critique of the pre-2003 law see Temkin, 2002.

5   For some brief (but perceptive) questions about the meaning of 'known personally' see Smith and Hogan, 2005: 721–722.

6   *R v Linekar* [1995] 2 WLR 237, [1995] Crim LR 321.

7   *R v Tabassum* [2000] 2 Cr App R 328, [2000] Crim LR 686.

8   See above, n 4.

liberal interpretation were to be adopted (following *Tabassum*[9]) then the absence of consent would be proved as a matter of law.

The former, narrow, interpretation is one for which I would argue. The fact that s 76(2)(a) does not apply in cases such as those set out above does not prevent the jury from using their common sense understanding of the meaning of consent (using the definition in s 74) and deciding whether or not it existed at the relevant time. They may, for example, conclude that the deception effectively prevented the complainant from exercising a *choice* whether to engage in penetrative intercourse with the defendant because it so substantially impeded his or her *freedom* and/or *capacity* to make that choice. If this is so they must, additionally, be satisfied that the defendant has the requisite fault requirement (an absence of reasonable belief in consent).[10] Alternatively, they may decide that the nature of the deception and/ or the context in which the deception occurred were such that it would be wrong to draw such a conclusion (in which case the question of fault does not arise because the *actus reus* is not established). If a broader interpretation as to the meaning of quality were adopted a person who intentionally failed to disclose the truth about his HIV positive status (as opposed to lying about it when asked) could conceivably be treated as engaging in an intentional deception[11] and be guilty of rape *even though* he reasonably believed that his partner would have consented to sex whether or not she or he knew the truth about his status. (For example, a man who failed to disclose his HIV positive status to a casual male partner with whom he has unprotected penetrative sex in a sauna might *reasonably* believe that the partner's willingness to have such sex in such a context[12] meant that he was consenting to such sex (an act of or with this quality); but if the wider interpretation of 'quality' were adopted, along with the expansive meaning of deception deployed elsewhere in the criminal law, then he would have no defence to a charge of rape.

It is significant that, to date, in none of the criminal cases involving HIV transmission in the UK has a rape charge been preferred against a defendant. This no doubt reflects the fact that the dominant view expressed in case law

---

9 See above, n 5.

10 S 1(2) SOA 2003.

11 This hypothesis derives by analogy from the definition and application of deception in the context of property offences, where it is well settled that it may be by words or conduct. A person's decision not to communicate information (here, known HIV positive status) could, if the analogy is correct, be treated as constituting deception by conduct as to the quality of the penetrative act (i.e. that it carried with it no risk of disease transmission). See, further, *R v Barnard* (1837) 7 C & P 784; *R v Rai* [2000] 1 Cr App R 242.

12 The jury's obligation to consider the context in which the belief is formed is, arguably, provided for in s 1(2) where it is stated that 'Whether a belief is reasonable is to be determined *having regard to all the circumstances*, including any steps A has taken to ascertain whether B consents' (emphasis added).

under the Sexual Offences Act 1956 suggested, more or less explicitly, that a narrow definition of 'quality' was preferable. While it is possible that cases decided under the SOA 2003 may result in a different position being taken, it is to be hoped that this will not happen. The wrong of rape (at at least as this is understood within law) is non-consensual penile penetration, not a negative 'quality' of such penetration in a sense expansive enough to include a disease known to the defendant and the subject of deception, or silence, by him.[13] While it may be necessary to retain a notion of quality that captures those who would prey on those so unworldly that they do not know what the act of penetration involves, and who attempt to take advantage of such unworldliness, it would be wrong in principle to stretch the meaning of 'quality' to such an extent that their conduct amounts to rape without further inquiry into context, motivation and fault.[14]

13　Those who disagree with this argument would have, I think, to provide strong reasons why intentional deception as to HIV status, or infection with another serious STI, differs from other 'qualities' of penile penetration so as to make the absence of consent a conclusive presumption. For example, it would be necessary for such people to accept that a married man who knows that a particular woman would not have sex with him if she knew he was married, and who lies about his marital status when asked by her (or, arguably, fails to disclose this fact), rapes that woman when they have intercourse. If the purpose of s 76(2)(a) of the SOA 2003 is to make rapists of those who intentionally deceive partners as to the quality of the act, and if 'quality' is argued to extend beyond the nature of the act of sexual penetration itself, then there is – in principle – no difference between gaining 'consent' by deception as to either marital or health status. To draw a distinction between the two, so that the former is not rape but the latter is, demands that one make the distinction not on the basis of the interest which the offence of rape is intended to protect (the right to choose how, when and with whom one expresses one's sexuality and bodily autonomy) but on the potential or realised physiological consequences of the deception. There is no basis in law, or arguably in principle, for such a distinction to be drawn.

14　Sentencers may, of course, wish to treat a rape defendant's HIV positive status as an aggravating factor when determining the nature and quantum of punishment. For this to be *prima facie* justifiable if transmission does *not* occur it would be necessary to treat penetration with a risk of exposure to infection as a particularly culpable kind of penetration, which would (if one is committed to a subjectivist model of fault) require (a) that the defendant was aware of his HIV positive status at the relevant time and (b) that he was aware that the kind of penetration concerned carried with it a risk of transmission (the risks associated with anal, vaginal and oral penile penetration differ, as do they when ejaculation occurs or a condom is used). Absent such knowledge there would be no legitimate basis on which to increase a defendant's sentence; and it is arguable that since there is no separate criminal offence of exposing someone to the risk of transmission in English law, the fact that a defendant is HIV positive should not in itself constitute an aggravating factor (even less so if the complainant was unaware of this fact). If transmission *does* occur, then the justification for an increased sentence is stronger; though it is again arguable that this should only be the case if the defendant was aware of his HIV positive status and of the risk of transmission by engaging in the particular form of penile penetration with which he is charged (For the level of sentencing in the signatory states of the European Convention on Human Rights, see Nyambe, 2007.)

Consent as a defence – the case of HIV transmission

In the crime of rape the absence of consent is a definitional element which the prosecution must establish if the offence is to be proved. Consent may also operate as a defence proper to charges involving non-fatal offences against the person, and it is in this sense that consent is particularly relevant in cases involving the transmission of HIV. This is so because a defendant charged with transmitting HIV to a sexual partner may admit both that he was reckless and that he was the cause of his partner's infection, but wish to argue that the partner either (a) consented to the infection itself or (b) by agreeing to have sex which carried with it the risk of transmission, consented to the risk of transmission occurring. If either of these lines of defence is admissible and, if so, successful, each will result in a not guilty verdict for the same reason that consent to penile penetration in cases of rape leads to an acquittal: what would have been an unlawful act is instead a lawful one. There is no *actus reus* present and therefore no crime has been committed. In the next section I will consider the specific way in which the appeal courts have dealt with the scope of consent in HIV transmission cases. Before doing so, however, it is important to understand the general approach they have adopted towards the availability or otherwise of the defence of consent in cases involving assault and bodily injury.

In Chapter 3 I suggested that the relaxation of the conditions necessary to establish the offence of assault in recent years could be explained by an increased popular concern with, and judicial sensitivity to, the threat which others pose to our physical and ontological security. The idea I sought to convey was that the courts, in tune (to this extent at least) with the risk society *zeitgeist*, had come to recognise that the meaning and causes of harm were now far more complex than they had been when the wrong of physical injury was understood essentially in terms of the immediate, direct, and unjustifiable violation of the body of a sovereign subject. The raised fist and broken nose of yesteryear has become the silent telephone call and psychological illness of today. This widening of the definition of assault as a response to popular and populist anxieties has, I would argue, been paralleled by a narrowing – or at least a continuing tight judicial circumscription – of the circumstances in which a person may legitimately and/or successfully raise consent as a defence when charged with an assault-based offence.

Briefly put, these circumstances are as follows. First, consent is a defence to common assault, but not to an assault that causes another bodily harm, whether serious or otherwise. An exception to the latter is made where the bodily harm is caused in certain specified contexts, such as dangerous exhibitions, recognised sporting activities and surgery.[15] No exception is made,

---

15 *Attorney General's Reference No 6 of 1980* [1981] QB 715.

despite the fact of consent, where the bodily harm arises in the context of sado-masochistic activity for the purposes of sexual gratification.[16] Second, a distinction is drawn by the courts between the intentional infliction of bodily harm (which will generally be unlawful, despite consent[17]), and the reckless infliction of injury (where consent may operate as a defence depending on the context and circumstances[18]). Third, of particular relevance in the HIV transmission cases, a distinction is drawn between consent to the infliction of serious bodily harm (where consent cannot operate as a defence) and consent to the risk of such harm occurring (where it may).[19] Finally, where consent is a defence that may be raised with respect to assault or the causing of bodily harm, or to the risk of harm, it is also a defence that the defendant *honestly believed* that the person assaulted or injured was consenting (even if this was not in fact the case).

It should be obvious even from this very brief summary that there is little coherence to the jurisprudence of consent as a defence in English criminal law.[20] Whether a person will be able to raise the defence where her actions cause bodily injury to another depends on the degree of harm in fact caused, and/or the context in which the injury was sustained, and/or her mental state at the relevant time, and/or whether (for policy reasons) the court is prepared to analogise the facts before them so as to bring them within the range of exceptions. If it is possible to discern any general principles informing the appellate courts' approach, it is one that could be said to start from a presumption in favour of allowing the defence, unless there exist compelling public policy reasons for denying it, such reasons including, for example, the cost to the public purse of treating the injured person, and the absence of any positive cultural value or significance of the activity in which injury occurred.[21] Because the default position is to allow the defence, the law may be said to be prioritising the liberal values of autonomy and self-determination. And because the law permits the defence to operate where, despite the absence of consent, the defendant honestly believes that it is present, it may be said to be affirming the orthodox subjectivism that pervades the English common law's approach to criminal liability more generally.

---

16 *R v Brown* [1994] 1 AC 212. Where injury (e.g. branding) is caused other than for the purposes of sexual gratification by a husband to a wife and with her consent, the Court of Appeal has held that no offence is committed: *R v Wilson* [1996] Cr App R 241.

17 Thus, the intentional causing of harm may be lawful in recognized sports such as boxing, and surgery – where 'injury' is necessary. See, further, Law Commission (1995), paras 4.29–4.40.

18 See *R v Barnes* [2004] EWCA Crim. 3246 (injury caused during football match).

19 *R v Dica* [2004] 2 Cr App R 28.

20 The absence of coherence is, some commentators have argued, reproduced in the Law Commission's attempts at providing a principled synthesis. See, for excellent and comprehensive critiques, Ormerod, 1994; Roberts, 1997.

21 For a fuller discussion of these ideas see Weait, 1996; 2005b.

However, the fact that the courts have resisted arguments in favour of expanding the range of contexts in which consent would render lawful those injuries that are otherwise unlawful (for example sado-masochistic sexual activity) suggests that they do wish to affirm the continuing importance of a paternalistic, welfare-oriented jurisdiction in which they act as *custos mores*, or moral custodians, of the public good. There is, therefore, an immanent tension in the law in which the right of legal subjects to choose how they wish to interact is subject to wider, policy-based and morally informed, notions of what the public interest demands.

Nowhere is this tension more evident than in the Court of Appeal's approach to consent in the context of HIV transmission liability. In neither *Dica*[22] nor *Konzani*[23] did the defendants deny that they were the cause of the complainants' infections; nor did they deny that they were reckless. In both cases the essence of their defence was that the complainants had consented to the risk of transmission (by agreeing to have unprotected sex), or, in the alternative, that the complainants' willingness to engage in such sex was the basis for an honest, albeit mistaken, belief that they were consenting. To understand the position that the Court has come to adopt on assertions of consent in these circumstances, and before exploring some of the difficulties with that position, it is necessary to look in some detail at the 'logic' behind it and at the cases in which that logic was applied.

At Mohammed Dica's first trial, the judge rejected counsel's attempt to raise the defence of consent, on the basis that the decision of the House of Lords in *R v Brown* had deprived the complainants 'of the legal capacity to consent to such serious harm'.[24] This ruling was explicable, on the basis that HIV infection was a serious harm which had been caused otherwise than in the context of one of the established exceptional categories (see above). As Judge LJ explained, having reviewed the decision in *R v Brown* and other analogous cases:[25]

> These authorities demonstrate that violent conduct involving the deliberate and intentional infliction of bodily harm is and remains unlawful notwithstanding that its purpose is the sexual gratification of one or both participants. Notwithstanding their sexual overtones, these cases were concerned with violent crime, and the sexual overtones did not alter the fact that both parties were consenting to the deliberate infliction of serious harm or bodily injury on one participant by the other. To date, as a matter of public policy, it has not been thought appropriate for such violent conduct to be excused merely because there is a private

22 *R v Dica* [2004] 2 Cr App R 28.
23 *R v Konzani* [2005] 2 Cr App R 198.
24 *R v Dica* [2004] 2 Cr App R 28, at [13].
25 *R v Boyea* [1992] 156 JPR 505; *R v Emmett* (unreported, June 18, 1999).

consensual sexual element to it. The same public policy reason would prohibit the deliberate spreading of disease, including sexual disease.[26]

There was, however, a distinction that needed to be drawn between the deliberate causing of serious bodily harm and the deliberate taking of risks that may and in fact do cause such harm. While it was settled and good law that the former was *prima facie* unlawful, and that absent any sound reasons to allow consent the defence should be denied, the latter was an immanent and inevitable fact of life. In Judge LJ's words:

> the impact of the authorities dealing with sexual gratification can too readily be misunderstood. It does not follow from them, and they do not suggest, that consensual acts of sexual intercourse are unlawful merely because there may be a known risk to the health of one or other participant. These participants are not intent on spreading or becoming infected with disease through sexual intercourse. They are not indulging in serious violence for the purposes of sexual gratification. They are simply prepared, knowingly, to run the risk – not the certainty – of infection, as well as all the other risks inherent in and possible consequences of sexual intercourse, such as, and despite the most careful precautions, an unintended pregnancy. At one extreme there is casual sex between complete strangers, sometimes protected, sometimes not, when the attendant risks are known to be higher, and at the other, there is sexual intercourse between couples in a long-term and loving, and trusting relationship, which may from time to time also carry risks.[27]

In short, people who take risks are not in the category of malevolent 'evil-doers' whom the Government had – in its 1998 White Paper – singled out as the only kind of people to whom liability for the transmission of serious disease should apply.[28] Rather they are merely doing what human beings do. Human beings have sex, and sex entails the taking of risks. It would, in the Court's view, be undesirable in the extreme to interpret the law in such a way that, for example, an HIV positive Roman Catholic husband would be committing a criminal offence when he had procreative sex with his wife. The couple's faith-based refusal to use prophylaxis, combined with a wish to conceive and a desire that HIV not be transmitted was not something with which the criminal law should concern itself, even if serious bodily harm was in fact caused. It is worth setting out the Court's reasoning on this point in full:

---

26 *R v Dica* [2004] 2 Cr App R 28 at [46].
27 Ibid, at [47].
28 Home Office, 1998. (See above, ch 1, pp 21–7.)

These, and similar risks, have always been taken by adults consenting to sexual intercourse. Different situations, no less potentially fraught, have to be addressed by them. Modern society has not thought to criminalise those who have willingly accepted the risks, and we know of no cases where one or other of the consenting adults has been prosecuted, let alone convicted, for the consequences of doing so.

The problems of *criminalising* the consensual taking of risks like these include the sheer impracticability of enforcement and the haphazard nature of its impact. The process would undermine the general understanding of the community that sexual relationships are pre-eminently private and essentially personal to the individuals involved in them. And if adults were to be liable to prosecution for the consequences of taking known risks with their health, it would seem odd that this should be confined to risks taken in the context of sexual intercourse, while they are nevertheless permitted to take the risks inherent in so many other aspects of everyday life, including, again for example, the mother or father of a child suffering a serious contagious illness, who holds the child's hand, and comforts or kisses him or her goodnight.

In our judgment, interference of this kind with personal autonomy, and its level and extent, may only be made by Parliament.[29]

The judicial refusal to deny the defence of consent in the context of intimate risk-taking is thus both pragmatic and principled: it would not only be impossible to police, it would amount to undemocratic judicial law-making. In itself this is an unremarkable manifestation of liberal legal reasoning, and welcome in the refusal effectively to deny the right of people to make choices in their private lives. What is more interesting and problematic about the Court's approach in *Dica* was its failure to engage in any detail with the finer points and wider implications of its reasoning. These may usefully be considered in terms of the nature of risk involved and the relevance of knowledge.

Knowledge and risk

In *Dica*, the Court of Appeal made it clear that it was a valid defence to a charge under s 20 of the OAPA 1861 where a person to whom HIV had been transmitted consented to the risk of HIV transmission. Whether that person did consent – or whether the defendant honestly believed that there was consent – are, on their face, simple questions of fact for the jury to determine having reviewed the evidence before them. The simplicity of the questions is, however, deceptive. When a jury is called upon to decide whether consent to

---

29 *R v Dica* [2004] 2 Cr App R 28, at [50]–[52].

the risk of transmission existed, or an honest belief was held, it will be doing so 'after the event'. Transmission will have occurred, and serious bodily harm (as the law views it) will have been caused. Furthermore, they will only be involved in a trial in which consent is in issue because the defendant has chosen to plead not guilty on consent grounds. They are therefore being invited to choose between different accounts of the same event, to choose (leaving aside the important question of credibility) between a narrative that takes the essential form 'I did nothing wrong, because they knew what might happen' and one which asserts 'I was wronged, because I had no idea that this might happen'. I have already argued that the way in which recklessness is interpreted will make it difficult for a defendant to argue that his risk-taking was justified, even where he honestly believes he was not at fault.[30] Here I want to suggest that it may be equally difficult for a defendant to succeed on consent grounds because of the way in which the Court of Appeal, despite its apparent concession to defendants in allowing the defence despite the fact of causing serious bodily harm, has treated the issue of knowledge.

Knowledge could be considered relevant to consent in the following two respects. First, it may be relevant to the question of whether the complainant consented to the degree of risk that in fact obtained at the relevant time (i.e. to the probability of infection associated with particular kinds of sexual intimacy with a person known by them to be HIV positive). Second, the existence, source, and reliability of a complainant's knowledge about the HIV positive status of a partner may be relevant to the question of whether she made an informed decision as to the risk she was taking. As for the first of these, the Court of Appeal appears to consider this to be irrelevant – if only by implication, since it is not a matter to which it addressed itself directly in either *Dica* or *Konzani*.[31] Although the probability of onward HIV transmission from an HIV positive partner varies substantially depending on the kind of sexual activity in which the parties are engaged (see Table 5.1), infection is

---

30 See above, Ch 4.

31 Although the relevance of probability is not addressed directly by the Court of Appeal in *Dica*, it has been a relevant consideration in those cases from which *Dica* is distinguished. In *R v Emmett* (unreported, June 18,1999) the Court held that where the appellant set fire to his partner's breasts with lighter fuel and almost asphyxiated her, the fact that he and she were, *per* Wright J, 'deeply involved in an energetic, very physical sexual relationship which both greatly enjoyed' did not mean that he should have been entitled to rely on her consent as a defence to a charge under s 47 of the OAPA 1861. In the Court's view the facts of the case were different in kind from those in *R v Wilson* [1996] 2 Cr App 241 (where a husband who branded his wife's buttocks with his initials had his s 47 conviction quashed) on the basis that the degree to which Mr Emmett had exposed his partner to the risk of unintended injury was unacceptably high. While the Court of Appeal in *Dica* may not specifically address the relevance or otherwise of the degree of risk to the question of consent in cases of reckless HIV transmission, there appears to be an implicit assumption that the magnitude of the risk makes no difference.

Table 5.1 The risk of HIV transmission following an exposure from a known HIV-positive individual[32]

Type of exposure	Estimated risk of HIV transmission per exposure (%)
Receptive anal intercourse	0.1–3.0
Receptive vaginal intercourse	0.1–0.2
Insertive vaginal intercourse	0.03–0.09
Insertive anal intercourse	0.06
Receptive oral sex (fellatio)	0–0.04

a zero-sum game. Either one is infected or one is not, and one has either consented to the risk of transmission, or one has not. There is no middle ground. An alternative approach would be to determine the presence or absence of consent based on the reasonableness of the previously HIV negative partner's estimation of the risk to which she believed herself to be exposed with a known HIV positive partner. Thus, the courts could investigate whether that partner believed the probability of infection to be high or low. They could, for example, direct juries to take consent as given and obtained if they were sure that the partner knew that being the receptive party in unprotected anal intercourse was a high-risk activity with an HIV positive man and agreed to this, but not otherwise. Or they could direct juries that consent should not be assumed where the partner had only agreed to a comparatively low-risk activity, such as receptive oral sex. That the courts have not taken this approach is to be welcomed. HIV may be transmitted during one incident of low-risk activity, or not transmitted during a number of incidents of high-risk activity. A person who consents to low-risk sex may in fact be putting themselves as at much risk on the relevant occasion as a person who consents to high-risk activities. To treat these as legally relevant distinctions would amount to accepting (a) that the individual and social responsibility of a person who knowingly risks infection by having unprotected sex, and is in fact infected, should be contingent on immanently unreliable predictive assessments of risk by them; and (b) that the criminal liability of the defendant should somehow depend on whether their partner's risk-taking was justifiable on this basis or not. Neither of these are morally defensible positions, nor ones that I believe the law should sanction.

Much more important, in practical terms, is the existence, source, and reliability of a complainant's knowledge of the HIV status of a partner with whom they engage in sex that could result in HIV transmission if that partner

32 This is adapted from Fisher *et al*, 2006: 82.

was, in fact, HIV positive. It is true that in *Dica*, the Court of Appeal expressed the view that a complainant's knowledge of the HIV status of a defendant charged under s 20 was to be distinguished from the question of whether or not there was consent to the risk of transmission; but this was because it wanted to avoid the conclusion that absence of knowledge equated to absence of consent. If it had held otherwise it would mean that a person who was ignorant of a partner's HIV positive status could not, as a matter of law, consent to the risk of infection; and if this were the case it would, logically, mean that they could not consent, in law, to the act through which transmission occurred (i.e. sexual intercourse) and would, therefore, be raped.[33]

The Court's distinction between knowledge and consent appears, at first glance, to be a sensible and defensible one. There is, however, a problem – one which stems from the way in which it approaches knowledge in this context. In a key passage of the judgment, Judge LJ holds as follows:

> The effect of this judgment in relation to s 20 is to remove some of the outdated restrictions against the successful prosecution of those who, knowing that they are suffering HIV or some other serious sexual disease, recklessly transmit it through consensual sexual intercourse, and inflict grievous bodily harm on a person from whom the risk is concealed and who is not consenting to it . . . If however, the victim consents to the risk, this continues to provide a defence under s 20. Although the two are inevitably linked, the ultimate question is not knowledge, but consent. We shall confine ourselves to reflecting that unless you are prepared to take whatever risk of sexually transmitted infection there may be, it is unlikely that you would consent to a risk of major consequent illness if you were ignorant of it. That said, in every case where these issues arise, the question whether the defendant was or was not reckless, and whether the victim did or did not consent to the risk of a sexually transmitted disease is one of fact, and case specific.

This, with respect, is rather muddy reasoning. It ensures (overturning *R v Clarence*) that consent to intercourse does not equate to consent to the risk of infection; but in addressing the relevance of knowledge it implicitly elides and equates concealment (active deception by the defendant) and ignorance

---

33 His reasoning is consistent with the position I argued for above – that the 'quality' of intercourse should not be interpreted so widely that it would mean that sexual intercourse with an HIV positive person could amount to rape under the SOA 2003. See also recent decision of the Court of Appeal in which it held that non-disclosure of known HIV status is not relevant to the question of whether a complainant consented to intercourse (and is thus irrelevant to the question of consent in the context of a prosecution for rape: *R v B* [2007] 1 Cr App R 29).

(of the complainant). These are not the same thing, and the difference between them is – I would suggest – critical. Certainly it is possible to argue that a person who is ignorant of a risk cannot consent to it (it would be bizarre to suggest that a person could consent to a risk of which he was unaware); but a person from whom a risk 'is concealed' (by the defendant) is not necessarily ignorant of it. It may be that the most reliable source of knowledge of a partner's HIV positive status is the partner himself, but not only did the Court indicate that knowledge as such was not the relevant consideration as regards the existence or otherwise of consent, it is also perfectly possible for someone to be aware of the risk of HIV (and other STI) transmission from other sources. A person may, for example, know that a partner has a previous sexual partner who is HIV positive; or that he is non-monogamous and has unprotected sex with other people; or that he comes from a group with a higher than average prevalence of HIV (such as gay men, or gay men living in London, or men from sub-Saharan Africa or the Ukraine, or injection drug users). That a partner from one of these groups has not actively disclosed his HIV status (or has 'concealed' it) does not, I suggest, mean that a person who has unprotected sex with him lacks knowledge of the risk of infection; and if that person does not lack knowledge of the risk of infection, it is possible to argue that when they consent to activities during which transmission may occur, that risk has been consented to (unless a more restrictive definition of consent is adopted, on which see below).

This problem – the specific relevance of the source of knowledge to the question of consent – was revisited by the Court of Appeal in *Konzani* where the sole issue for consideration was whether the trial judge had, on his reading of *Dica*, misdirected the jury at Mr Konzani's trial as to the meaning of consent. It will be recalled, from Chapter 2, that the judge's direction had emphasised that the defence of consent was unavailable unless the alleged consent was 'consciously' or 'willingly' given. It is worth recalling the relevant part of the direction:

> . . . the Prosecution must make you sure that at the time of being so infected with the virus the young woman in question, whichever it was, did not willingly consent to the risk of suffering that infection. Note that I use the phrase 'to the risk of suffering that infection' and not merely just to suffering it. That is an important point which [defence counsel] rightly drew to your attention in his speech to you this morning. He put it this way, it is whether she consented to that risk, not consented to being given the disease which is, as he put it graphically, a mile away from the former.
>
> That is right, but note that I use the word 'willingly' in the phrase 'willingly consent' and I did that to highlight that the sort of consent I am talking about means consciously, that is to say thinking about the matter at the time as opposed to either not giving it any thought at all or having a theoretical or general awareness of life's risks.

Counsel for the appellant argued that this part of the direction, and other elements of it, were deficient because of the failure to explain that the defence was available as a matter of law where a person honestly believed that the partner to whom he had transmitted HIV had consented to the risk of transmission, even if this belief was an unreasonable one.

The Court was unwilling to accept this argument.[34] Although it agreed that an honest belief in consent would, as a general rule, provide a defence,[35] in this context 'the defendant's honest belief must be concomitant with the consent which provides a defence'.[36] The Court expressed the view that there was a fundamental difference between running a risk (which some, at least, of the complainants' evidence suggested they were conscious of doing),[37] and *consenting* to a risk (which Mr Konzani's failure to disclose known HIV status prevented them from doing). As a result there was no legally recognised consent in respect of which Mr Konzani could have had any belief, honest or otherwise.

This, it is suggested, is faulty logic. In *Dica* the Court of Appeal had held simply that a person would have a defence if the complainant consented to the risk of transmission. It is at least arguable that a person who agrees to have unprotected sex with a person about whose HIV status they are uncertain consents to the risk of transmission by the very act of agreeing to have unprotected sex with that person. In *Konzani*, the Court of Appeal seems to have decided that there was a need to explain in categorical terms that this is *not* how it wanted *Dica* to be interpreted. It did so by reinforcing the connection between recklessness, consent and disclosure, and explaining that the allegation in *Dica* had been that the accused:

> behaved recklessly on the basis that knowing that he was suffering from the HIV virus, and its consequences, and knowing the risks of its transmission to a sexual partner, he concealed his condition from the complainants, leaving them ignorant of it.[38]

This, it is suggested, is a somewhat radical interpretation of recklessness, one that extends its meaning well beyond conscious, unjustifiable, risk-taking. Instead, in this context at least,[39] the Court appears to be saying that

---

34 This section is drawn from Weait, 2005c.
35 This is the case in the context of offences against the person. The law has now changed in the context of sexual offences so that belief in consent must now be reasonable if it is to provide a defence (Sexual Offences Act 2003): see above, pp 165–9.
36 *R v Konzani* [2005] 2 Cr App R 198 at [45].
37 See the extracts of the complainants' evidence in *R v Konzani*, extracted in Ch 2 at [12]–[14], [19]–[20] and [25]–[28].
38 *R v Konzani* [2005] Cr App R 198 at [41].
39 In most cases concerning non-fatal offences against the person, where recklessness is sufficient to establish liability, the presence or absence of disclosure is not an issue.

recklessness comprises the additional element of non-disclosure; and because non-disclosure results in ignorance, a person infected by the non-discloser cannot consciously or willingly consent to the risk of transmission. Logically therefore, the defence is not available.[40]

The decision of the Court of Appeal in *Konzani* will appease those who reject the argument that people who recklessly transmit HIV should be able to rely on the defence of consent where their partner(s) are aware of the risk of transmission but to whom no disclosure has been made.[41] However, it is suggested that those who do approve of the decision should acknowledge the fact that they are in danger of reinforcing the idea, contrary to the philosophy behind most HIV prevention campaigns, that we bear no responsibility for our own health. This is because in confirming that the defence is available only where there is consent to risk (or an honest belief in such consent) the Court is implicitly saying that those who do not willingly consent to the risk, but who willingly choose to *run* the risk, are not to be held responsible for the consequences of doing so. Moreover, those who would identify with the Court's reasoning need to recognise that this necessarily means agreeing that disclosure by a partner is the only relevant source of knowledge for the purposes of being able consciously to consent to the risk of transmission, despite the fact that there are other ways in which conscious knowledge of risk can be gained by those to whom HIV is transmitted.

Those arguments – or ones along these lines – are not, however, ones that found favour with the Court. Where a person discloses his known HIV positive status to a partner who, in receipt of this information, agrees to have unprotected sex it is submitted that it is wrong in principle to assert that a criminal act has been committed if that partner is thereby infected. But the question of whether a partner's *non*-disclosure ought automatically to mean that a criminal act has been committed is not so easy to sustain. The reason for this is as follows. The Court of Appeal held in both *Dica* and *Konzani* that

---

40 This interpretation is supported by the Court's approval of the Lord Chief Justice's interpretation of *R v Dica* in the case of *R v Barnes* ([2005] 1 WLR 910). There his Lordship said, at [10], 'This Court held [in *Dica*] that the man would be guilty of an offence contrary to Section 20 of the 1861 Act if, being aware of his condition, he had sexual intercourse with [the complainants] without disclosing his condition. On the other hand, this Court considered that he would have a defence if he had made the women aware of his condition, but with this knowledge because they were still prepared to accept the risks involved and consented to having sexual intercourse with him.' It is worth recording that the Lord Chief Justice sat on the panel that heard the appeal in *R v Dica*, and that Judge LJ, who delivered the judgment in *R v Dica*, also delivered the judgment in *R v Konzani*.

41 It is also a position that has been accepted in terms by the Supreme Court of Canada: 'Without disclosure of HIV status there cannot be a true consent. The consent cannot simply be to have sexual intercourse. Rather it must be consent to have intercourse with a partner who is HIV-positive. True consent cannot be given if there has not been a disclosure by the accused of his HIV-positive status. A consent that is not based upon knowledge of the significant relevant factors is not a valid consent' (*R v Cuerrier* (1998) 127 CCC (3d) 1 at 50).

consent to the risk of transmission should provide the person who recklessly transmits HIV with a defence. In *Konzani* the Court made it clear that such consent had to be 'willing' or 'conscious' and that this was, in effect, not possible if the infecting partner had failed to disclose known HIV positive status at the relevant time. In its words:

> If an individual who knows that he is suffering from the HIV virus conceals this stark fact from his sexual partner, the principle of her personal autonomy is not enhanced if he is exculpated when he recklessly transmits the HIV virus to her through consensual sexual intercourse. On any view, the concealment of this fact from her almost inevitably means that she is deceived. Her consent is not properly informed, and she cannot give an informed consent to something of which she is ignorant.[42]

The problematic approach to autonomy is explored below. For the moment it is simply important to note that in using the language of deception the Court is able to reinforce the link between (a) non-disclosure and fault (of the person who transmits HIV), and (b) non-disclosure and ignorance (of the person to whom HIV is transmitted). And in so doing it effectively denies the possibility that a person to whom disclosure is *not* made may still be sufficiently knowledgeable about the risk of transmission to warrant the conclusion that he or she did in fact consent to it.

It is important to add 'effectively' as a qualification because the Court in *Konzani* did in fact concede that there might arise situations in which a person may not have directly disclosed his HIV positive status, but the circumstances are such that (a) the partner to whom he transmits HIV could give a legally recognised consent, or (b), they provide the basis for a claim that he honestly believed his partner to have consented. In the words of the Court:

> By way of an example, an individual with HIV may develop a sexual relationship with someone who knew him while he was in hospital, receiving treatment for the condition. If so, her informed consent, if it were indeed informed, would remain a defence, to be disproved by the prosecution, even if the defendant had not personally informed her of his condition. Even if she did not in fact consent, this example would illustrate the basis for an argument that he honestly believed in her informed consent. Alternatively, he may honestly believe that his new sexual partner was told of his condition by someone known to them both. Cases like these, not too remote to be fanciful, may arise.[43]

---

42 *R v Konzani* [2005] 2 Cr App R 198 at [42].
43 *R v Konzani* [2005] 2 Cr App R at [44].

While this may appear to be a significant concession, the Court's choice of examples demonstrates its rejection of any argument based on *general* knowledge about the risks associated with unprotected sexual intercourse with a person about whose HIV status one is uncertain. Both of the hypotheticals are ones where there has, in effect, been disclosure – either through context (the hospital treatment setting) or through a third party. As such, these concessions are extremely limited in scope and suggest that even where a person adverts consciously to the possibility that a non-disclosing sexual partner may be HIV positive, such conscious advertence should not provide the person who transmits HIV to them with a defence. Voluntary disclosure of known HIV positive status to sexual partners may be the ethically defensible practice, and is a cornerstone of much HIV prevention work; but as is apparent elsewhere in the criminal law, what is ethically indefensible is not a sufficient condition for the imposition of criminal liability.[44] Legitimate concern may be raised about the criminalisation of the individual who transmits HIV where those who have been infected are, despite non-disclosure, well aware of the potential harm to which they may be subjecting themselves by agreeing to have sex that carries the risk of transmission. The transmission of HIV should be seen first and foremost as a public health issue and that everyone, not just those who are HIV positive, has a responsibility for minimising the spread of the virus. To impose criminal liability on those who recklessly transmit HIV or STIs to people who are in a position to protect themselves against infection, and elect not to, sends a message that people are, and should be, entitled to assume that their partners will ensure that transmission does not occur. The very fact that the virus has spread so dramatically in recent years among the sexually active demonstrates that this is simply not the case.

Autonomy

Given the importance of the principles at stake, the judgment of the Court of Appeal in *Konzani* is intellectually disappointing. Any principled justification that may be said to exist is to be found in one critical passage, referred to above, where the Court explains that a complainant's 'personal autonomy is not enhanced if [the defendant] is exculpated when he recklessly transmits the HIV virus to her through consensual sexual intercourse'. What might this mean, and what merit does it have as a justification for imposing

---

44 For example, X is married. X fails to disclose this fact to Y, with whom he has sexual intercourse. Y would not have had sexual intercourse with X had this fact been disclosed to her. Y has not been raped, because she has not been deceived as to X's identity or as to the nature of the act. X's failure to disclose is something that would have materially affected Y's decision. Y's autonomy has, it is arguable, been violated – or at the very least not respected; and yet this violation is not seen as a harm with which the criminal law should concern itself.

criminal liability via the denial of a defence based on honest belief in consent?

Autonomy means, literally, self-government. In the context of law generally, and in the context of the law as it relates to sexual offences and offences against the person in particular, it suggests the right of a person to be free from unwarranted and unwanted physical interference. Thus the essence of rape law, in which the absence of consent is definitional of the *actus reus*, is that no legal wrong is done if consent exists, because the partner with whom a person has sexual intercourse is exercising his or her autonomy rather than having it infringed or violated; and where consent operates as a defence to a charge of assault, or causing bodily harm, it reflects the law's recognition that there exists a sphere (albeit one circumscribed by public policy considerations) in which people should be entitled to freedom from liability because to hold otherwise would result in a significant and unjustified diminution of essential human freedoms. It is of critical importance to recognise the distinction. In the former (rape) example the reason why the law does not criminalise the putative defendant is that there is no legally recognised harm committed. However in the latter (assault) example the law protects a putative defendant from criminal liability not on the basis that no recognisable harm has been caused, but because of the context in which it has taken place. It follows that in such circumstances the law is not, at least *prima facie*, concerned with protecting, or indeed 'enhancing' the autonomy of the person harmed, but rather with protecting the person who harms from the imposition of unjustified liability. Put simply, it is his autonomy (in the sense of his right to be free from unwarranted interference and condemnation by the state) that the law is concerned to protect.

If the principles underpinning this argument are sound then any departure from them demands strong and careful justification. With respect, the Court of Appeal in *Konzani* not only departs from them but fails to provide any such justification. The Court indicates that a complainant's autonomy is not enhanced by exculpating a person who recklessly harms her by transmitting HIV (and, by implication, that it is enhanced by denying such a defendant the right to assert an honest belief in her consent to the risk of such harm). In so doing it starts from the premise that, in the context of non-fatal offences against the person at least, it is the autonomy of the person harmed that it is the law's function to protect. However, if this were so then those who recklessly harm people should be denied the defence of consent on the basis of honest belief or otherwise, irrespective of the context in which such harm occurs; and yet case law demonstrates that this is not the case. Without explicitly acknowledging this difficulty, the Court identifies the failure of a person to disclose his known HIV positive status, and the deception that is thereby practised on a partner to whom he transmits HIV, as the basis for making the distinction. The non-discloser may not assert an honest belief in his partner's consent, because the fact of non-disclosure renders her 'consent' un-informed, legally nugatory, and therefore not one on which he is, or should be, entitled to rely. This line of reasoning is emphasised in the Court's second reference to the autonomy of a complainant, when it states that this is:

> not normally protected by allowing a defendant who knows that he is suffering from the HIV virus which he deliberately conceals, to assert an honest belief in his partner's informed consent to the risk of the transmission of the HIV virus. Silence in these circumstances is incongruous with honesty, or with a genuine belief that there is an informed consent. Accordingly, in such circumstances the issue either of informed consent, or honest belief in it will only rarely arise: in reality, in most cases, the contention would be wholly artificial.[45]

What is to be made of the Court's deployment of autonomy in this way? While it no doubt has a certain intuitive appeal, it is submitted that the consequences of this line of reasoning are such that it should be rejected.

The Court in *Dica* recognised that people should be entitled in principle to consent to the risks associated with sexual intercourse because to deny them this right (and the correlative defence such a right provides those who expose them to such risks) would amount to an infringement of autonomy that only Parliament should sanction. In *Konzani*, however, the Court has made it clear that only an informed consent, grounded in knowledge gained from direct or indirect disclosure of a partner's HIV positive status, amounts to consent for these purposes. In effect, therefore, the cumulative *ratio* of the two cases is not that a person should be entitled to consent to the risks associated with sexual intercourse, but that she should be entitled to consent to such risks as have been directly or indirectly disclosed to her. It is only in the latter context that a defendant's claim of honest belief in consent can, and should, be legally recognised. If this is indeed the *ratio*, a number of consequences follow.

First, in emphasising that it is only in the most exceptional of cases that non-disclosure to a sexual partner by an HIV positive person will be 'congruent' with an honest belief, the Court has, in effect, imposed a standard of reasonable belief in cases where there has been an absence of disclosure. This may be consistent with legislative developments in the law of rape, but if such is the trajectory the law should follow, then it is submitted that this should be for Parliament to decide, not – with respect – the Court of Appeal. Second, the Court has, also in effect, imposed a positive duty of disclosure on people who know they are HIV positive (and who wish to avoid potential criminal liability) before they have sex which carries the risk of transmission. Since

45 *R v Konzani* [2005] 2 Cr App 198 at [42].

there is no reason in principle why this positive duty should be limited to HIV (which is, for those able to access treatment at least, a manageable if life-limiting condition), it should be assumed that it applies to all those who are aware that they are suffering from a serious STI. Given that chlamydia may, if untreated in a woman, lead to infertility, that hepatitis B can lead to severe liver damage, and that syphilis – if untreated – can result in significant mental and physical impairment, it is presumably safer to assume that this positive duty now applies to all those who have been diagnosed with these, and other potentially serious, diseases who wish to avoid the possibility of prosecution and imprisonment. Third, in the absence of any indication to the contrary by the Court, disclosure as a precautionary principle ought presumably to be adopted by those that are infected with serious or potentially serious contagious diseases. A passenger with SARS or avian influenza may very well be aware that on an intercontinental flight there could be elderly people or others with impaired immune systems (including, it should be added, people living with HIV). Such people's autonomy is certainly not 'enhanced' if the passenger is able to assert that he honestly believed they would consent to being infected by a virus that results in their developing pneumonia; nor is it 'normally protected', where, knowing that he is suffering from a condition that can cause such an effect, he conceals this information. These consequences of the Court's reasoning may be thought more or less fanciful; but the point is, surely, that in using the language of autonomy so loosely, and in failing to specify precisely what the justification for, and scope of, the decision in *Konzani* is, the Court of Appeal has delivered a judgment, and settled the law, in a way that fails abjectly to deal with the core issues which its subject matter raises.

The meaning and significance of disclosure

He [Feston Konzani] knew what it meant, of course, didn't he? It means you have got a future ahead of you of serious illness followed by an early death, because HIV is a terrible thing, isn't it, members of the jury? It doesn't get much worse, you might think, and that is in reality simply not the sort of thing you consent to catching, is it? Again, you may think about it yourselves but it is at the top of the list of things you would want to be told by a prospective sexual partner, isn't it, 'I am HIV positive. Have sex with me and you're taking your life, or putting your life in very substantial risk indeed.'[46]

So far in this chapter I have sought to provide a detailed critique of the way in which English law has approached the inter-related issues of consent and

46 See Ch 2.

knowledge in cases involving HIV transmission. In that discussion, disclosure of HIV status plays an important but obscure part: important because it is evident that, absent disclosure, it will be all but impossible for a defendant to raise the defence of consent successfully; obscure, because this effect of the Court of Appeal's reasoning has come about despite the fact that there is – in English law – no legal obligation to disclose one's HIV status to a sexual partner.[47] In the final section of this chapter I want to consider more closely the meaning and significance of disclosure – not just in the law concerning transmission liability but more generally for people living with HIV. For if the notion of responsibility is problematic anywhere in this area, it is arguably most problematic here.

Disclosure as confession

In the first volume of his *History of Sexuality*, Michel Foucault emphasises the central place that confession, and the technologies of the confessional, have had in the production of truth (Foucault, 1978: 58). In contrast to those earlier times in which an individual relied on others to testify or bear witness on his behalf, the confession – in its religious. criminal justice and other institutionalised manifestations – gradually came to be the principal means by which the individual 'was authenticated by the discourse of truth he was able or obliged to pronounce concerning himself' (ibid). Just as significantly, and inevitably, the confession came to be 'inscribed at the heart of the procedures of individualization' (ibid: 58–9). The responsible subject of modernity is one whose autonomy is in part realised through, and manifest in, confession. To tell the truth about oneself is a necessary condition of responsibility – whether in one's relations with others or before the law. As Foucault further explains:

> The confession . . . plays a part in justice, medicine, education, family relationships, and love relations, in the most ordinary affairs of everyday life, and in the most solemn rites; one confesses one's crimes, one's sins, one's thoughts and desires, one's illnesses and troubles; one goes about telling, with the greatest precision, whatever is most difficult to tell. One confesses in public and in private, to one's parents, one's educators, one's doctor, to those one loves; one admits to oneself, in pleasure and in pain, things it would be impossible to tell anyone else, the things people write books about. One confesses – or is forced to confess.
>
> (Ibid: 59)

---

47 The position is different in, for example, Canada. See the Supreme Court case of *R v Cuerrier* (1998) 127 CCC (3d) 1 (SCC), and the detailed commentary by Richard Elliott (Elliott, 1999).

For the person living with HIV, this account of confession and its universality may ring particularly true. In private, there is the admission, or confession to self, that one is HIV positive – or that this is one's fear in the absence of confirmed clinical diagnosis. In public there is there is the decision whether to express this fear or knowledge to others, whether those others be acquaintances or intimates. Before the law, as subject of law, there is – as we have seen – the implicit obligation to confess one's HIV positive status, or (more strongly) one's HIV positive identity, to certain others if one is to avoid social condemnation, moral censure and state punishment: if one is to remain, and be, responsible. This is, of course, because a person's HIV positive status is something that he can, potentially, share with others. The very thing that an HIV positive person may deny about himself, or be unwilling, scared or cautious to confess, to disclose, to others is something that those others have an investment in him revealing. For, as Foucault explains, the confession is:

> a ritual that unfolds within a power relationship, for one does not confess without the presence (or virtual presence) of a partner who is not simply the interlocutor but the authority who requires the confession, prescribes and appreciates it, and intervenes in order to judge, punish, forgive, console, and reconcile . . .
>
> (Ibid: 61–2)

The sexual partner to whom an HIV positive diagnosis is not revealed, and is subsequently infected may intervene in any or all of these ways. For the purposes of this book, what is important is that such a partner has, through the medium of the criminal law, and because of the law's approach to disclosure, the opportunity to put in motion a process that may result in her infector's conviction and immediate imprisonment.

The wrong of non-disclosure of HIV status

Common sense, often but not necessarily a good guide to what is right, tells us that a person who has the potential to harm others should alert others to that possibility so that those others may decide for themselves whether, and if so to what extent, they are willing to accept the risk of such harm. Such common sense is no doubt embedded in the deep psychology of, and instinct for, survival. We (the as yet unharmed) have an investment in them (the potential harmers) taking responsibility for preventing our transfiguration. Such common sense is also reflected in the common law's linear and unidirectional approach to causation, one that (simplistically put) identifies as the cause of a consequence the action but for which things would have remained the same.[48]

---

48 The *locus classicus* of the common law approach to causation is Hart and Honoré, 1985.

We assume, and the law assumes along with us, that – bar unforeseen events – things will change predictably, if they change at all. It is the thing that may be directly associated with the unexpected that we tend to treat as the cause of the unexpected: put more strongly, it may be argued that it is only the unexpected and unanticipated that we tend to treat as having causes at all.[49] We also tend, intuitively, to seek and focus upon – where there is the option to do so – an agential cause of events in the world. Where human beings are, or may be, implicated in outcomes, especially adverse ones, we (and the law) are more than ready to identify their contribution and, where morally justified, to blame them for those outcomes.[50]

Applied to the present context, these principles and intuitions suggest that disclosure is the 'right thing to do', since it enables others to avoid being infected; that the cause of infection where it happens is properly identified as the HIV positive partner (not the virus); and that failure to disclose is, in some sense, bound up with the adverse consequence which HIV infection represents. These interrelated positions, or claims, are ones that are – as we have seen – manifested in English criminal law's complicated approach to the relevance of HIV status disclosure cases where consent is raised as a defence.

To this extent, intuition and common sense are in tune with the courts' approach to non-disclosure of HIV status, and with the moral philosophical and liberal political traditions that underpin the criminal law, both here and in other jurisdictions with a common law heritage. It is irrelevant, as a matter of *principle*, that there exists empirical evidence suggesting no necessary correlation between disclosure to a partner and subsequent safer sex with that partner (see, for example, Marks and Crepaz, 2001; Serovich and Mosack, 2003; Simoni and Pantalone, 2004). The fact that some HIV positive people do not disclose their status and yet engage in unsafe sex with a partner (Marks, Richardson and Maldonado, 1991; Stein *et al*, 1998; Ciccarone *et al*, 2003), represents a form of deception that denies that partner's moral personhood:

> . . . powerful arguments can be made that withholding information about one's HIV infection from a sex partner is morally disrespectful and treats

49 We do not ask why the aircraft landed safely; we ask why it crashed.
50 A person parks their car on a hill and neglects to put on the handbrake. They get out, and the car rolls down the hill, resulting in damage to a neighbouring car parked further down. Ask a group of people what caused the damage to the neighbouring car, and most if not all will answer 'because the person forgot to put the handbrake on'. It is rare that someone will answer 'gravity'. Similarly, a woman builds a dam across a stream and the stream stops flowing. Ask the person who arrives after the dam is constructed why the stream is not flowing, and they will answer, 'because she built a dam'; but if the woman is merely standing by the stream, and ask the person who arrives at the same spot why the stream is flowing, it is extremely unlikely that he will answer, 'because she didn't build a dam'. It is our intervention, or lack of it, in the world that we treat as relevant and meaningful causes.

the other as a means to one's own end (pleasure or some other satisfaction, or avoidance of discomfort) rather than as a moral agent – a
human being – who is entitled to make his or her own decisions about
sexual risk.

(Bruner, 2004: 20)

Within a legal system informed by Kantian morality, one in which people are
to be treated as ends in themselves, it is irrelevant that HIV positive people
may choose to engage in low risk sexual activity rather than to disclose
(Rooney and Taylor, 1997; Keogh *et al*, 1999; Davis, 2001); or that they are
more likely to disclose to those with whom they have longer and more intimate relationships than to casual or anonymous partners (Rooney and Taylor,
1997; Wolitski *et al*, 1998; Keogh *et al*, 1999; Davis, 2001; Klitzman and
Bayer, 2003; Ciccarone *et al*, 2003). And within criminal law, the rules of
which articulate values and general standards of behaviour (including those
of prudence and honesty) against which we may all be legitimately judged, it
matters not one wit that HIV positive people (in particular gay men and men
who have sex with men) may believe that others have a responsibility to
protect themselves (Cusick and Rhodes, 1999; Stephenson *et al*, 2003), or that
they sometimes find it difficult or inappropriate to raise the topic of HIV in
sexual and intimate contexts (Keogh and Beardsell, 1997; Keogh *et al*, 1998,
1999; Derlega *et al*, 2000; Green and Sobo, 2000; Greene *et al* 2003; Sheon
and Crosby, 2004).

It does not matter that people living with HIV and AIDS may avoid disclosure for fear of rejection (Perry *et al*, 1994; Simoni *et al*, 1995; Moneyham
et al, 1996; Gielen *et al*, 1997; Kilmarx *et al*, 1998; Levy *et al*, 1999); or
because of concerns about stigma and discrimination (Limandri, 1989;
Moneyham *et al*, 1996; Gielen *et al*, 1997; Derlega, *et al*, 2002; Petrak *et al*,
2001), privacy and confidentiality (Perry *et al*, 1994; Simoni *et al*, 1995;
Moneyham *et al*, 1996), the desire to protect the feelings of others (Levy *et al*,
1999; Petrak *et al*, 2001) or even because of worries about abuse and violence
(Gielen *et al*, 1997; Gielen *et al*, 2000). What matters, instead, is that the
failure to tell the truth precludes the exercise of a partner's autonomy, and
prevents the co-operation that is necessary for trust and for the flourishing of
human relationships:

When the freedom of choice that secrecy gives one person limits or destroys that of others, it affects not only his own claims to respect, but
theirs. Because it eludes interference, secrecy is central to the planning of
every form of injury to human beings.

(Bok, 1982: 26)

The English criminal law's approach to disclosure – one of common sense
imbued both with a readily comprehensible morality and a faultless liberal

logic – is an immediately appealing one. When the judge in Feston Konzani's trial directed the jury that for the defence of consent to be successful, they had to be sure that the complainants' consent was 'willing and conscious', and when the Court of Appeal affirmed that direction, it is indisputable that their approach would chime with the views of many, if not most, people. The Court may not have been able to invent an obligation to disclose where none existed in law, but by affirming that a belief in consent absent disclosure was not congruent with an honest belief (the only kind that matters), it managed to bring in by the back door a *de facto* obligation on HIV positive people to disclose their status to sexual partners in order to avoid a criminal conviction and almost certain imprisonment if transmission in fact occurs.

To the extent that the Court's approach corresponds with popular sentiment it is, of course, democratically defensible. But it is also, I would argue, an approach whose limitations and potential for injustice are substantial, and which should therefore be subjected to close and careful scrutiny. More specifically, in the context of this book, it is important to recognise that it is an approach whose intuitive appeal reflects certain assumptions about knowledge, reason, choice, and action – categories of thought which are themselves the product, and constitutive, of a particular liberal-political and moral-philosophical model of what it is to be human, and what it is to be responsible. It is an approach that ignores the lived experience of HIV positive people, the real and documented difficulties they may face in disclosing to intimates, and the fact that what matters in the long run is not disclosure as such but the prevention of onward transmission. Because, as the law currently stands, liability may only be imposed if transmission in fact occurs, it is inevitable that juries will be evaluating the conduct of people who have already – in legal terms – caused bodily harm. Such people are thus, irrespective of their (reasonable) belief that safer sex is more important than disclosure, necessarily people who have a high hurdle to leap if they are to satisfy their (probably HIV negative) peers that they did nothing wrong.

One, perfectly reasonable, response to explanations for non-disclosure revealed in the literature would be that they are simply irrelevant to the question of responsibility (i.e. liability) because they amount to motive – and motive is irrelevant to liability. The person who steals out of greed is as much a thief as the person who steals because she is starving, and so the person who fails to disclose because of privacy concerns, or because of a fear of violence by a partner is as responsible as the person who fails to disclose his HIV status because, for selfish reasons, he wants unprotected sex with a partner who he believes will refuse this if his status is known. Viewed in a purely ethical light, it is difficult to deny the strength of this argument. Just as non-maleficence is a central principle informing the physician's duty to a patient, so it may be argued that an HIV positive person's duty to a sexual partner is to do them no harm. Similarly, a Kantian commitment to the categorical imperative would demand that the truth be told. Others should not be treated as means to one's own ends. The law, however, is not (and can never, nor should not, be) an institution that effects such principles or imperatives *tout court*. If it were so then intentional killings would always be murder (which the defences of provocation and self-defence demonstrate is not the case) and – arguably – neither an honest nor a reasonable belief in consent would be treated as a defence to rape. The point is that the criminal law makes allowances. These allowances may take the form of justification (as in the 'concession to human frailty' that provocation provides) and provide a partial defence; or of excuse (as in self-defence) and provide a full one.

However, as things currently stand, 'being responsible' in the English criminal law relating to the reckless transmission of HIV entails a *de facto*, if not *de jure*, obligation to disclose known HIV status. Although it is the practising of safer sex that minimises the risk of transmission and not the fact of disclosure, it is the latter that has been established as a key determinant of liability in cases where transmission has occurred. Coupled with a failure on the part of the Court of Appeal to clarify whether the use of condoms will preclude a finding of recklessness, and a refusal to accept that general knowledge of the risks associated with unprotected sex is relevant to the question of whether consent exists, this emphasis on disclosure is one that affirms a model of responsibility based on the principles of liberalism at the expense of the lived experience of people with an HIV positive diagnosis. Never mind that the HIV positive woman who fails to disclose because she fears violence or the loss of economic support will be sent to jail if she infects a male partner who would not agree to using a condom even if asked to do so. Her failure to respect his interests, irrespective of her attempts to be responsible in a way that is manageable for her, means that she may legitimately be subject to public censure and punishment. To the extent that the defence is available in principle, but not in practice, its concession to human fallibility – and the protection it is intended to provide – is all but illusory.

And this is, of course, only to be expected. The criminal law denies – or, put more strongly and accurately, must deny – the relevance of people's lived experience of what it is to be responsible and of their ability to behave responsibly in particular contexts, at particular times, with particular people and with regard to particular behaviours. It must deny the relevance of such experience and such ability because to do otherwise would result in an infinitely individuated mode of criminal adjudication that would undermine the very function of a legal system within a liberal democratic polity – which is to establish and sustain a set of behavioural standards that apply equally to all, and against which all may legitimately be judged. In the context of criminal law's response to the sexual transmission HIV this means that a person's actual ability to discuss HIV positive status with partner(s), the nature of the relationship between that person and the partner (for example, husband and wife, casual sex partners, client and sex worker), the respective gender and sexual orientation of the partners, and the context in which viral transmission occurs (for example, matrimonial bed, sauna, or brothel) are all irrelevant to the question of liability for such transmission. They may not be irrelevant for the purposes of deciding whether to prosecute a particular incident of transmission (it may not be thought to be in the public interest, or there may be evidential difficulties), or for determining questions of culpability at the sentencing stage in the event of a guilty verdict; but for the purposes of establishing whether the HIV positive defendant *was* responsible for transmitting the virus to someone else, and whether that defendant should be held responsible *for* doing so (which are the issues that inform questions of criminal liability in this context), these factors can, and must, be ignored.

For some people this is not a problem, it is the solution. Within the paradigmatic mode of legal reasoning it is necessary to essentialise, i.e. to translate (and by doing so abstract and reduce) facts in the world to elements that can be 'read' by law. If we accept, without question, that HIV transmission is a harm with which the criminal law should be concerned, that the cause of such harm can be located in the actions of a particular agent, that the requisite fault element is established if there exists proof of a specified mental state with respect to transmission on the agent's part, and that the only way of avoiding liability (if all these elements are present) is the existence of a legally recognised defence, then it is inevitable that people aware of their HIV positive status who transmit HIV to their partners will be treated as responsible for doing so. But, and this is critical, such a conclusion is only inevitable *if* one frames one's thinking about responsibility by applying the internal and inexorable logic of the criminal law, and by accepting the philosophical principles and established analytical categories upon which it is based.

In the next, and final, chapter I will consider some of the limitations of that logic in the context of HIV transmission. Here I simply want to conclude with some basic but important observations. The first is that the Court of Appeal's emphasis on non-disclosure may have negative public health consequences. For example, because there is a *de facto* requirement for an HIV-positive person to disclose prior to sex (in case transmission occurs, a case is brought against them, and they want to argue that there was consent to the risk of transmission) this may provide a disincentive for an HIV positive person who has not disclosed, especially in the context of casual sex, *to* disclose in the event of condom failure if condoms have been used. Disclosure in the event of such failure is important so that a partner may, if it is clinically indicated, access post-exposure prophylaxis (treatment that may, if taken quickly, be effective in preventing HIV from taking hold in the body (Fisher *et al*, 2006). Equally important, the emphasis on non-disclosure may result in false and dangerous assumptions about the HIV status of one's sexual partner. To the extent that the Court has indicated that disclosure is necessary to avoid criminal liability it is not inconceivable that some people may (wrongly) assume that sexual partners who say nothing about their HIV status must therefore be HIV negative – why would they risk criminal liability? – and fail to take precautions against transmission, or to ask that precautions are taken. The second observation is more jurisprudential and less practical, but no less important for that. The function of disclosure in cases involving the reckless transmission of HIV is to enable the court to determine whether the person to whom HIV was transmitted may be treated as someone who has given consent to the risk of transmission (and is therefore not properly characterised as the victim of a crime who has been harmed), or whether the defendant honestly believed that there was such consent (and is therefore not properly characterised as the perpetrator of a crime). As such, in cases where HIV positive people who are aware of their diagnosis infect others, disclosure operates as a critical marker of (legal) responsibility. But whereas the mere fact of disclosure operates (and can only operate as) a decontextualised, atemporal, signifier for law,[51] it operates as a far more complex indicator of responsibility for those living with HIV and AIDS and who must determine whether, and if so how, to disclose to people with whom they have, or anticipate, an intimate physical relationship. This means that it is important to reflect, as I have sought to do here, on what disclosure means for HIV positive people. If the decision not to disclose is understood simply as a rational, selfish and self-serving choice made by people who want to 'use' others as means to their own ends, and which denies them the right to make informed choices of their own, the justification for punishing such people is, at least in a criminal justice system informed by Kantian retributivism, a strong one. If, however, the decision not to disclose is not properly characterised in this way then the justification is significantly weaker. Put more strongly, it may be possible to argue that not disclosing may – under certain conditions, for some people – be appropriately understood as either a responsible or reasonable course of action, and that to punish such people who transmit HIV without first disclosing their status to those whom they infect *using non-disclosure as a reason to do so* is unjustifiable.

51 It is important to recognise that whereas law treats disclosure as something that either has, or has not, happened, it is better understood as a process that – where it occurs – may take place over time. It may also involve the use of non-verbal cues, and be either oblique ('we need to use condoms') or direct ('I am HIV positive'). As a result, some people living with HIV may subjectively believe that they have disclosed but be treated as if they have not. Similarly, a person to whom disclosure has been made may not recognise it as such, or understand the implications. Given that liability for reckless transmission may only be avoided if there is consent to risk, disclosure *per se* may not provide an HIV positive person with a defence.

Chapter 6

Responsibility, HIV transmission and the criminal law

> Finding and using the implicit and explicit theories that inform the personal, political, and educational approaches to preserve the lives of sexual dissidents is not just an immediate project: *it is our lives*.
>
> (Patton, 1996: 139)

Introduction

What, then, is it to be responsible in the time of AIDS? What are the justifications for and problems with deploying the criminal law against people who transmit HIV to those with whom they are engaged in acts of sexual intimacy? And what does the use of criminal law in this context reveal to us about the law itself? This book has been an attempt if not to answer those questions then at least to address them in a sustained and critical way. In this last chapter it is not my intention to review in detail everything that has already been said. Instead, I want first to summarise the key themes that have emerged during the discussion before concluding with some reflections on the way in which the criminal law approaches, and constructs, the subject of responsibility.

The first theme, explored in Chapter 1, is that there is a necessarily complicated relationship between the human rights of people living with HIV and AIDS and the public interest in minimising the spread of the virus. In the United Kingdom, as in western continental Europe, North America, and Australasia we are fortunate in having a lower prevalence of HIV and AIDS than in regions that are poorer, that exist in states of more or less permanent conflict, and where migration for survival is a fact of life. In these regions, where access to HAART and basic health services cannot be assumed, living with HIV and AIDS is a fight for survival: whether or not a person living with HIV or AIDS should be sent to prison, or subjected to compulsory isolation or detention, for infecting another or because they pose a risk to others is a subsidiary concern. But in the developed west and north, where PLHA have – at least in theory, if not always realised in practice – an expectation that care and treatment will be available, questions about criminalising transmission and the legitimacy of exercising other coercive state powers are, in a sense, a luxury that can be explored.[1] The consequence of that exploration has been to affirm, as a matter of general principle, that PLHA constitute a vulnerable population for whom human rights protection is critically important, but that those rights are not absolute and may be limited or qualified for the wider 'public good'. The difficulty, or tension, arises in jurisdictions such as England and Wales because the debates about the relationship between health and human rights in the context of HIV and AIDS, in which the promotion of human rights has come to be recognised as positively correlated with minimising the spread of the epidemic, have centred on the importance of rights in those areas of the world in which HIV prevalence is high and human rights protection traditionally low. This means that in this country, where (subject to some egregious exceptions[2]) human rights are protected and access to treatment is available, it is easier to focus on the secondary issue of responsibility for transmission and on the techniques that can, and should, be used to regulate, control and censure those who infect others. By this I do not mean to suggest that questions concerning responsibility are not worth asking – this whole book has been an attempt to demonstrate why they are. Rather, I mean that we are in the 'fortunate' position of being able to turn political and jurisprudential attention to the moral obligations of people living with HIV, and the ways in which these may legitimately be enforced *via* legislation and through the development of legal principles in case law, instead of having, perforce, to focus that attention on the more basic concerns that affect people living with HIV and AIDS elsewhere in the world.

The political and jurisprudential attention to which I have referred provided the raw material for the rest of the book. In Chapter 2 I sought, through a detailed analysis of the trial of Feston Konzani, to demonstrate how the law in this area works in practice, and to highlight the ways in which the concepts of responsibility, consent and disclosure are articulated in the messy, complicated, and emotionally charged context of a criminal court. The criminalisation of HIV transmission, as I hope that analysis demonstrated, is not merely an intellectual puzzle whose solution lies in the application of rareified legal principle to facts, but a subject that engages real people, with

---

1 It is, of course, only those who have a right to remain in the jurisdiction who typically have access to any free care and treatment that may be available. In England and Wales National Health Service treatment is available to those whose asylum claims are pending, but not to those whose have failed (see the NHS (Charges to Overseas Visitors) Charging Regulations 1989, and the NHS (Charges to Overseas Visitors) Charging (Amendment) Regulations 2004). Furthermore, the House of Lords has made it clear that returning someone to a country where there are difficulties in accessing HIV treatment does not constitute inhuman and degrading treatment for the purposes of Art 3 of the ECHR: *N (FC) (Appellant) v Secretary of State for the Home Department (Respondent)* [2005] UKHL 31.

2 See above, n 1.

real concerns. In Chapter 3 I explored the key issues of harm and causation. There I sought to explain that, while it is possible to conceive of HIV as a bodily injury with which law may legitimately be concerned, it is important to reflect on why that is, and that there may different, equally legitimate, ways of comprehending the 'harm' that infection represents. I also set out, in some detail, the technical problems that may be associated with proving transmission and, I hope, explained how there is the potential for miscarriages of justice if the science of transmission is not fully understood by those with responsibility for processing cases in the criminal justice system. Chapter 4, the most theoretically dense part of the book, was an attempt to explain why it was that, after twenty years of the epidemic, the criminal law finally caught up with people who recklessly transmit HIV to their partners. Briefly stated, the thesis put forward was as follows. HIV positive people represent the paradigm Other of risk society, and recklessness the paradigm fault. Those who are reckless with respect to HIV transmission are those who represent one of the most significant threats to our physical and ontological security. The criminal law of assault in England and Wales had, during the course of the epidemic, developed in such a way that it became possible to criminalise those who harm others in ways less immediate and direct than had previously been necessary in order to secure a conviction. As a result, it became legally possible, and to impose liability on those who transmit HIV to others. Those who recklessly transmit HIV became, as a result, a legitimate focus for the criminal law and could justifiably be censured and punished for the injury they caused their partners.

The purpose of Chapter 5 was, through a close reading the Court of Appeal's reasoning in *Dica* and *Konzani*, to explain the complex inter-relationship between consent, knowledge and disclosure. In those judgments, the Court came to affirm that while there was no legal obligation to disclose known HIV positive status to a partner to whom HIV might be transmitted, it was 'incongruous' for a defendant to raise the defence of consent, or a mistaken belief in consent, in the absence of disclosure. In reaching this conclusion the Court affirmed, in terms, the moral obligation to disclose and the dangers of not doing so. It is irrelevant, for the purposes of establishing liability through the effective denial of the defence of consent to those who remain silent or lie, what the reasons for non-disclosure may be; and it is irrelevant that there is no necessary correlation between disclosure and the practising of safer sex. What matters, in the last analysis, is the violation of the autonomy of the person to whom the virus is transmitted and the denial of their right to make a willing and conscious choice about the risks they are prepared to take.

Being responsible before the law[3]

As a process, rather than an outcome (Urban Walker, 1997), living, or attempting to live, a life of integrity necessarily involves interactions with others; and these interactions may have both positive and negative consequences for those involved. Similarly, the response of others (both human and institutional) to that life and those interactions may be critical to the point of judgment and proscription. It is also, I would argue, important to recognise that the extent to which a person is able to live such a life will, in part, be contingent on their socio-economic and civil status, and the (often) multiple and complex relationships of dependency, care and obligation that they have with others.

Put in more concrete terms particularly relevant to the concerns of this book, people may be honest, open and communicative with intimate partner(s) in some respects and contexts but not in others. If it is a new relationship they may withhold information about known HIV positive status until they have established sufficient trust, or if it is an established one withhold such information for fear of rejection (and of any negative material consequences for them and/or their dependants); and for their partner(s) this may be information which they wish to have, while for some it may be information about which they would prefer to remain ignorant (Greene *et al*, 2003; Klitzman and Bayer, 2003). In each of these situations, from each person's perspective, the meaning, value and – importantly – the implications of embodied autonomy vary.

For feminists, and for other critical theorists of law, the very notion of autonomy is, of course, problematic. On the one hand it is a pre-condition of agency, and therefore of potential utility in challenging oppressive and patriarchal socio-economic structures; on the other it is a value that has traditionally served to occlude or deny the importance of the relational, the (inter-)dependent, and the affective and whose socio-cultural effects have included the political prioritisation of the individual as a bearer of rights *contra mundum*. Among others, Jennifer Nedelsky has argued that the extent to which autonomy has any value or meaning, or is able to serve any feminist political or legal objective, is contingent on acknowledging its dependency on the corporeal and relational realities of human life (Nedelsky, 1989a; 1989b). For her, and for a number of feminist scholars who have used or been influenced by her work (see, for example, Friedman, 1997; Lacey, 1998), autonomy is a valuable analytical resource only to the extent that its linkage to the physical and psychic domains is recognised. Only then can it contribute effectively to the possibility of a feminist politics in which a person's integrity is fully recognised, and a legal system that is alert, sensitive and responsive to the felt experience of those whose integrity is violated or compromised by others.

3 The remaining part of this chapter is drawn largely from Weait, 2007.

These insights have been hugely influential, and form an important counter-point to the dominant liberal tradition which sees autonomy as having to do almost exclusively with 'objective' reality and the mental realm. They have also provided a theoretical position from which legal reform, especially in the field of sexual offences and domestic violence, has been able to develop (and, indeed, from which such reform can be constructively criticised). There remain, however, difficulties for advocates of this theoretical position when a person's expression of embodied autonomy, of their integrity, appears to undermine rather than to sustain or nourish the embodied autonomy of those with whom they are in relations of intimacy, of dependency, or of love, care and affection (Inness, 1992) – in other words, where it results in what might be termed harm. This is particularly so for the HIV positive person, whose attempts to live such a life may not always be successful and who may, as a result of failing effectively to communicate with, or to take care of, partners be the source of an infection for which there is treatment (where available) but no cure. How are these people to be judged? On what basis are they to be held responsible before the law?

The vast majority of those criminal law theorists who have engaged with the idea of responsibility have adopted (more or less uncritically) a moral-philosophical framework which takes the responsible agent as the foundational unit of analysis (see, for example, Moore, 1997; Tadros, 2005). This means that when engaging in discussions of what it is to be responsible their focus and emphasis – whether or not they are engaging in critique or criticism – are centred on the capacities and/or characters that human beings *qua* individuated agents possess, or on the choices they make. According to these analytical approaches being (held) responsible requires either (a) a set of capacities – including (but not limited to) cognitive skills, self- and other-awareness, foresight of consequences resulting from willed action, and an understanding of right and wrong; (b) that the person chose (consciously) to act in a particular way, and that the choice was freely made; or (c) that her conduct was in some way expressive of her character. Irrespective of one's preferred mode of analysis a person's capacities, choices or character are thus both constitutive *of* agency *and* a basis on which their exercise or expression – or non-exercise and non-expression – can be (morally) evaluated. Put another way, the individual agent, her actions, and the consequences that they (are seen to) produce provide the conceptual framework within which theories of responsibility are built; and responsibility provides the conceptual framework within which the actions of individual agents are, and may legitimately be, judged. Legal theorists for whom capacity, choice and character provide an adequate, if ever refinable, basis for thinking about responsibility and those for whom such analytical categories provide a point of critical departure are both therefore caught in an ultimately self-referential mode of reasoning about what being, and being held, responsible means.

More importantly, and this is the nub of my argument, this kind of theorising, whatever its particular concern and focus, takes the criminal law as a given, and – whether explicitly or implicitly – asserts that the conduct, consequences and people with which it is concerned can be and are appropriately analysed and critiqued in terms both of the criminal law's own institutionalised logic and the moral and political traditions within which it is embedded. Because of this, such theorising – while important in enabling us better to understand that logic and the principles which inform it – is necessarily constrained in its understanding of what 'being responsible' means. My argument is that while we may learn much about the criminal law's construction of responsibility from such theorising, because the criminal law is itself a conservative institution the function of which is not to liberate but to repress, censure and condemn, it precludes us from thinking differently, laterally and imaginatively about the very conduct, consequences and people that are the objects of its repression, censure and condemnation. The fact that criminal law cannot, as I hope I have shown, respond adequately to people's lived experience of responsibility, or be responsive to difference and specificity, does not mean that radical critics – feminist and otherwise – who think that this is problematic are ham-strung. Far from it. It is my contention that we can use the very constraints and limitations of criminal law as the justification for arguing, should there be the desire and the political will to do so, that criminalising certain conduct, consequences and people may be unhelpful, counter-productive and unjustifiable. Put more strongly, it is my contention that with respect to some conduct, some consequences and some people, *being responsible* as lawyers, whether theorists or practitioners, entails recognising the importance and value of developing sound and defensible arguments for – or at the very least opening our minds to – decriminalisation. The fact that we inhabit a society governed by the constraints of *realpolitik* and deafened by the clamour of populist retributivism, in which an ever more extensive and punitive system of criminal law is understood as *the* mechanism that can provide *the* solution, does not mean that we should allow our imaginations to rot.

It is not possible to talk about what being *responsible* means without first being clear about *being* responsible. In the context of law and legal theory this necessarily entails addressing the question of legal subjectivity. Only subjects of law are legally accountable at law. Therefore, being held to account depends on first satisfying the conditions necessary to be treated as a 'legal subject'. In the context of criminal law – these conditions are framed in terms of identity and capacity (understood in terms of cognitive functioning and willed action), and organised around certain rebuttable presumptions. Thus, an adult human being is presumed to operate with a set of mental capacities that link conduct (and any consequences of that conduct) to volition, and unless – by virtue of immaturity or mental impairment – it is not possible to make that link, *prima facie* liability is established. A second condition of (criminal) liability is, in keeping with the principles of 'orthodox subjectivism', a requirement that the legal subject exhibit fault of a kind necessary for the offence (which will typically set out the fault requirements) to be made out. Such fault, expressed usually in terms of intention, recklessness or knowledge (whether with respect to conduct, consequences or circumstances), expresses – for want of a better term – the *moral dimension* of legal subjectivity. A legal subject that meets the primary capacity condition will only be treated as responsible (i.e. criminally liable) if they also exhibit, through voluntary action, certain morally significant states of mind with respect to that action. Those states of mind (intention, recklessness, etc) provide, where present, justification for the moral condemnation that criminal liability represents. They, along with the capacity condition, also reflect the particular moral philosophical and liberal political heritage that underpins contemporary Anglo-American criminal law. From a philosophical perspective they represent a Kantian commitment to treating people as ends, not means. To be treated as a responsible subject is to have one's humanity acknowledged and respected. To be held responsible for those actions which define subjectivity in these terms is to have that subjectivity affirmed (see, for example, Gardner, 2003). From a liberal political perspective, these states of mind and the presumption of capacity are constitutive of personhood. Personhood depends on freedom of action and on individual self-realisation. To be held personally responsible is to have one's autonomy – *the* central liberal value – respected.

One of the most important aspects of *legal* subjectivity in the criminal context is that its meaning is established through the process of adjudication. Adjudication is based on reconstruction. The legal settlement of conflict, where this concerns the determination of liability for the conduct or consequences that have brought about such conflict, provides the occasion for identifying the rights and responsibilities of the legal subject. While the nature of such subjectivity may be a necessary and prior inquiry when determining legal claims relating to status and entitlement, in a world without dispute there would be no need to determine (*via* a retrospective analysis of the capacities and character manifested in *this* person's behaviour on *that* occasion) the conditions or criteria that should and must be met before responsibility for acting in a particular way, or for bringing about particular effects, can be established. A consequence of this is that the legal subject that is constructed through adjudication (at trial and on appeal) is one that is necessarily embedded within the social, economic, and political processes and values that have contributed over time to the development, and informed the values, of adjudicative procedure and reasoning. This means that the legal subject of adjudication is one that can only be framed – in our legal system – within the logic of due process under the rule of law. As such, *legal* subjectivity, and the responsibilities it entails, are (and must be) of a kind that only make sense *for the law* if they are premised on assumptions of equality, generality, and neutrality. And, it follows, the construction of subjectivity and responsibility *through* law can only provide an account of subjectivity and responsibility *for* law, and this account is one that will inevitably occlude the reality, and deny the relevance of, inequality, specificity and partiality.

Taken together, our moral-philosophical, liberal-political and due process inheritance have combined to produce an idealised model of the rational, prudent person whose self-fulfilment and self-realisation depends on respect for autonomy, on choices that are freely made, and on relationships – whether of an economic, political, social or intimate nature – that are entered into voluntarily, as an expression of individual will. This dominant model of personhood, which finds expression in the discourse of legal reasoning about subjectivity, necessarily produces an account of responsibility that further distances it from the diversity and uniqueness of people's individual, relational and social experience. The responsible subject is responsible *for* (and *only* for) that behaviour and those effects that can be identified with the necessary criteria of personhood (rational choices freely made within a coherent and internalised moral universe as the result of deliberative cognitive processing) (see, further, Hart, 1968); and the responsible subject may thus only legitimately be *held* responsible (and, in the context of criminal law, punished), where his actions and their effects manifest – or may be interpreted as – a failure to exercise the responsibility that defines him as a subject of, and for, law. Understood in this way, it is not merely the adjudicative process that has the (inevitable and necessary) effect of denying the legal subject's humanity (*it* has none to deny); such denial is a consequence of that process being informed by the very values that provide *its* content. Law is necessarily reductivist. People are, and must be, reduced to persons. Responsibility is, and must be, reduced to the quality that defines persons. To be held responsible is to have one's personhood respected and one's legal subjectivity acknowledged; and to have one's personhood respected and one's legal subjectivity acknowledged implies an acceptance of the account of responsibility on which these depend.

For critical criminal law theorists this descriptively thin but normatively potent account of subjectivity and responsibility is one that poses interrelated significant theoretical, methodological and – critically – political challenges. These challenges stem from the fact that endogenous critiques which focus on doctrinal inconsistency in the treatment of subjectivity and responsibility may, while exposing incoherence, end up simply highlighting that incoherence; and exogenous critiques which seek to evaluate their legal meaning in light of social 'facts', cultural traditions, psychological insights, ethical values or political ideologies run the risk of reducing law to, or criticising it for being, something it is not (nor can ever be). This is not to suggest that it is theoretically futile to argue that the inherent (and inescapable) contradictions in the criminal law's treatment of responsibility are the result of a positivising project that seeks, but necessarily fails, to exclude questions of communal morality and human sociality from questions of liability (see, for example, Norrie, 1998; 2000); nor that it is unimportant to emphasise the way in which a pervasive legal rhetoric of rationality serves to provide a legitimating gloss on interpretations and decisions that serve dominant socio-economic interests (see, for example Kelman, 1980–81); nor that it is fruitless to point to the fact that for the criminal law to acknowledge the 'real world', and to renounce its conceptual formalism, would (because such formalism is necessary for the individualised blaming function that is criminal law's essence) be both undesirable and logically impossible (Seidman, 1996). Such critical insights, along with those which emphasise the historically contingent and socially constructed nature of legal subjectivity (see, for example, Norrie, 1993; Lacey, 2001a; 2001b) and the extent to which is determined by procedural and evidential rules (see, for example, Farmer, 1996) have provided an important and necessary foil to those whose work affirms, whether implicitly or explicitly, the dominant liberal and/or moral-philosophical conceptual heritage in criminal law theorising (see, for example, Hart, 1968; Moore, 1997; Horder, 2004; Tadros, 2005).

The same is true of specifically feminist theorising about the criminal law. Feminist legal theory has ensured that sex and gender are acknowledged as a (and for some such theorists *the*) critical issues for any legal scholarship that seeks to contribute to the broader political goal of eliminating unjustified discrimination against people on identity grounds. But, like critical legal scholarship more generally, it too has had to confront subjectivity and responsibility as these are understood within law for law. As far as subjectivity is concerned, the brightest illumination that feminist scholars have shone into the dark recesses of conventional legal scholarship is the fact that law's subjects (or objects, depending on one's point of view) have bodies – bodies which (depending on their sex) bleed, gestate, give birth, nurture, have the capacity for pleasure and pain, connect with other bodies in conflict, love and sex, bodies which work, live and die (see, generally, Naffine and Owens, 1997). This insight has done much to alert other than the most unreconstructed in the legal academy to the differential impact that law – neutral, impartial and therefore 'fair' – has in fact had, and continues to have, on differently sexed/gendered human beings. And it is, I think, an insight that can also help us understand the way in which the law responds to those, like people living with HIV and AIDS, whose bodies are 'abnormal'. But the assertion and (partial) recognition of sexed/gendered human embodiment, while it has been critical to, and (in certain contexts) effective as part of, the feminist political project of asserting equality on grounds of status – in, for example, employment – it has been a far more complex and vexed project within the sphere of legal reasoning and adjudication.

The reason for this is that the subject of legal reasoning (the woman, the man, the person living with HIV) as far as questions of liability are concerned is necessarily without substantive, or biographical, content. It is important to be clear here. I do not mean that liberal legal reasoning is incapable of articulating and accommodating difference and specificity (whether that be in matters of gender, race, sexuality, HIV status etc). Indeed, it is one of the reasons for liberalism's continued domination in the indus-trialised West as a political philosophy and/or mode of governance (Dean, 1999) that it has managed to recognise and give at least partial effect through legislation to the claims of marginalised groups. Rather, what I mean to suggest is that this recognition and the effecting of these claims is successful (where it is) at the level, and as the result of, political struggle within liberal democratic polities. They do not (and cannot, I believe) succeed – as I hope I have explained – within the confines of liberal legal reasoning itself.

Concluding observations

The criminal law's approach to the question of responsibility is one based on a model of subjectivity that will, and must, deny the specificity of individual human experience. For those, like me, who have been brought up within a democratic polity, who take the rule of law as both a given and as funda-mental, who are the product of a legal education whose source material manifests values informed by a tradition of liberalism, and whose conduct is judged according to a set of particular philosophical assumptions about what it is to be a person, it requires a significant leap of imagination (or, possibly, a complete suspension of disbelief) to be able to question the premises that underpin what it is to be, and be held, responsible in such a society at such a time. Those premises deny – or at the very least marginalise – the relevance of my gender (male), my class (middle), my sexuality (gay), my colour (white), my ethnicity (Caucasian), and my political status (British citizen). They ignore – or at the very least marginalise – the relevance of time in which I am living, my biography, my relationships, my character, and my political and spiritual beliefs. They are premises which assume that the individual human being is the locus – or at the very least the starting point – of any inquiry, but demand a prior distillation of homeopathic intensity. For the theoretician of responsibility wedded to the articulation and/or elaboration of the con-ventional account, the richness, variety and complexity of what it is to live as a human being is abstracted to a set of cognitive processes, volitions and choices. The object (and subject) of the inquiry – who becomes, through this process of abstraction, simply an agent – is assumed to have a moral com-pass; but it is a moral compass whose origin, range, and content is treated as a given and which functions simply as a means of evaluating the agent's conduct against the (same) moral compass that all other agents, whether individually or collectively, are assumed to possess.

If I am correct in my assertion that a criminal law informed by these moral, philosophical and political principles will, and must, have these effects; and if it is accepted that those effects may have adverse consequences both for indi-viduals attempting to live responsible lives, and for public health more gener-ally (to the extent that the criminalisation of HIV transmission may have adverse effects on the management and control of the epidemic) then it seems to me that there are – as I suggested earlier – two choices. The first is to reflect the reality of individual experience in adjudicative processes concerned with determinations of responsible subjectivity. This, I believe to be politically unrealistic since it would mean dismantling the most fundamental premises and values that inform the rule of law. This is not to argue – let me be clear – that political projects which seek to address the adverse *effects* of adjudication should not be pursued. Such projects are important and can lead to beneficial outcomes for people whose interests the law fails to recognise and protect. Rather, it is simply to suggest that attempts to seek substantive justice for individual human beings by particularising the legal subject are doomed to failure. The second choice, and one that I believe could serve to promote a more authentic and socially beneficial approach to the meaning, practice and expression of responsibility than that which the law constructs and reinforces, is to decriminalise the reckless transmission of HIV. This, to be sure, is a radical suggestion which will be rejected by those who believe that the function of the criminal law is to articulate the moral sentiment of a society that (a) treats HIV infection as a harm, (b) views unjustifiable risk-taking and non-disclosure as reprehensible, and (c) constructs the person to whom HIV is transmitted as a victim. For those who subscribe to such a view – and I am under no illusions as to their prevalence – decriminalisation is unthinkable; and such people are unlikely to be converted by any argument, least of all that which I advance here. Nevertheless, I do think it is important to question the premises upon which this view is based. First, those who accept the legitimacy of criminalisation need to recognise that it is based on an individualised model of fault and conduct that ignores the fact that HIV exists in populations and that its transmission occurs between people. Each person who transmits HIV to another is someone who was him- or herself infected. If HIV is understood as a social fact rather than merely as a quality or characteristic of individuals it becomes legitimate to develop responses to transmission that centre on the social consequences and benefits of any intervention (such as human rights sensitive public health provisions) rather than on the censure of particular people. Such consequentialist thinking is, no doubt, anathema to those committed to a Kantian analysis of responsibility; but I would argue, if our principal concern is (as I think it must be) the eradication of this dreadful virus through the prevention of onward transmission, that such an analysis has the potential to do us more harm than good. Second, the approach that the criminal law has adopted towards responsibility for transmission is one that will deny the relevance of particular individuals' attempts to behave responsibly (by practising safer sex rather than disclosing status, for example). To the extent that it does so, it undermines those attempts and ignores the very real impediments and barriers to behaving as the law demands. Third, criminal law (unlike tort law) is not concerned with fault allocation. If a defendant meets the conditions for liability he will be held responsible; if not, he will be absolved. And yet there are strong, public health centred, arguments that emphasise the importance of joint and shared responsibility for sexual health (see, for example, Gostin, 1989). To the extent that the criminalisation of reckless transmission establishes a perpetrator/victim dyad – even in cases where the 'victim' was aware of the risks she was taking when she engaged in unprotected sex *despite* the lack of disclosure – the law is serving to undermine this important public health message. Finally, an argument for the decriminalisation of reckless HIV transmission is emphatically *not* an argument for the decriminalisation of all reckless conduct that harms the interests of others. Legal reasoning in the common law tradition is grounded in analogy. As such, it is tempting to deploy a general account or analysis in other contexts. While it may be that the pragmatic approach I have advocated here may have application elsewhere, that is for others to judge; and some may argue that the wider implications of the position I take here is one that would, if applied in other contexts, have morally and politically unsupportable effects. I am not, however, arguing for a principle of general application. What I am arguing is that where the negative social impact of criminalisation in a particular context has the potential to outweigh any social benefits it might achieve (as I believe is the case here) it is legitimate to question whether criminalisation is, as a matter of principle, always and in every case defensible and justifiable.

I want to end this book by reminding ourselves of what we must not forget. HIV transmission occurs between human beings. Those human beings may be male or female masculine or feminine, hetero-, homo- or bisexual. They may be infants, adolescents, or adults. They may be mothers, fathers or carers. They may be orphans. They may belong to any ethnic, religious, or national group. They may be in marital, casual, committed or commercial sexual relationships with others. They may be HIV negative or HIV positive. They may know their HIV status, have unconfirmed beliefs or be ignorant about it, or not have given it a moment's thought. They may consider themselves to be 'at risk', or immune. They may know or believe, rightly or wrongly, their sexual partner(s) to be HIV positive, or HIV negative. They may understand the way in which HIV is transmitted, be unsure, or ignorant. Those who have contracted HIV may have been infected decades ago and be asymptomatic, or they may have been infected last year and have been diagnosed as suffering from an AIDS-related illness. They may have contracted HIV through maternal-fetal or perinatal transmission, a blood transfusion, needle sharing in the course of injecting drug use, consensual sexual intercourse or rape. They may have taken no precautions against transmission, or attempted unsuccessfully to protect themselves. They may have a high or negligible viral load. They may have access to care, treatment, advice and support, fail to take advantage of these where they are available, or be denied such services. They may know the identity of the person who infected them, or neither know nor care. They may feel ashamed, empowered, stupid or unlucky (or all of these things).

They may voluntarily disclose their HIV positive status to those with whom they have sex of a kind that poses a risk of transmission, or stay silent. They may tell the truth if asked, or they may lie. They may not care about infecting others, or they may take every precaution against doing so. They may feel responsible for their infection, or that someone else is responsible for infecting them.

The point to be made is this: HIV affects everyone, whether they are positive or negative, and whether they know this or not. It affects them in different ways, in different contexts and for different reasons. Those who are HIV negative may, unless they take precautions against transmission in situations where that is a risk, become infected; those who are HIV positive may, unless they take precautions, infect others. There is, therefore, for those in each category a responsibility, both to themselves and to others, to minimise the risk of onward transmission. This simple truth of prevention, central to safer sex and health promotion initiatives in the field of HIV and AIDS, nevertheless fails to capture – as the variety of experience, attitudes, emotions and statuses described above demonstrate – what being responsible means and entails, both for people living with HIV/AIDS and those at risk of infection. Nor does it give any indication of how people, individually or in their relations with others, are able to put, or are prevented from putting, their understanding of what being responsible means into practice. Put more simply, being responsible in the time of AIDS is both critically important and deeply problematic; and it is something that the criminalisation of reckless transmission fails abjectly to address.

References

Adam, BD, Sears, A and Schellenberg, EG (2000) 'Accounting for unsafe sex: Interviews with men who have sex with men', *Journal of Sex Research*, 37: 24–36

AIDSFONDS (2004) *Detention or Prevention? A Report on the Impact and Use of Criminal Law on Public Health and the Position of People Living with HIV*, Amsterdam: AIDS FONDS

Albert J, Wahlberg, J, Leitner, T, Escanilla, D and Uhlen, M (1994) 'Analysis of a rape case by direct sequencing of the HIV-1 pol and gag genes', *Journal of Virology*, 68: 5918–5924

Alcabes, P (2006) 'Heart of darkness: AIDS, Africa, and race', *Virginia Quarterly Review*, Winter: 5–9

Alldridge, P (1993) 'Sex, lies and the criminal law', *Northern Ireland Legal Quarterly*, 44: 250–268

Allen, MJ (1996) 'Look who's stalking: seeking a solution to the problem of stalking', *Web Journal of Current Legal Issues*, 4

Alonzo, AA and Reynolds, NR (1995) 'Stigma, HIV and AIDS: An exploration and elaboration of a stigma trajectory', *Social Science and Medicine*, 41: 303–315

Altman LK (1994) 'AIDS mystery that won't go away: did a dentist infect 6 patients?', *New York Times*, (5 July 1994) Available at <http://querynytimescom/gst/fullpagehtml?sec=health&res=9C02E0DB1E3CF936A35754C0A962958260> (accessed May 20 2007)

Altman, D (1984) 'AIDS: The Politicization of an Epidemic', *Socialist Review*, 14: 93–109

Amaro, H (1995) 'Love, sex, and power: considering women's realities in HIV prevention', *American Psychologist*, 50: 437–447

Ashford, B (2006) 'The thought she might have been HIV positive never entered my head', *IC South London* (June 20 2006)

Ashworth, A (1997) 'Sentencing', in M Maguire, R Morgan and R Reiner (eds) *The Oxford Handbook of Criminology*, Oxford: Oxford University Press

Ashworth, A (2000) 'Is criminal law a lost cause?', *Law Quarterly Review*, 116: 225–256

Ashworth, A (2003) *Principles of Criminal Law* (4th ed), Oxford: Oxford University Press

Baer, J *Our Lives Before the Law: Constructing a Feminist Jurisprduence*, Princeton: Princeton University Press (1999)

Bayer R (1989) *Private Acts, Social Consequences: AIDS and the Politics of Public Health*, New York City: The Free Press

Bayer, R (1996) 'AIDS prevention: sexual ethics and responsibility', *New England Journal of Medicine*, 334: 1540–42

BBC (2004) *HIV bigamist jailed for infections*, available at <http://newsbbccouk/1/hi/england/merseyside/3389735stm> (accessed May 20 2007)

BBC (2005) *Man infected woman, 82, with HIV*, available at <http://newsbbccouk/1/hi/england/devon/4543152stm> (accessed May 20 2007)

Beccaria, C (1966) *On Crimes and Punishments*, Indianapolis: Bobbs-Merrill

Beck, U (1992a) 'From industrial society to the risk society: questions of survivial, social structure and ecological environment', *Theory, Culture and Society*, 9: 97–123

Beck, U (1992b) *Risk Society: Towards a New Modernity*, London: Sage

Beck, U (1996) 'Risk society and the provident state', in S Lash, B Szerszinski and B Wynne (eds), *Risk, Environment and Modernity: Towards a New Ecology*, London: Sage

Beck, U 'The reinvention of politics: towards a theory of reflexive modernization', in U Beck, A Giddens and S Lash (eds), *Reflexive Modernization: Politics, Tradition and Aesthetics in the Modern Social Order*, Cambridge: Polity Press

Beck, U and Beck-Gernsheim (1995) *The Normal Chaos of Love*, Cambridge: Polity Press

Beltran, ED, Ostrow, DG and Joseph, JG (1993) 'Predictors of sexual behavior change among men requesting their HIV-I antibody status: The Chicago MACS/CCS cohort of homosexual/bisexual men' *AIDS Education and Prevention*, 5: 185–195

Bentham, J (1962) 'An Introduction to the Principles of Morals and Legislation', in J Bowring (ed), *Collected Works*, Vol 1, New York: Russell

Bentham, J (1995) *The Panopticon Writings*, M Bozovic (ed), London: Verso

Bernard, E (2005) *Welsh woman given two year sentence in reckless HIV transmission case: widespread media misreporting*, (July 19 2005) available at <http://wwwaidsmapcom/en/news/09E20EF5–1067–48FC–A1D1–DF79B6C6FE2Aasp> (accessed May 20 2007)

Bernard, E (2007) *Criminal HIV Transmission*, London: National AIDS Manual

Bernard, E Azad, Y, Geretti, A-M, van Damme, AM and Weait, M (2007) *HIV Forensics: The Use of Phylogenetic Analysis as Evidence in Criminal Investigation of HIV Transmission*, London: National AIDS Manual and National AIDS Trust

Berridge V (1996) *AIDS in the UK: The Making of Policy, 1981–1994*, Oxford: Oxford University Press

Bersani, L (1988) 'Is the rectum a grave?' in D Crimp (ed) *AIDS: Cultural Analysis/Cultural Activism*, Cambridge: MIT Press

Bessant, C (2004) 'Domestic violence law – punishment or protection?', *Family Law* 34: 750

Bhaskar, R (1993) *Dialectic: the Pulse of Freedom*, London: Verso

Bibeau, G and Pedersen, D (2002) 'A return to scientific racism in medical and social sciences: the case of sexuality and the AIDS epidemic in Africa' in N Nichter and M Lock (eds) *New Horizons in Medical Anthropology: Essays in Honor of Charles Leslie*, Routledge: New York

Bingman, CR, Marks, G and Crepaz, N (2001) 'Attributions about one's HIV infection and unsafe sex in seropositive men who have sex with men', *AIDS and Behavior*, 5: 283–289

Birch, CJ, McCaw, RF, *et al* (2000) 'Molecular analysis of human immunodeficiency virus strains associated with a case of criminal transmission of the virus', *Journal of Infectious Diseases*, 182: 941–944

Bird, S and Leigh Brown, A (2001) 'Criminalisation of HIV transmission: implications for public health in Scotland', *British Medical Journal*, 235: 1174–1177

Blackstone, W ((1830)(1979)) *Commentaries*, (vol 3) Chicago: Chicago University Press

Bloor, M (1995) *The Sociology of HIV Transmission*, London: Sage

Bok, S (1978) *Lying: Moral Choices in Public and Private Life*, New York: Pantheon Books

Bok, S (1982) *Secrets: On the Ethics of Concealment and Revelation*, New York: Pantheon Books

Boulton, M, McLean, J, Fitzpatrick, R and Hart, G (1995) 'Gay men's accounts of unsafe sex', *AIDS Care*, 7: 619–630

Bourdain, A (2001) *Typhoid Mary: An Urban Historical*, Bloomsbury: New York

Bronitt, SH (1992) 'Criminal liability for the transmission of HIV/AIDS', *Criminal Law Journal*, 16: 85–93

Bronitt, SH (1994) 'Spreading disease and the criminal law', *Criminal Law Review*, 21–34

Bruner, D (2004) 'High-risk sexual behavior and failure to disclose HIV infection to sex partners: how do we respond?', *AIDS & Public Policy Journal*, 19(1/2): 11–36

Buchanan, DR, Poppen, PJ and Reisen, CJ (1996) 'The nature of partner relationship and AIDS sexual risk-taking in gay men', *Psychological Health*, 11: 541–555

Budowle, B and Harmon R (2005) 'HIV legal precedent useful for microbial forensics', *Croat Med J*, 46(4): 514–521

Burris, S, Beletsky, L, Burleson, JA, Case, P and Lazzarini, Z (2007) 'Do criminal laws influence HIV risk behavior? An empirical trial, *Temple University Beasley School of Law Research Paper No 2007–03* (Arizona State Law Journal, forthoming)

Burris, S, Dalton, HL, Miller, JL and the Yale AIDS Law Project (1993) *AIDS Law Today: A New Guide for the Public*, New Haven: Yale University Press

Campbell, CA (1995) 'Male gender roles and sexuality: implications for women's AIDS risk and prevention', *Social Science and Medicine*, 41: 197–210

Cane, P (2002) *Responsibility in Law and Morality*, Oxford: Hart Publishing

Carter, M (2006a) *London woman jailed for infecting partner with HIV – police actively investigated her sexual history to find past partners*, (June 19 2006) available at <http://wwwaidsmapcom/en/news/13B0B7DF–38E3–41B6–8FC5–3F089A7A8B6Dasp> (accessed May 20 2007)

Carter, M (2006b) *40 month sentence in first gay case of reckless HIV transmission in England* (August 4 2006), available at <http://wwwaidsmapcom/en/news/43C0C178–DA22–464D–9065–8BC403A53ABBasp> (accessed May 20 2007)

Castel, R (1991) 'From dangerousness to risk' in G Burchell, C Gordon and P Miller (eds), *The Foucault Effect: Studies in Governmentality*, London: Harvester-Wheatsheaf

CDC (1981) 'Pneumocystis Pneumonia – Los Angeles', *Morbidity and Mortality Weekly Report*, 30: 250–252

CDC (1990) 'Possible transmission of human immunodeficiency virus to a patient during an invasive dental procedure', *Morbidity and Mortality Weekly Report*, 39: 489–93

Chalmers, J (2002) 'Criminalizing HIV transmission', *Journal of Medical Ethics*, 28: 160–163

Chalmers, J 'Sexually Transmitted Diseases and the Criminal Law', *The Juridical Review*, 5: 59–78

Chambers, DL (1994) 'Gay men, AIDS and the code of the condom', *Harvard Civil Rights-Civil Liberties Law Review*, 29: 353–385

Chapman, S (2004a) 'BIGAMIST GAVE HIV TO LOVER; Bogus asylum seeker guilty of infecting city woman with virus', *Liverpool Echo*, (January 9 2004), available at <http://wwwhighbeamcom/doc/1G1–112067400html> (accessed May 23 2007)

Chapman, S (2004b) ' "Danger to women" jailed for six years', *IC Liverpool*, (January 13 2004), available at <http://icliverpoolicnetworkcouk/0100news/0100regional news/tm_method=full%26objectid=13810737%26siteid=50061-name_pagehtml> (accessed May 23 2007)

Ciccarone, DH, Kanouse, DE, Collins, RL, Miu, A, Chen, JL, Morton, SC, and Stall, R (2003) 'Sex without disclosure of positive HIV serostatus in a US probability sample of persons receiving medical care for HIV infection', *American Journal of Public Health*, 93(6): 949–954

Cieselski, C, Marianos, D, Ou, CY (1992) 'Transmission of human immunodeficiency virus in a dental practice', *Annals of Internal Medicine*, 116: 798–805

Clear, T and Cadora, E (2001) 'Risk and community practice', in K Stenson and RR Sullivan (eds), *Crime, Risk and Justice: The Politics of Crime Control in Liberal Democracies*, Cullompton: Willan Publishing

Closen, ML (1984) 'The Arkansas criminal HIV exposure law: statutory issues, public policy concerns and constitutional objections', *Arkansas Law Review*, 46: 921–983

Cochran, S and Mays, VM (1990) 'Sex, Lies and HIV', *New England Journal of Medicine*, 322: 774–775

Cohen, S (1972) *Folk Devils and Moral Panics*, London: MacGibbon and Kee

Coker R (2003) 'Public health impact of detention of individuals with tuberculosis: a systematic literature review', *Public Health*, 117: 281–87

Coker, R (2006) 'Communicable disease control and contemporary themes in public health law', *Public Health*, 120: 23–29

Conaghan, J (1996) 'Gendered harm and the law of tort', *Oxford Journal of Legal Studies*, 16(3): 407–431

Conaghan, J (2002) 'Law, harm and redress: a feminist perspective', *Legal Studies* 22(3): 319–339

Council of Europe (2006) *HIV/Aids in Europe* (Doc 11033, September 27 2006) (Report of the Social, Health and Family Affairs Committee)

Council of Europe (2007) *HIV/Aids in Europe* (Parliamentary Assembly Resolution 1536, adopted January 25 2007)

CPS Cleveland (2003–4) *Annual Report*, available at <http://wwwcpsgovuk/ publications/docs/areas/2004/ar2004clevelandpdf> (accessed May 20 2007)

Crawford, R (1994) 'The boundaries of the self and the unhealthy other: reflections on health, culture and AIDS', *Social Science and Medicine*, 38: 1347–1365

Crepaz, N and Marks, G (2001) 'Are negative affective states associated with HIV sexual risk behaviors? A meta-analytic view', *Health Psychology*, 20: 291–299

Crepaz, N and Marks, G (2003) 'Serostatus disclosure, sexual communication and safer sex in HIV-positive men', *AIDS Care*, 15: 379–387

Crimp, D (2002 (1987)) *AIDS: Cultural Analysis / Cultural Activism*, Cambridge: MIT Press

Crimp, D (2002) *Melancholia and Moralism: Essays on AIDS and Queer Politics*, Cambridge, MA: MIT Press

Cusick, L and Rhodes, T (1999) 'The process of disclosing positive HIV status: findings from qualitative research', *Culture, Health and Sexuality*, 1: 3–18

Cusick, L and Rhodes, T (2000) 'Sustaining sexual safety in relationships: HIV positive people and their sexual partners', *Culture, Health and Sexuality*, 2: 472–488

Daily Mirror (2006) *Death of jailed HIV sex fiend*, Daily Mirror (May 26 2006)

Daly, M (1973) *Beyond God the Father: Toward a Philosophy of Women's Liberation*, Boston: Beacon Press

Daly, M (1978) *Gyn/Ecology: the Metaethics of Radical Feminism*, Boston: Beacon Press

Daly, M (1993) *Pure Lust: Elemental Feminist Philosophy*, Boston: Beacon Press

Dan-Cohen, M (2002) *Harmful Thoughts: Essays on Law, Self and Morality*, Princeton: Princeton University Press

D'Angelo, RJ, McGuire, JM, Abbott, DW and Sheridan, K (1998) 'Homophobia and perceptions of people with AIDS', *Journal of Applied Social Psychology*, 28: 157–170

Davidovich, U, de Wit, JBF and Stroebe, W (2004) 'Behavioral and cognitive barriers to safer sex between men in steady relationships: implications for prevention strategies', *AIDS Education and Prevention*, 16: 304–314

Davis, MDM (2001) 'HIV prevention rationalities and serostatus in the risk narratives of gay men', *Sexualities*, 5(3): 281–299

De Bruyn, M (1992) 'Women and AIDS in Developing Countries', *Social Science and Medicine*, 34: 249–262

De Rosa, CJ and Marks, G (1998) 'Preventive counseling and HIV-positive men and self-disclosure of serostatus to sex partners: New opportunities for preventio', *Health Psychology*, 17: 224–231

de Vroome, EMM, Stroebe, W, Sandfort, TGM, de Wit, JBF and Van Griensven, GJP (2000) 'Safer sex in social context: Individualistic and realtional determinants of AIDS-preventive behavior among gay men', *Journal of Applied Social Psychology*, 30: 2322–2340

Dean, M (1999) *Governmentality: Power and Rule in Modern Society*, London: Sage

Decker, AM (1998) 'Comment: criminalizing the intentional or reckless exposure to HIV: a wake-up call to Kansas, *University of Kansas Law Review* 46: 333–35

Dennis, I (1997) 'The critical condition of criminal law', *Current Legal Problems*, 50: 213–49

Department of Health (2001) *Better prevention, better services, better sexual health – The national strategy for sexual health and HIV*, London: Department of Health

Department of Health (2007) *Review of Parts II, V and VI of the Public Health (Control of Disease) Act 1984: A Consultation*, London: Department of Health

Derlega, VJ, Winstead, B and Greene, K, (2002) 'Perceived HIV-related stigma and HIV disclosure to relationship partners after finding out about the seropositive diagnosis', *Journal of Health Psychology*, 7: 415–432

Derlega, VJ and Winstead, BA (2001) 'HIV-infected persons' attributions for the disclosure and nondisclosure of the seropositive diagnosis to significant others' in V Manusov, and JH Harvey (eds), *Attribution, Communication Behavior, and Close Relationships* New York: Cambridge University Press

Derlega, VJ, Winstead, BA and Folk-Barron, L (2000) 'Reasons for and against disclosing HIV-seropositive test results to an intimate partner: a functional perspective' in S Petronio (ed) *Balancing the Secrets of Private Disclosures*, Mahwah: Lawrence Erlbaum Associates

Derlega, VJ, Winstead, BA, Greene, K, Serovich, JM and Elwood, WN (2002) 'Perceived HIV-related stigma and HIV disclosure to relationship partners after finding out about the seropositive diagnosis', *Journal of Health Psychology*, 7: 415–432

Devine, PG, Plant, EA and Harrison, K (1999) 'The problem of "us" versus "them" and AIDS stigma', *American Behavioural Scientist*, 42: 1212–1228

Dine, J and Watt, B (1998) 'The transmission of disease during consensual sexual activity and the concept of associative autonomy, *Web Journal of Current Legal Issues*, 4

Dodds, C, Weatherburn, P, Hickson, F, Keogh, P, Nutland, W (2005) *Grievous Harm: Use of the Offences Against the Person Act 1861 for Sexual Transmission of HIV*, London: Sigma Research

Douglas, M (1966 (2002)) Purity *and Danger: An Analysis of Concepts of Pollution and Taboo*, London: Routledge & Kegan Paul

Douglas, M (1992) *Risk and Blame: Essays in Cultural Theory*, London: Routledge

Duff, RA (1990) *Intention, Agency and Criminal Liability*, Oxford: Blackwell

Dwyer, J (1993) 'Legislating AIDS away: The limited role of legal persuasion in minimizing the spread of HIV', *Journal of Contemporary Health Law and Policy*, 9: 169

Elias, N (1939 (1994)) *The Civilizing Process*, Oxford: Blackwell

Elliott, R (1997) *Criminal Law and HIV/AIDS: Final Report*, Montreal: Canadian Legal Network and Canadian AIDS Society

Elliott, R (1999) *After* Cuerrier: *Canadian Criminal Law and the Non-Disclosure of HIV-Positive Status*, Canadian Toronto: HIV/AIDS Policy Network

Elliott, R (2002) *Criminal Law, Public Health and HIV Transmission: A Policy Options Paper*, Geneva: UNAIDS

Ericson, R and Heggarty, KD (1997) *Policing the Risk Society*, Oxford: Clarendon Press

Erni, JN (1994) *Unstable Frontiers: Technomedicine and the Cultural Politics of 'Curing' AIDS*, Minneapolis: University of Minnesota Press

Ewald, F (1986) *L'Etat Providence*, Paris: Grasset et Fasquelle

Ewald, F (1991) 'Insurance and risks', in G Burchell, C Gordon and P Miller (eds), *The Foucault Effect: Studies in Governmentality*, London: Harvester-Wheatsheaf

Ewald, F (1993) 'Two infinities of risk', in B Massumi (ed), *The Politics of Everyday Fear*, Minneapolis: University of Minnesota Press

Ewing, AC (1929) *The Morality of Punishment*, London: Kegan Paul

Ezzy, D (2000) 'Illness narratives: time, hope and HIV', *Social Science and Medicine*, 50: 605–617

Farmer, L (1996) *Criminal Law, Tradition and Legal Order: Crime and the Genius of Scots Law 1747 to the Present*, Cambridge: Cambridge University Press

Fee, E and Krieger, N (1993) 'Understanding AIDS: historical interpretation and the limits of biomedical individualism', *American Journal of Public Health*, 83: 1477–1486

Feinberg, J (1984) *Harm to Others*, Oxford: Oxford University Press

Fenton, B (2006) *Woman with HIV who deliberately took a string of lovers is jailed*, (21/06/06) available at <http://wwwtelegraphcouk/news/mainjhtml?xml=/news/2006/06/20/naids20xml> (accessed May 20 2007)

Fettner, AG (1988) 'Bad Science Makes Strange Bedfellows', *Village Voice*, 25

Fisher, M, Benn, P, Evans, B, Pozniak, A, Jones, M, MacLean, S, Davidson, O, Summerside, J and Hawkins, D (2006) 'UK Guideline for the use of post-exposure prophylaxis for HIV following sexual exposure', *International Journal of STD & AIDS*, 17: 81–92

Foucault, M (1979) *Discipline and Punish*, London: Allen Lane

Foucault, M (1981) *The History of Sexuality, Volume One: An Introduction*, Harmondsworth: Penguin

Foucault, M (1988) 'Technologies of the self', in LH Martin, H Gutman, and P Hutton, *Technologies of the Self: A Seminar with Michel Foucault*, London: Tavistock

Fox, N (1999) 'Postmodern reflections on "risks", "hazards" and life choices', in D Lupton (ed), *Risk and Sociocultural Theory: New Directions and Perspectives*, Cambridge: Cambridge University Press

Frankowski, S (ed) (1998) *Legal Responses to AIDS in Comparative Perspective*, The Hague: Kluwer

Fresco, A (2006a) 'HIV infected woman may have infected dozens', *The Times* (June 20 2006)

Fresco, A (2006b) 'HIV Infected woman may have infected dozens', *The Times* (online version) (June 20 2006) available at <http://wwwtimesonlinecouk/tol/news/uk/crime/article676594ece> (accessed December 15 2006)

Friedman, M (1997) 'Autonomy and social relationships', in DT Meyers (ed) *Feminists Rethink the Self*, Boulder, Colorado: Westview Press

Gagnon, J and Simon, W (1973) *Sexual Conduct: The Social Sources of Human Sexuality*, New York: Aldine de Gruyter

Gardner, J (2003) 'The mark of responsibility', *Oxford Journal of Legal Studies*, 23: 157–171

Garfield, S (1994) *The End of Innocence: Britain in the Time of AIDS*, London: Faber

Giddens, A (1990) *The Consequences of Modernity*, Cambridge: Polity Press

Giddens, A (1991) *Modernity and Self-Identity*, Cambridge: Polity Press

Giddens, A (1998) 'Risk society: the context of British politics', in J Franklin (ed), *The Politics of Risk Society*, Cambridge: Polity Press

Gielen AC, O'Campo, P, Faden, RR, and Eke, A (1997) 'Women's disclosure of HIV status: experiences of mistreatment and violence in an urban setting' *Women Health*, 25(3): 19–31

Gielen, AC, McDonnell, KA, Burke, JG, and O'Campo, P 'Women's lives after an HIV-positive diagnosis: disclosure and violence', *Maternal and Child Health Journal*, 4(2): 111–120

Gleeson, K (2005) 'The problem of Clarence, brutal at his best: James Fitzjames Stephen and the doctrine of sexual inequality', *Nottingham Law Journal*, 14: 1–16

Goffmann, E (1963) *Stigma: Notes on the Management of Spoiled Identity*, New York: Prentice Hall

Goffmann, E (1969) *The Presentation of Self in Everday Life*, London: Penguin

Gostin, LO (1989) 'The politics of AIDS: compulsory state powers, public health and civil liberties', *Ohio State Law Journal*, 49(4): 1017–1058

Gostin, LO (2003) *The Aids Pandemic: Complacency, Injustice, and Unfulfilled Expectations*, Chapel Hill: University Of North Carolina Press

Gottlieb, M S R, Schroff, R and Schanker, H M (1981) '*Pneumocystis carinii* pneumonia and mucosal candidiasis in previously healthy homosexual men', *New England Journal of Medicine*, 305: 1425–31

Graham, S, Weiner, B, Giuliano, T and Williams, E (1993) 'An attributional analysis of reactions to Magic Johnson', *Journal of Applied Social Psychology*, 23: 996–1010

Gray, J (1983) *Mill on Liberty: A Defence*, London: Routledge and Kegan Paul

Gray, J (1995) *Liberalism* (2nd edn), Buckingham: Open University Press

Green, G and Sobo, EJ (2000) *The Endangered Self: Managing the Social Risks of HIV*, London: Routledge

Greene, K, Derlega, VJ, Yep, GA, and Petronio, S (2003) *Privacy and Disclosure of HIV in Interpersonal Relationships: A Sourcebook for Researchers and Practitioners*, Mahwah: Lawrence Erlbaum Associates

Gross, A (2006) *The Parliamentary Assembly of the Council of Europe as source of inspiration for a Parliamentary Dimension of the United Nations* (Statement to the General Assembly of the United Nations 61st Session, October 20 2006) available at <http://wwwandigrossch/html/site495htm> (accessed May 20 2007)

Grosz, E (1994) *Volatile Bodies: Toward a Corporeal Feminism*, Sydney: Allen & Unwin

Hacking, I (1990) *The Taming of Chance*, Cambridge: Cambridge University Press

Haigh, R, and Harris, D (eds) (1995) *AIDS: A Guide to the Law*, (2nd edn), London: Routledge

Hall, R and Longstaff, L, 'Defining consent', *New Law Journal* (1997), 840

Hall, S, Critchley, C, Jefferson, T *et al* (1978) *Policing the Crisis*, London: Macmillan

Halpin, A (2004) *Definition in the Criminal Law*, Oxford: Hart Publishing

Hart, HLA (1968) *Punishment and Responsibility*, Oxford: Oxford University Press

Hart, HLA and Honoré, A (1985) *Causation in the Law* (2nd edn), Oxford: Oxford University Press

Haver, W (1997) *The Body of this Death: Historicity and Sociality in the Time of AIDS*, Stanford: Stanford University Press

Hays, RB, Kegeles, SM and Coates, TJ (1997) 'Unprotected sex and HIV risk-taking among young men within boyfriend relationships', *AIDS Education and Prevention*, 1: 314–329

Hays, RB, McKusick, L, Pallack, L, Hilliard, R, Hoff, C and Coates, TJ (1993) 'Disclosing HIV seropositivity to significant others', *AIDS*, 7: 425–431

Health Protection Agency (2006) *A Complex Picture: HIV and other Sexually Transmitted Infections in the United Kingdom*, London: Health Protection Agency, available at <http://wwwhpaorguk/publications/2006/hiv_sti_2006/defaulthtm> (accessed May 20 2007)

Heise, LL and Elias, C (1995) 'Transforming AIDS prevention to meet women's needs: A focus on developing countries', *Social Science and Medicine*, 40: 931–943

Herek, GM and Capitiano, JP (1999) 'AIDS and stigma and sexual prejudice', *American Behavioural Scientist*, 42: 1130–1147

Herring, J (2006) *Criminal Law: Text, Cases and Materials*, (2nd edn) Oxford: Oxford University Press

Home Office (1998) *Violence: Reforming the Offences Against the Person Act 1861*, London: Home Office

Hood, R and Shute, S (1996) 'Protecting the public: automatic life sentences, parole and high-risk offenders', *Criminal Law Review*, 788–800

Horder, J (1994) 'Rethinking non-fatal offences against the person', *Oxford Journal of Legal Studies*, 14(3): 335–351

Horder, J (1998) 'Reconsidering psychic assault', *Criminal Law Review*, 392–403

Horder, J (2004) *Excusing Crime*, Oxford: Oxford University Press

Hudson, B (2004) *Justice in the Risk Society*, London: Sage

Hutchinson, JF (2003) 'HIV and the evolution of infectious diseases', in G Ellison, M Parker and C Campbell (eds), *Learning from HIV and AIDS*, Cambridge: Cambridge University Press

Hyde, A (1997) *Bodies of Law*, Princeton, NJ: Princeton University Press

Inness, JC (1992) *Privacy, Intimacy and Isolation*, New York: Oxford University Press

Intergovernmental Committee on AIDS, Legal Working Party (1991) *Legislative Approaches to Public Health Control of HIV-Infection*, Canberra: Department of Community Services and Health

Jaffe HW, McCurdy, JM, Kalish, ML, *et al* (1994) 'Lack of HIV transmission in the practice of a dentist with AIDS', *Annals of Internal Medicine*, 121(11): 855–859

James, R, Azad, Y and Weait, M (2007) *Are the people prosecuted for HIV transmission in the criminal courts representative of the UK epidemic? HIV Medicine* 8 (Supplement 1): 42 (Poster presentation, British HIV Association Annual Conference, Edinburgh 2007)

Jareborg, N (1995) 'What kind of criminal law do we want?', in A Snare (ed), *Beware of Punishment*, Oslo: Pax Forlag

Kadish, S (1967) 'The crisis of overcriminalization', *Annals of the American Academy of Political and Social Science*, 374:157–170

Kalichman, SC, Heckman, T and Kelly, JA (1996) 'Sensation seeking as an explanation for the association between substance use and HIV-related risky sexual behavior', *Archives of Sexual Behaviour*, 25: 141–154

Kalichman, SC, Kelly, J A and Rompa, D (1997) 'Continued high-risk sex among HIV-seropositive gay and bisexual men seeking HIV prevention services', *Health Psychology*, 16: 369–373

Kane, S and Mason, T (2001) 'AIDS and criminal justice', *Annual Review of Anthropology*, 30: 457–479

Katz, MH, Schwarcz, SK, Kellogg, TA, Klausner, JD, Dilley, JW and Gibson, S (2002) 'Impact of highly active antiretroviral treatment on HIV serocoincidence among men who have sex with men: San Francisco', *American Journal of Public Health*, 92: 388–394

Kelman, M (1980/81) 'Interpretive construction in the substantive criminal law', *Stanford Law Review*, 33: 591

Kenny, CS (1902) *Outlines of Criminal Law*, Cambridge: Cambridge University Press

Keogh, P and Beardsell, S (1997) 'Sexual negotiation strategies of HIV positive gay men: a qualitative approach', in P Aggleton, PM Davies and G Hart (eds), *AIDS: Activism and Alliances*, London: Taylor and Francis

Keogh, P, Holland, P and Weatherburn, P (1998) *The Boys in the Backroom: Anonymous Sex Among Gay and Bisexual Men*, London: Sigma Research

Keogh, P, Weatherburn, P, and Stephens, M (1999) *Relative Safety: Risk and Unprotected Anal Intercourse Among Gay Men Diagnosed with HIV*, London: Sigma Research

Kesby, M, Fenton, K, Boyle, P and Power, R (2003) 'An agenda for future research on HIV and sexual behaviour among African migrant communities in the UK', *Social Science and Medicine*, 57: 1573–1592

Kilmarx, P *et al*, 'Experiences and perspectives of HIV-infected sexually transmitted disease clinic patients after post-test counselling', *Sexually Transmitted Diseases*, 25 (1998) 28

King, E (1994) *Safety in Numbers: Safer Sex and Gay Men*, London: Routledge

King, JL (2004) *On the Down Low: A Journey Into the Lives of 'Straight' Black Men Who Sleep With Men*, New York: Random House

Kippax, S, Crawford, J, Davis, M, Rodden, P and Dowsett, G (1993) 'Sustaining safe sex: A longitudinal study of a sample of homosexual men', *AIDS*, 7: 257–263

Kippax, S, Noble, J, Prestage, G, Crawford, J M, Campbell, D and D, B (1997) 'Sexual negotiation in the AIDS era: Negotiated safety revisited', *AIDS*, 11: 191–197

Klitzman, R (1999) 'Self-disclosure of HIV status to sexual partners: A qualitative study of issues faced by gay men', *Journal of the Gay and Lesbian Medical Association*, 3: 39–49

Klitzman, R and Bayer, R (2003) *Mortal Secrets: Truth and Lies in the Age of AIDS*, Baltimore: Johns Hopkins University Press

Kramer, L (1994) *Reports From the Holocaust*, New York: St Martin's Press

Kristeva, J (1982) *Powers of Horror: An Essay on Abjection*, New York: Columbia University Press

Kulstad, R (1986) *AIDS: Papers from 'Science', 1982–1985*, Washington, DC: American Association for the Advancement of Science

Lacey, N (1998) *Unspeakable Subjects*, Oxford: Hart Publishing

Lacey, N (2001a) 'In search of the responsible subject: history, philosophy and criminal law', *Modern Law Review*, 64(3) 350–371

Lacey, N (2001b) 'Responsibility and modernity in criminal law', *Journal of Political Philosophy*, 9(3): 249–277

Lacey, N (2001c) 'Beset by boundaries: The Home Office review of sex offences', *Criminal Law Review*, 3–14

Laurie, GT (1991) 'AIDS and criminal liability under Scots law', *Journal of the Law Society of Scotland*, 36: 312

Law Commission (1993) '*Offences against the Person and General Principles*', (Report No 218), London: HMSO

Law Commission (1995) *Consent in the Criminal Law* (Consultation Paper No 139), London: HMSO

Lazzarini, Z, Bray, S and Burris, S (2002) 'Evaluating the impact of criminal laws on HIV risk behavior', *Journal of Law, Medicine and Ethics*, 30: 239–253

Leary, MR and Schreindorfer, L S (1998) 'The stigmatization of HIV and AIDS: Rubbing salt in the wound', in VJ Derlega and AP Barbee (eds), *HIV and Social Interaction*, Thousand Oaks: Sage

Lederer, R (1987) 'Origin and spread of AIDS: Is the West responsible?' *Covert Action*, 28: 43–54

Lederer, R (1988) 'Origin and spread of AIDS: Is the West responsible', *Covert Action*, 29: 52–65

Lemey P, van Dooren, S, van Laetham, K *et al* (2005) 'Molecular testing of multiple HIV-1 transmissions in a criminal case' *AIDS*, 19(15): 1649–1658

Leonard, A (1998) *AIDS Legal Bibliography* (unpublished manuscript), available at <http://wwwqrdorg/qrd/browse/aidslegalbibliography> (accessed May 22 2007)

Leone, C and Wingate, C (1991) 'A functional approach to understanding attitudes toward AIDS victims', *Journal of Social Psychology*, 131: 761–768

Levy, A, Laska, F, Abelhauser, A *et al* (1999) 'Disclosure of HIV seropositivity', *Journal of Clinical Psychology*, 55(9): 1041–1049

Limandri, BJ (1989) 'Disclosure of stigmatizing conditions: the discloser's perspective', *Archives of Psychiatric Nursing*, 3: 69–78

Locke, J (1988 (1690)) *Two Treatises of Government*, Cambridge: Cambridge University Press

Luhmann, N (1993) *Risk: A Sociological Theory*, New York: Aldine de Gruyter

Lupton, D (1999) *Risk*, London: Routledge

Lynch, A (1978) 'Criminal liability for transmitting disease', *Criminal Law Review*, 612–625

McBarnet, D (1981) *Conviction*, London: Macmillan

McConville, M, Sanders, A and Leng, R (1991) *The Case for the Prosecution: Police Suspects and the Construction of Criminality*, London: Routledge

McGuire, AL (1999) 'Comment: AIDS as a weapon: criminal prosecution of HIV exposure', *Houston Law Review*, 36(5):1787–817

Machuca, R Jorgensen, LB, Theilade, P (2001) 'Molecular investigation of transmission of human immunodeficiency virus type 1 in a criminal case', *Clin Diagn Lab Immunol*, 8(5): 884–90

MacKinnon, CA (1982) 'Feminism, Marxism, method, and the state: An agenda for theory', *Signs: Journal of Women in Culture and Society*, 7(3): 515–544

MacKinnon, CA (1987) *Feminism Unmodified*, Cambridge, MA: Harvard University Press

MacKinnon, CA (1983) 'Feminism, Marxism, method, and the state: Toward feminist jurisprudence', *Signs: Journal of Women in Culture and Society*, 8(4): 635–658

Mamcli, PA (2000) 'Managing the HIV/AIDS pandemic: paving a path into the future of international law and organization', *Law & Policy*, 22: 202–225

Mann, J (1997) 'Medicine and public health, ethics and human rights', *Hastings Center Report*, 27(3): 6–14

Mansergh, G, Marks, G and Simoni, JM (1995) 'Self-disclosure of HIV infection among men who vary in time since seropositive diagnosis and symptomatic status', *AIDS*, 9: 639–644

Mansergh, G, Marks, G, Colfax, G, Guzman, R, Rader, M and Buchbinder, S (2002) ' "Barebacking" in a diverse sample of men who have sex with men', *AIDS*, 16: 653–659

Marks G, and Crepaz, N (2001) 'HIV-positive men's sexual practices in the context of self-disclosure of HIV status', *Journal Of Acquired Immune Deficiency Syndromes*, 27(1): 79–85

Marks, G, Bingman, CR and Duval, TS (1998) 'Negative affect and unsafe sex in HIV-positive men', *AIDS and Behavior*, 2: 89–99

Marks, G, Richardson, JL and Maldonado, N (1991) 'Self-disclosure of HIV infection to sexual partners', *American Journal of Public Health*, 81(10): 1321–1322

Marks, S and Ellison, GTH (2003) 'Postscript: reflections on HIV/AIDS and history', in GTH Ellison, M Parker and C Campbell (eds) *Learning from HIV and AIDS* (Vol 15), Cambridge: Cambridge University Press

Markus, M (1999) 'A treatment for the disease: criminal HIV transmission / exposure laws', *Nova Law Review*, 23: 847–79

Marshall, WE (2005) 'AIDS, race and the limits of science', *Social Science and Medicine*, 60: 2515–2525

Martin, R (2006) 'The exercise of public health powers in cases of infectious disease: human rights implications', *Medical Law Review*, 14(1): 132–143

Mason, HRC, Marks, G, Simoni, JM, Ruiz, MS and Richardson, JL (1995) 'Culturally sanctioned secrets? Latino men's nondisclosure of HIV infection to family, friends and lovers', *Health Psychology*, 14: 6–12

Massumi, B (1993) 'Everywhere you want to be: introduction to fear', in B Massumi (ed), *The Politics of Everyday Fear*, Minneapolis: University of Minnesota Press

Metts, S (1989) 'An exploratory investigation of deception in close relationships', *Journal of Social and Personal Relationships*, 6: 495–512

Metzker, ML, Mindell, DP, Liu, XM *et al* 'Molecular evidence of HIV-1 transmission in a criminal case', *Proceedings of the National Academy of Science*, 99(22): 14292–14297

Mill, JS (1972) *Utilitarianism, On Liberty and Considerations on Representative Government*, ed H B Acton, London: Everyman

Miller, J (2005) 'African immigrant damnation syndrome: The case of Charles Ssenyonga', *Sexuality Research and Social Policy*, 2(2): 31–50

Moatti, J-P, Hausser, D and Agrafiotis, D (1997) 'Understanding HIV risk-related behaviour: a critical overview of current models', in L van Campenhoudt, M Cohen, G Guizzardi and D Hausser (eds), *Sexual Interactions and HIV Risk*, London: Taylor & Francis

Mondragon, D, Kirkman-Liff, B and Schneller, ES (1991) 'Hostility to people with AIDS: Risk perception and demographic factors', *Social Science and Medicine*, 32: 1137–1142

Moneyham, L, Seals, B, Demi, A, Sowell, R, Cohen, L and Guillory, J (1996) 'Experiences of disclosure in women infected with HIV', *Health Care for Women International*, 17: 209–221

Monk, D (1998) 'Education about HIV/AIDS in the English classroom: political conflict and legal resolution, *Children and Society*, 12: 295–305

Moore, M (1997) *Placing Blame*, Oxford: Clarendon Press

Moore, M *Placing Blame*, Oxford: OUP (1997)

Moulton, J, Sweet, DM, Temoshok, L and Mandel, JS (1987) 'Attributions of blame and responsibility in relation to distress and health behavior change in people with AIDS and AIDS-related complex', *Journal of Applied Social Psychology*, 17: 493–506

Myers G (1994) 'Molecular investigation of HIV transmission', *Annals of Internal Medicine*, 121(11): 889–890

Naffine, N (1990) *Law and the Sexes: Explorations in Feminist Jurisprudence*, London: Allen and Unwin

Naffine, N (1994) 'Possession: Erotic love in the law of rape', *Modern Law Review* 57(1): 10–37

Naffine, N and Owens, R, (eds) (1997) *Sexing the Subject of Law*, London: Sweet and Maxwell

Nagel, T (1998) 'Concealment and exposure', *Philosophy and Public Affairs* 27: 3–30

Nedelsky, J (1989a) 'Law, boundaries and the bounded self', *Representations*, 30: 162–189

Nedelsky, J (1989b) 'Reconceiving autonomy: Sources, thoughts and possibilities', *Yale Journal of Law and Feminism*, 1: 7–36

Nedelsky, J (1993) 'Reconceiving rights as relationship', *Review of Constitutional Studies*, 1: 1–26

Niccolai, L, Dorst, D and Myers, L (1999) 'Disclosure of HIV status to sexual partners: Predictors and temporal patterns', *Sexually Transmitted Diseases*, 26: 280–285

Norrie, A (1991) *Law, Ideology and Punishment*, Dordrecht: Kluwer

Norrie, A (1996) 'The limits of justice: Finding fault in the criminal law', *Modern Law Review*, 59: 540–556

Norrie, A (1998) ' "Simulacra of Morality"? Beyond the Ideal / Actual Antinomies of Criminal Justice' in RA Duff (ed) *Philosophy and the Criminal law*, Cambridge: Cambridge University Press

Norrie, A (1999) 'After *Woollin*', *Criminal Law Review*, 532–544

Norrie, A (2000) *Punishment, Responsibility, and Justice: A Relational Critique*, Oxford: Oxford University Press

Norrie, A (2001) *Crime, Reason and History: A Critical Introduction to Criminal Law* (2nd edn), London: Butterworths

Norrie, A (2005) 'Closure and critique: antimony in modern legal theory' in A Norrie, *Law and the Beautiful Soul*, London: Glasshouse Press

Nyambe, M (2006) *Criminalisation of HIV transmission in Europe: A rapid scan of the laws and rates of prosecution for HIV transmission within signatory States of the European Convention of Human Rights*, London: GNP+ and Terrence Higgins Trust

Nyberg, D (1993) *The Varnished Truth: Truth Telling and Deceiving in Ordinary Life*, Chicago: Chicago University Press

O'Connor, C (2006) 'Law and Disorder', *Positive Nation*, 126 (October)

O'Donovan, K (1985) *Sexual Divisions in Law*, London: Weidenfeld and Nicolson

O'Malley, P (2004) *Risk, Uncertainty and Government*, London: Glasshouse Press

Oliver, K (1993) *Reading Kristeva: Unraveling the Double-Bind*, Bloomington: Indiana University Press

Ormerod, D (1994) 'Consent and offences against the person: Law Commission Consultation Paper No 134', *Modern Law Review*, 57: 928–940

Ormerod, D (2005) *Smith & Hogan: Criminal Law* (11th edn), Oxford: Oxford University Press

Ormerod DC, and Gunn MJ (1996) 'Criminal liability for the transmission of HIV', *Web Journal of Current Legal Issues*, 1

Ou, CY, Cieselski, CA, Myers, G, *et al* 'Molecular epidemiology of HIV transmission in a dental practice', *Science*, 256: 1165–1171

Packer, H (1969) *The Limits of the Criminal Sanction*, Stanford: Stanford University Press

Patton, C (1985) *Sex and Germs: the Politics of AIDS*, Boston: South End

Patton, C (1990) *Inventing AIDS*, New York: Routledge

Patton, C (1996) *Fatal Advice: How Safe-Sex Advice Went Wrong*, Durham: Duke University Press

Perry, SW, Card, CA, Moffatt Jr, M, Ashman, T, Fishman, B and Jacobsberg, LB (1994) 'Self-disclosure of HIV infection to sexual partners after repeated counseling', *AIDS Education and Prevention*, 6: 403–411

Perry, SW, Ryan, J and Fogel, K (1990) 'Voluntarily informing others of positive HIV test results: Patterns of notification by infected gay men', *Hospital and Community Psychiatry*, 41: 549–551

Peters, L, den Boer, DJ, Kok, G and Schaalma, HP (1994) 'Public reactions towards people with AIDS: An attributional analysis', *Patient Education and Counseling*, 24: 323–335

Peterson, C (1996) 'Deception in intimate relationships', *International Journal of Psychology*, 31(6): 279–288

Petrak, JA, Doyle, A-M, Smith, A, Skinner, C and Hedge, B (2001) 'Factors associated with self-disclosure of HIV serostatus to significant others', *British Journal of Health Psychology*, 6: 69–79

Pillay, D and Fisher, M (2007) 'Primary HIV infection, phylogenetics, and antiretroviral prevention', *The Journal of Infectious Diseases*, 195: 924–926

Pool, H (2006) *Porter's real crime: she slept with black men*, (June 21 2006), available at <http://wwwguardiancouk/g2/story/0,,1802230,00html> (accessed May 20 2007)

Porter, D and Porter, R (1988) 'The Enforcement of Health: The British Debate' in E Fee and D Fox (eds) *AIDS: The Burdens of History*, Berkeley: University of California Press

Prestage, G, Van de Ven, P, Grulich, A, Kippax, S, McInnes, D and Hendry, O (2001) 'Gay men's casual sexual encounters: Discussing HIV and using condoms', *AIDS Care*, 13: 277–284

Pryor, JB, Reeder, GD and Landau, S (1999) 'A social-psychological analysis of HIV-related stigma: A two factor theory', *American Behavioural Scientist*, 42: 1193–1211

Pryor, JB, Reeder, GD and McManus, J (1991) 'Fear and loathing in the workplace: Reaction to AIDS-infected co-workers', *Personality and Social Psychology Bulletin*, 17: 133–139

Pryor, JB, Reeder, GD, Vinacco, R and Kott, TL (1989) 'The instrumental and symbolic functions of attitudes towards people with AIDS', *Journal of Applied Social Psychology*, 19: 377–404

Rawls, J (1999) *A Theory of Justice* (Revised Edition), Oxford: Oxford University Press

Reddy, S (1996) 'Claims to expert knowledge and the subversion of democracy: The triumph of risk over uncertainty', *Economy and Society*, 25(2): 222–254

Reiner, R (1997) 'Media made criminality' in M Maguire, R Morgan and R Reiner (eds) *The Oxford Handbook of Criminology* (2nd edn), Oxford: Oxford University Press

Rhodes, T and Cusick, L (2002) 'Accounting for unprotected sex: Stories of agency and acceptability', *Social Science and Medicine*, 55: 211–226

Roberts, P (1997) 'The philosophical foundations of consent in the criminal law, Oxford Journal of Legal Studies, 17(3): 389–414

Robertson, J (2005) 'HIV man accused of infecting girlfriend', *The Scotsman*, (April 27, 2005) available at <http://newsscotsmancom/edinburghcfm?id=447242005> (accessed May 20 2007),

Rollins, J (2004) *AIDS and the Sexuality of Law: Ironic Jurisprudence*, Basingstoke: Palgrave Macmillan

Rooney, M and Taylor, S (1997) *Sexual Health Promotion Needs of HIV Positive Gay Men*, London: Health First

Rose, N (1989) *Governing the Soul*, London: Routledge

Rose, N (1993) 'Government, authority and expertise in advanced liberalism', *Economy and Society*, 22: 283–299

Rose, N (1996a) 'Governing "advanced liberal democracies" ', in A Barry, T Osborne and N Rose (eds), *Foucault and Political Reason*, London: UCL Press

Rose, N (1996b) 'The death of the "social"? Refiguring the territory of government', *Economy and Society*, 25: 327–356

Rosenblum, NL (1978) *Bentham's Theory of the Modern State*, Cambridge: Harvard University Press

Rubenstein, W, Eisenberg, R and Gostin, LO (1996) *The Rights of People who are HIV Positive : The Authoritative ACLU Guide to the Rights of People Living with HIV Disease and AIDS*, Carbondale: Southern Illinois University Press

Rubin, G (1984) 'Thinking sex: Notes for a radical theory of the politics of sexuality', in C Vance (ed), *Pleasure and Danger: Exploring Female Sexuality*, London: Routledge & Kegan Paul

Ryan S (2007) 'Risk-taking, recklessness and HIV transmission: accommodating the reality of sexual transmission of HIV within a justifiable approach to criminal liability, *Liverpool Law Review* (forthcoming)

Ryan, S (2006) 'Reckless transmission of HIV: Knowledge and culpability', *Criminal Law Review*, 981–992

Sanders A (1997) 'From suspect to trial', in M Maguire, R Morgan and R Reiner (eds) *The Oxford Handbook of Criminology*, Oxford: Oxford University Press

Schnell, DJ, Higgins, DL, Wilson, RM, Goldbaum, RM, Cohn, D and Wolitski, R (1992) 'Men's disclosure of HIV test results to male primary sex partners', *American Journal of Public Health*, 82: 1675 1676

Sears, N and McIntyre, S (2006) *HIV test anguish for dozens of men after jailing of Aids attacker*, (June 21, 2006) available at <http://wwwdailymailcouk/pages/live/articles/news/newshtml?in_article_i   =391687&in_page_id=1770&in_a_source=> (accessed May 20 2007)

Sedgwick, EK (1990) *Epistemology of the Closet*, Berkeley: University of California Press

Seidman, S (1996) 'Points of intersection: discontinuities at the junction of criminal law and the regulatory state', *Journal of Contemporary Legal Issues*, 7: 97

Sentencing Advisory Council (2005) *Assaults and Other Offences Against the Person*, (Consultation) London: Sentencing Advisory Council

Sentencing Guidelines Council (2005) *Assaults and other Offences Against the Person*, available at <http://wwwsentencingguidelinesgovuk/consultations/closed/indexhtml> (accessed May 23 2007)

Serovich, JM and Mosack, KE (2003) 'Reasons for HIV disclosure or nondisclosure to casual sexual partners', *AIDS Education and Prevention*, 15(1): 70–80

Sheon, N and Crosby, GM (2004) 'Ambivalent tales of HIV disclosure in San Francisco', *Social Science and Medicine*, 58: 2105–2118

Shilts, R (1987) *And the Band Played On: People, Politics and the AIDS Epidemic*, New York: St Martin's Press

Shriver, CM (2001) 'State approaches to criminalizing the exposure of HIV: Problems in statutory construction, constitutionality and implications', *Northern Illinois University Law Review*, 319

Siegel, K, Lune, H and Meyer, I (1998) 'Stigma management among gay/bisexual men with HIV/AIDS', *Qualitative Sociology*, 21: 3–24

Simoni, J and D Pantalone, (2004) 'Secrets and safety in the age of AIDS: Does HIV disclosure lead to safer sex?', *Topics in HIV Medicine*, 12(4): 109–118

Simoni, JM, Demas, P and Mason, H (2000) 'HIV disclosure among women of African descent: Associations with coping, social support and psychological adaptation', *AIDS and Behavior*, 4: 147–148

Simoni, JM, Mason, H and Marks, G (1995) 'Women's self-disclosure of HIV infection: Rates, reasons and reactions', *Journal of Consulting and Clinical Psychology*, 63: 474–478

Simoni, JM, Mason, HRM and Marks, G (1997) 'Disclosing HIV status and sexual orientation to employers', *AIDS Care*, 9: 598–599

Smith, JC and Hogan, B (1999) *Criminal Law*, Oxford: Oxford University Press

Smith, KJM (1991) 'Sexual etiquette, public interest and the criminal law', *Northern Ireland Legal Quarterly*, 42: 309–341

Sparks, R (2001) ' "Bringin' it all back home": Populism, media coverage and the dynamics of locality and globality in the politics of crime control', in K Stenson and RR Sullivan (eds) *Crime, Risk and Justice: The Politics of Crime Control in Liberal Democracies*, Cullompton: Willan Publishing

Spencer, JR (2004a) 'Liability for reckless infection: part 1', *New Law Journal*, 384

Spencer, JR (2004b) 'Liability for reckless infection: part 2', *New Law Journal*, 448

Spencer, JR (2004c) 'Reckless Infection in the Court of Appeal: *R v Dica*', *New Law Journal*, 762

St Lawrence, JS, Husfeldt, BA, Kelly, JA, Hood, HV and Smith, S (1990) 'The stigma of AIDS: Fear of disease and prejudice toward gay men', *Journal of Homosexuality*, 19: 85–99

Stein, MD, Freedberg, KA, Sullivan, LM, Savetsky, J, Levenson, SM, Hingson, R, and Samet, JH (1998) 'Sexual ethics: disclosure of HIV-positive status to partners', *Archives of Internal Medicine*, 158: 253–257

Stempel, R, Moulton, J and Moss, A (1995) 'Self-disclosure of HIV-I antibody test results: The San Francisco General Hospital cohort', *AIDS Education and Prevention*, 7: 116–123

Stenson, K and Edwards, A (2001) 'Rethinking crima control in advanced liberal government: the "third way" and the return of the local', in K Stenson and RR Sullivan (eds), *Crime, Risk and Justice: The Politics of Crime Control in Liberal Democracies*, Cullompton: Willan Publishing

Stephenson, JM, Imrie, J, Davis, MMD, Mercer, C, Black, S, Copas, AJ, Hart, GJ, Davidson, OR, and Williams, IG (2003) 'Is use of antiretroviral therapy among homosexual men associated with increased risk of transmission of HIV infection?', *Sexually Transmitted Infections*, 79: 7–10

Sullivan, KM and Field MA (1988) 'AIDS and the coercive power of the state', *Harvard Civil Rights-Civil Liberties Law Review* 23(1): 139–198

Syrota, G 'A radical change in the law of recklessness?', [1982] *Criminal Law Review*, 97

Tadros, V (2005) *Criminal Responsibility*, Oxford: Oxford University Press

Tauber, AI (1994) *The Immune Self: Theory or Metaphor?*, Cambridge: Cambridge University Press

Temkin, J (2002) *Rape and the Legal Process* (2nd edn), Oxford: Oxford University Press

Temkin, J and Ashworth A (2004) 'The Sexual Offences Act 2003: (1) rape, sexual assault and the problems of consent', *Criminal Law Review*, 328–346

Tong, R (1989) *Feminist Thought: A Comprehensive Introduction*, London:

Traynor, L and Roughley, L (2006) 'Jail for for lover who gave HIV to girlfriend', Liverpool Echo (September 22, 2006) available at <http://icliverpoolicnetwork couk/0100news/0100regionalnews/tm_objectid=17802351&method=full&siteid= 50061&headline=jail-for-lover-who-gave-hiv-to-girlfriend-name_pagehtml> (accessed May 20 2007)

Treichler, P (1988) 'AIDS, homophobia and biomedical discourse: an epidemic of signification', in D Crimp (ed) *AIDS: Cultural Analysis, Cultural Activism*, Cambridge: MIT Press

Treichler, PA (1999) 'AIDS and HIV infection in the third world: A first world chronicle', in PA Treichler *How to Have Theory in an Epidemic: Cultural Chronicles of AIDS*, Durham, NC and London: Duke University Press

Treichler, PA (1999) 'AIDS, Africa and cultural theory', in PA Treichler *How to Have Theory in an Epidemic: Cultural Chronicles of AIDS*, Durham, NC and London: Duke University Press

UNAIDS (2002) *Criminal Law, Public Health and HIV Transmission: A Policy Options Paper*, UNAIDS: Geneva

UNAIDS (2002) *Criminal Law, Public Health and HIV Transmission: A Policy Options Paper*, UNAIDS: Geneva

UNCHR (1989) *Report of an International Consultation on AIDS and Human Rights, Geneva, 26 to 28 July 1989* (HR/PUB/90/2)

UNCHR (1998) *HIV/AIDS and Human Rights: International Guidelines*, United Nations: New York and Geneva

United Nations (1995) *E/CN4/1995/45 (Report of the 51st Session)*

Urban Walker, M, (1997) 'Picking up Pieces: Lives, Stories and Integrity', in DT Meyers (ed), *Feminists Rethink the Self*, Boulder, CO: Westview Press

van Campenhoudt, L, Cohen, M, Guizzardi, G, and Hausser D (eds) (1997), *Sexual Interactions and HIV Risk*, London: Taylor & Francis

Waldby, C (1996) *AIDS and the Body Politic: Biomedicine and Sexual Difference*, London: Routledge

Walzer, M (1983) *Spheres of Justice: A Defense of Pluralism and Equality*, New York: Basic Books

Warburton, D (2004) 'A critical review of English law in respect of criminalising blameworthy behaviour by HIV+ individuals', *Journal of Criminal Law*, 68(1) 55–78

Watchirs, H (2003) 'AIDS Audit – HIV and human rights: an Australian pilot, *Law & Policy*, 25(3): 244–268

Watney, S (1986 (1994)) 'AIDS, "Moral Panic" Theory and Homophobia' in S Watney, *Practices of Freedom*, London: Rivers Oram Press

Watney, S (1987 (1997)) *Policing Desire*, (3rd edn), London: Cassell

Watney, S (1988 (1994)) 'The spectacle of AIDS', in S Watney *Practices of Freedom*, London: Rivers Oram Press

Watney, S (1989 (1994)) 'Missionary positions: AIDS, "Africa", and race', in S Watney *Practices of Freedom*, London: Rivers Oram Press

Watney, S (1994) *Practices of Freedom*, London: Rivers Oram Press

Weait, M (1996) 'Fleshing it out', in L Flynn and L Bentley (eds) *Law and the Senses*, London: Pluto Press

Weait, M (2001) 'Taking the blame: Criminal law, social responsibility and the sexual transmission of HIV', *The Journal of Social Welfare and Family Law*, 23(4): 441–457

Weait, M (2004) 'Dica: Knowledge, consent and the transmission of HIV', *New Law Journal*, 448

Weait, M (2005a) 'Criminal law and the sexual transmission of HIV: *R v Dica*', *Modern Law Review*, 68(1): 120–133

Weait, M (2005b) 'Harm, consent and the limits of privacy', *Feminist Legal Studies*, 13: 97–122

Weait, M (2005c) 'Knowledge, autonomy and consent: *R v Konzani*', *Criminal Law Review*, 763–772

Weait, M (2007) 'On being responsible', in V Munro and CF Stychin (eds) Sexuality and Law: Feminist Engagements, Abingdon: Routledge-Cavendish

Weait, M and Azad, Y (2005) 'The Criminalization of HIV Transmission in England and Wales: Questions of Law and Policy', *HIV/AIDS Policy and Law Review*, 1–12

Weiner, B (1993) 'On sin versus sickness: A theory of perceived responsibility and social motivation', *American Psychologist*, 48: 957–965

Weiner, B, Perry, RP and Magnusson, J (1988) 'An attributional analysis of reactions to stigmas', *Journal of Personality and Social Psychology*, 55: 738–48

Wellings, K (1988) 'Perceptions of Risk: Media Treatment of AIDS', in P Aggleton and H Homans (eds) *Social Aspects of AIDS*, New York: Falmer

Wells, C (1997) 'Stalking: the criminal law response', *Criminal Law Review*, 463–470

Wenger, NS, Kusseling, FS, Beck, K and Shapiro, MF (1994) 'Sexual behavior of individuals infected with the human immunodeficiency virus: the need for intervention', *Archive of Internal Medicine*, 154: 1849–1854

Wertheimer, A (2003) *Consent to Sexual Relations*, Cambridge: Cambridge University Press

West, R (1988) 'Jurisprudence and Gender', *University of Chicago Law Review* 55(1): 1–72

West, R (1997) *Caring for Justice*, New York: New York University Press

WHO (2006) Report of the WHO European Region Technical Consultation on the Criminalization of HIV and other Sexually Transmitted Infections, Copenhagen: World Health Organization Available at <wwweurowhoint/aids> (accessed May 20 2007)

Williams, G (1981) 'Recklessness redefined', *Cambridge Law Journal*, 40: 252

Williams, L (2006) *HIV acquittal 'first of many'*, (August 20 2006) available at <http://wwwthisislocallondoncouk/displayvar8856170hiv_acquittal_first_of_manyphp> (accessed May 20 2007)

Wolf, LE and Vezina, R (2004) 'Crime and punishment: Is there a role for criminal law in HIV prevention policy?', *Whittier Law Review*, 25: 821–886

Wolitski, R, MacGowan, RJ, Higgins, DL and Jorgensen, CM (1997) 'The effects of HIV counseling and testing on risk-related practices and help-seeking behavior', *AIDS Education and Prevention*, 9: 52–67

Wolitski, R, Valdisserri, R, Denning, P and Levine, W (2001) 'Are we headed for a resurgence of the HIV epidemic among men who have sex with men?' *American Journal of Public Health*, 91: 883–888

Wolitski, RJ, Reitmeijer, CAM, Goldbaum, GM, and Wilson, RM (1998) 'HIV serostatus disclosure among gay and bisexual men in four American cities: General patterns and relation to sexual practices', *AIDS Care*, 10(5): 599–610

Worth, H, Reid, A and McMillan, A (2002) 'Somewhere over the rainbow: Love, trust and monogamy in gay relationships', *Journal of Sociology*, 38: 237–253

Yeo, M (1991) 'Sexual ethics and AIDS: A liberal view' in C Overall and WP Zion (eds) *Perspectives on AIDS: Ethical and Social Issues*, Toronto: Oxford University Press

Yirrel, DL, Robertson, P, Goldberg, J, McMenamin, J, Cameron, S, Leigh Brown, AJ (1997) Molecular investigation into outbreak of HIV in a Scottish prison, *British Medical Journal*, 314: 1446–1450

Zedner, L (1997) 'Victims', in M Maguire, R Morgan and R Reiner (eds) *The Oxford Handbook of Criminology*, Oxford: Oxford University Press

Index